D1290124

Humor and Psyche
Psychoanalytic Perspectives

HUMOR AND PSYCHE
Psychoanalytic Perspectives

edited by
JAMES W. BARRON

THE ANALYTIC PRESS

1999   Hillsdale, NJ   London

Set in Sabon 10/12 and Bernhard Modern by EvS Communication Networx,
Pt. Pleasant, NJ

Published by The Analytic Press, Inc.
101 West Street, Hillsdale, New Jersey 07642
www.analyticpress.com

Library of Congress Cataloging-in-Publication Data

Humor and psyche : psychoanalytic perspectives / edited by James W.
Barron.
        p.   cm.
    Includes bibliographical references and index.
    ISBN 0-88163-257-0
    1. Psychoanalysis. 2. Wit and humor—Psychological aspects.
I. Barron, James W., 1944-   .
BF175.H85 1999
  152.4′3—dc21

for Library of Congress   98-33349
                                                               CIP

Printed in the United States of America
10 9 8 7 6 5 4 3 2 1

To Mia Lesley Barron
For her Dramatic Appreciation of the Human Comedy

Contents

Contributors

Ronald Baker, M.R.C. Psych., Training and Supervising Psychoanalyst, British Psychoanalytical Society; Member, Royal College of Psychiatrists.

Barnaby B. Barratt, Ph.D., D.H.S., Training and Supervising Analyst, Michigan Psychoanalytic Institute; Professor of Family Medicine, Psychiatry and Behavioral Neurosciences, Wayne State University.

James W. Barron, Ph.D. (editor), Senior Associate in Psychology, Department of Psychiatry, Harvard Medical School and Supervising Psychologist, Beth Israel Deaconess Medical Center, Boston, Massachusetts; Faculty, Massachusetts Institute for Psychoanalysis and Psychoanalytic Institute of New England, East.

Professor Martin S. Bergmann, Clinical Professor of Psychology, New York University Post Doctoral Program in Psychoanalysis and Psychotherapy; Training and Supervising Psychoanalyst, New York Freudian Society.

Judith Dupont, M.D., Associate Member, Association Psychanalytique de France (Paris); Literary representative of Sándor Ferenczi.

Stuart Feder, M.D., Clinical Associate Professor of Psychiatry, Albert Einstein College of Medicine; Faculty, New York Psychoanalytic Institute.

Peter L. Giovacchini, M.D., Training and Supervising Analyst and Founder of the Center for Psychoanalytic Studies, Chicago; Professor Emeritus, University of Illinois College of Medicine, Department of Psychiatry.

James S. Grotstein, M.D., Clinical Professor of Psychiatry, University of
California at Los Angeles School of Medicine; Private Practice, West Los
Angeles.

W. W. Meissner, S.J., M.D., University Professor of Psychoanalysis, Boston College; Training and Supervising Analyst, Boston Psychoanalytic
Institute.

F. Robert Rodman, M.D., Member, Los Angeles Psychoanalytic Society
and Institute; Editor, "The Spontaneous Gesture: Selected Letters of D.
W. Winnicott."

Jean Sanville, Ph.D., Supervising and Training Analyst, Los Angeles Institute and Society for Psychoanalytic Studies; Author, *The Playground
of Psychoanalytic Therapy.*

Acknowledgments

The idea for this book germinated from conversations with Ellen Handler Spitz, whose exploration of linkages between art and psyche serves as an exemplary model of interdisciplinary study. Another generous source of inspiration has been Warren Poland, whose creative character combines seriousness of purpose with lightness of spirit. I am also grateful to Paul Stepansky for recognizing the timeliness and relevance of this new look at humor and psyche and for providing me with the opportunity to bring this project to completion.

Humor and Psyche
Psychoanalytic Perspectives

Introduction

OBJECTIVE

More than 70 years have elapsed since Freud wrote his last essay on humor, time for an indepth reappraisal of the role of humor in psychic life. Humor is inextricably related to the origin and development of psychoanalytic theory which in turn has deepened our understanding of the dynamics of humor. *Humor and Psyche*[1] systematically examines that unique relationship. In the realm of technique, psychoanalysts typically regard humor with suspicion and ambivalence. With considerable justification, they see humor as sometimes helpful, facilitating the therapeutic relationship and the treatment process, but also as potentially destructive, subject to misuse and abuse. Several authors in this book address themselves to the important task of sorting out the positive and negative manifestations of humor in the treatment setting. Humor also leaves its

---

[1] As Bulfinch (1970, pp. 89–90) points out, the same Greek word, *psyche,* has multiple meanings and can be used to refer to mind or soul as well as to a butterfly, the archetypal symbol of metamorphosis, transformation, and transcendence. Bulfinch also calls our attention to the artistic representations of Psyche as a beautiful maiden with the wings of a butterfly. In referring to humor, Freud frequently emphasized its transformative and transcendent (over harsh realities) qualities.

imprint on the formation and expression of character in general and on creative capacities in particular. *Humor and Psyche* explores these domains as well.

Despite the richness of humor and its relevance to theory and technique, as well as to character and creativity, for many years psychoanalysts, with some notable exceptions (e.g., Kris, 1938), simply relegated it to the periphery of psychoanalytic concerns or focused on the dangers of humor in the psychoanalytic situation (e.g., Kubie, 1971). *Humor and Psyche* strives for a more balanced perspective and considers humor in a fuller context.

Although Bergmann and other authors included in this book examine historical and contemporary contributions to the psychoanalytic literature on humor, which I will not repeat here, I will cite one outstanding example. Winnicott's (1971) highly original ideas of playing in transitional space open new theoretical pathways to explore humor in child development, in the treatment situation, and in larger cultural contexts.

Over the past decade we have witnessed the beginning of a healthy corrective to the previous neglect or underappreciation of the value of humor in the psychoanalytic situation, perhaps most clearly articulated by Poland (1990, 1996), who describes humor as potentially facilitating the therapeutic encounter, which in turn can enhance the capacity to view oneself and one's world with mature humor. Bollas (1995) explores the early determinants of the capacity for humor which, he suggests, derives from the mother's ability to transform the infant's ordinary misery into amusement and, ultimately, to contribute to dreams and free associations: "Mothers 'crack up' their babies, thus establishing a precedent for other types of cracking up, such as the one that occurs when the self breaks down in a dream or the deconstruction of speech in the process of free association" (p. 7).

ORIGIN

Although Freud explored similarities and differences among the comic, irony, wit, puns, jokes, and humor, in my introductory remarks I refer generically to humor in limning its fundamental characteristics. In developing his topographic theory of the mind, Freud unexpectedly found himself exploring the domain of humor. While examining his own dreams and those of his patients, he noted that they frequently contained humorous or comic elements such as puns and jokes. In "The Interpretation of Dreams" (1900) and in "Jokes and Their Relation to the Unconscious" (1905), he demonstrated that the manifest content of dreams and jokes yields pleasure through their disguised expression of unconscious wishes, resulting in a partial lifting of repression and an economic expenditure of psychic energy. Moreover, he took pains to show that such underlying mechanisms as condensation, displacement, reversals into opposites, and substitute formation operate in dreamwork and jokework.

Much later, after articulating his structural theory in "The Ego and the Id" (1923), Freud once again turned his attention to the topic of humor (1927) and described the unique relationship of the superego to the ego:

> If it is really the super-ego, which, in humour, speaks such kindly words of comfort to the intimidated ego, this will teach us that we still have a great deal to learn about the nature of the super-ego. Furthermore, not everyone is capable of the humorous attitude. It is a rare and precious gift, and many people are even without the capacity to enjoy humorous pleasure that is presented to them. And finally, if the super-ego tries, by means of humour, to console the ego and protect it from suffering, this does not contradict its origin in the parental agency [p. 166].

Without responsive parental caretaking, the infant is easily overwhelmed by the terrors of its helpless, dependent state. Similarly, without the consolation and protection of the superego, the ego is easily intimidated and condemned to suffer.

The superego's benevolent attitude toward the ego helps generate humor that is likely to be soothing and comforting. A harsher superego contributes to humor that is more likely to be biting or attacking or perhaps leads to the suppression of humor altogether. Humor bears the unique imprint not only of the individual's instinctual endowment, complementary meshing of primary and secondary process, and compromise formations, but also of the individual's history of internalized object relations.

OVERVIEW

The first section of *Humor and Psyche* focuses on historical and theoretical perspectives. After describing the pervasive influence of Jewish humor on Freud's attitudes and associations, Bergmann proceeds to explicate Freud's theory of humor from the topographic frame of reference in "Jokes and Their Relation to the Unconscious" (1905) and from the structural frame in "Humour" (1927). Bergmann notes that the post-Freudian analytic literature on humor deals with the developmental acquisition of the capacity for humor, the nature of humor itself, and the role of humor in the analytic process. He observes that these contributions rarely have gone beyond the theoretical parameters set by Freud but that new approaches to the understanding and use of humor in the psychoanalytic situation are starting to evolve, such as those of Rose (1969), Chasseguet-Smirgel (1988), and Poland (1996).

Sanville's unifying theme is the inseparability of humor and play, which she initially views from historical and literary perspectives. After highlighting critical aspects of Freud's formulations of jokes, humor, and the comic, she synthesizes relevant contributions of recent theorists, with particular reference to Winnicott. "A sense of humor would be, in Winnicott's terms, evidence of freedom, the opposite of the rigidity of defenses that characterize illness." Sanville provides brief clinical vignettes illustrating the role of humor in the treatment of children and adolescents and concludes her chapter with a more extensive case presentation of the treatment of a man toward the end of his life in which humor and play were vital components of the therapeutic encounter.

From a postmodernist perspective, Barratt views one intriguing aspect of humor, the phenomenon of the crack, as exemplified by an excerpt from the writings of George Orwell. Barratt links this phenomenon with intimations of insufficiency and incapacity, with meanings paradoxically existing within and beyond human discourse, and ultimately with castration and death—ineluctable companions of every human endeavor.

After exploring both classical and contemporary psychoanalytic views, Grotstein creatively plays with a synthesis of the ideas of several theorists and extends their application to the realm of humor. Grotstein makes use of Bion's description of the integration and complementarity of primary and secondary processes in the production of humor, and he builds on Lacan's basic premise that the unconscious is socially, linguistically, and semiotically structured; capable of a sophistication of a high order; able to transform syntax; and generate the complex, surprising narratives of dreams and jokes. In his vignettes, Grotstein focuses on the unique properties of humor, including its cognitive and affective poetic compression and its capacity to help both participants in the therapeutic encounter to decenter and entertain new perspectives.

The second section of this book deals with the relationship of humor to various aspects of the therapeutic process. After a thoughtful examination of the literature, Baker defines what in his view constitutes the appropriate use of humor in the psychoanalytic situation: "Humor must approximate an interpretation, in particular a transference interpretation and, as such, must always be offered prudently." While reaffirming the importance of abstinence and neutrality, Baker maintains that, when used appropriately, humor functions as a condensed language of transference interpretation closely linked to the patient's preconscious and unconscious. He also points out the dangers of the misuse of humorous remarks as countertransference enactments. There is an interesting tension between Baker's wariness about the use of humor in any form in working with very disturbed patients and Giovacchini's belief that humor can be used judiciously in some cases with patients who have regressed to primitive mental states. Baker emphasizes that, to be effective, humor must emerge in the context of an intact treatment alliance with the analyst closely attuned to the patient.

After recalling the chilling interactions with humorless analysts in the course of his analytic training, Giovacchini focuses on the enlivening effects of humor on the therapeutic process. Expanding upon the ideas of Winnicott, Giovacchini suggests that humor, which both lives in and helps to preserve the transitional space essential for effective treatment, is a developmental achievement like the capacity to play. Without that well-developed capacity, the analyst is severely limited in his or her self-analytic efforts, particularly with regard to empathic awareness of countertransference enactments. Giovacchini also points out the linkages between humor and creativity in the therapeutic process.

Meissner demonstrates that humor is always overdetermined and reflects multiple aspects of meaning and motive. He assesses the role and function of humor for both therapist and patient along three dimensions: transference–countertransference, real relation, and therapeutic alliance. Meissner concludes that humor enacted within the transferential sphere or the real relationship will most likely have deleterious effects, whereas humor expressed within the framework of the alliance is likely to enhance the efficacy of treatment.

The last section of *Humor and Psyche* explores the relationship of humor to character and creativity. Judith Dupont's essay, deftly translated by Susan Fairfield, focuses on the central role of humor in Freud's and Ferenczi's 25-year correspondence comprising nearly 1250 letters. By carefully examining the content and style of Freud's and Ferenczi's use of humor, Dupont reveals important aspects of their characters, theoretical predispositions, and vicissitudes of their conflictual, creative relationship.

Rodman, whose earlier work (1987) has become essential reading for scholars and clinicians interested in deepening their understanding of Winnicott's pioneering contributions, begins his chapter in *medias res* with excerpts from previously unpublished letters of Winnicott. Rodman artfully demonstrates the interweaving of Winnicott's comic spirit, capacity for play, and his innovations as a psychoanalytic theorist of the first rank.

In an interdisciplinary tour de force, Feder examines the role of humor in the creative process, exemplified by the music of American composer Charles Ives. He reveals the defensive aspects of Ives's humor, his denial of his underlying seriousness of purpose and affective intensity.

Feder traces the close connection of Ives's humor to his ongoing conflicts over bisexuality, to his conflictual identifications with his father, and to his incomplete mourning following the death of his father. Although Ives referred to his composition as a *scherzo* (joke), Feder uncovers the multiple layers of meaning condensed within Ives's humor, which is an inextricable part of Ives's creative process and product.

SUMMARY

As the contributors to *Humor and Psyche* clearly demonstrate, humor belongs not in the margins but in the center of psychoanalytic thought and practice. While psychoanalysts have understandably been concerned with the ways in which humor can distort the treatment process, they have, until quite recently, been reluctant to explore the ways in which humor can enhance that process. Psychoanalytic approaches can also contribute significantly to the understanding of humor as a complex developmental achievement. When the capacity for humor is severely limited, psychic life is correspondingly narrowed and comparatively impoverished. Humor infuses psychotherapy and other human endeavors with vitality, playfulness, and creativity.

REFERENCES

Bollas, C. (1995), *Cracking Up: The Work of Unconscious Experience.* New York: Hill & Wang.

Bulfinch, T. (1970), *Bulfinch's Mythology.* New York: Harper & Row.

Chasseguet-Smirgel, J. (1988), The triumph of humor. In: *Fantasy, Myth and Reality: Essays in Honor of Jacob A. Arlow,* ed. H. Blum et al. Madison, CT: International Universities Press, pp. 197–213.

Freud, S. (1900), The interpretation of dreams. *Standard Edition,* 4 & 5. London: Hogarth Press, 1953.

——— (1905), Jokes and their relation to the unconscious. *Standard Edition,* 8:9–236. London: Hogarth Press, 1960.

——— (1923), The ego and the id. *Standard Edition,* 19:12–66. London: Hogarth Press, 1961.

——— (1927), Humour. *Standard Edition,* 21:159–166. London: Hogarth Press, 1961.

Kris, E. (1938), Ego development and the comic. In: *Psychoanalytic Explorations in Art.* New York: International Universities Press, 1952, pp. 204–216.

Kubie, L. S. (1971), The destructive potential of humor in psychotherapy. *Amer. J. Psychiatr.,* 127:861–866.

Poland, W. S. (1990), The gift of laughter: On the development of a sense of humor in clinical analysis. *Psychoanal. Quart.*, 59:197–225

———— (1996), *Melting the Darkness: The Dyad and Principles of Clinical Practice.* Northvale, NJ: Aronson

Rodman, F. R. (1987), *The Spontaneous Gesture: Selected Letters of D. W. Winnicott.* Cambridge, MA: Harvard University Press.

Rose, G. J. (1969), King Lear and the use of humor in treatment. *J. Amer. Psychoanal. Assn.*, 17:927–940.

Winnicott, D. W. (1971), *Playing and Reality.* New York: Basic Books.

PART I

Historical and Theoretical Perspectives

1

The Psychoanalysis of Humor and Humor in Psychoanalysis

MARTIN S. BERGMANN

On my bookshelf I see the 24 volumes of the *Standard Edition* of Freud's writings. For years these volumes have been subjected to rough use, and on most the gold letters have dimmed and the covers are torn. Not all volumes, however, have fared that badly. Among those that look pristine is Volume 8, "Jokes and Their Relation to the Unconscious" (1905a). No class has ever asked me to teach this book, and I wonder for a moment whether I ever made use of it. Then I recall that in 1976, when I published a paper dealing with Freud's Jewish identity, I did refer to it. There I explained Freud's interest and enjoyment of Jewish jokes.

> The Jewish joke, a unique creation of the Jews, requires no adherence to Judaism in any organized sense, and can, therefore, become a vehicle for the expression of feelings of solidarity for those who have retained a sense of belonging, without religious or national affiliation (p. 118).

Readers of "the Interpretation of Dreams" (1900) could not miss the point that Freud was a Jew. However, in that book being a Jew was experienced by Freud as a burden. It stood in the way of his becoming a

Read before the Postdoctoral students of Adelphi University as the Carol Feder Memorial Lecture, April 15, 1998.

professor. It illustrates the role of anti-Semitism in shaping Freud's attitude toward his father Jacob and his subsequent selection of Hannibal as his hero. In "Totem and Taboo" Freud (1913) excluded any reference to Jewish history. When Freud wrote "Moses and Monotheism" (1939), one of his main points was that Moses was an Egyptian and therefore not a Jew. By contrast, the joke book can be called the most Jewish of Freud's writings.

JEWISH HUMOR

In his letters to Fliess (Masson, 1985), Freud compared himself and Fliess to two *Schnorrers* (Yiddish for beggars). Dividing a province between them, Freud claimed psychology and Fliess biology. Freud's letter to Fliess on June 22, 1897, contained a strange phrase: "I must admit that I have recently started a collection of profound Jewish stories." The German equivalent is: "*Ich will gestehen, dass ich in letzter Zeit eine Sammlung tiefsinniger jüdischer Geschichten angelegt habe*" (Masson, 1986, p. 271). "I must admit" is a strange way of reporting what one would ordinarily assume was an honorable and even pleasurable activity. I interpret this to mean that the idea of writing a Jewish joke book evoked resistance in Freud. The joke book was published 10 years later with most of the Jewish emphasis eliminated.

Oring (1984) singled out one category of jokes, that of the Jewish *Schnorrer*:

> A *Schnorrer*, who was allowed as a guest into the same house every Sunday, appeared one day in the company of an unknown young man who gave signs of being about to sit down to the table. "Who is this?" asked the householder. "He's been my son-in-law," was the reply, "since last week. I've promised him his board for the first year" [Freud, 1905a, p. 112].

Since the joke book contains many such *Schnorrer* jokes, Oring believes that they belong to what he called Freud's unconscious biography. As a student, and even later in life, Freud accepted gifts from various acquaintances. The need to pay those debts was difficult. Oring (1984, p. 15) cites a letter of Freud's to his bride, written on August 18, 1883, where he described an attempt to borrow a guilden in order to loan it to a friend. In that letter he refers to his benefactors, his Hebrew teacher, Hammerschlag, his colleagues at the Brücker Institute, and Breuer as his "bankers." He writes that he was at first ashamed to accept these offers from his friends. He wrote to Martha that he decided to accept his indebtedness to good men of his own faith without feeling a sense of personal obligation. This attitude is typical of the Jewish *Schnorrer* who does not regard the gift he receives as charity, but feels entitled to it.

Jokes were used by Freud to master difficult situations. When he was confronted with the difficulty of becoming a professor (because he was a Jew), he collected Jewish jokes. When his sons were at the front facing death, he collected war jokes.

The famous letter to Fliess on September 21, 1897, in which Freud informed his friend that he had lost faith in his erotica, contains a Jewish saying:

> The expectation of eternal fame was so beautiful, as was that of certain wealth, complete independence, travels, and lifting the children above the severe worries that robbed me of my youth. Everything depended upon whether or not hysteria would come out right. Now I can once again remain quiet and modest, go on worrying and saving. A little story from my collection occurs to me: "Rebecca, take off your gown; you are no longer a bride" (p. 266).

It is amusing that this story was so difficult for the editor to decipher that Anna Freud's authority was required for explanation. Freud compared his lot to that of the former bride who refuses to accept that she is no longer a bride.

In "The Interpretation of Dreams" (1900), Freud shows how Jewish jokes emerged spontaneously when he was free associating:

> An impecunious Jew had stowed himself away without a ticket in the fast train to *Karlsbad*. He was caught, and each time tickets were inspected he was taken out of the train and treated more and more severely. At one of the stations on his *via dolorosa* he met an acquaintance, who asked him where he was traveling to. "To Karlsbad," was his reply, "if my constitution can stand it." My memory then passed on to another story: of a Jew who could not speak French and had been recommended when he was in Paris to ask the way to the rue Richelieu. Paris itself had for many long years been another goal of my longings; and the blissful feelings with which I first set foot on its pavement seemed to me a guarantee that others of my wishes would be fulfilled as well. "Asking the way was a direct allusion to Rome, since all roads lead to Rome" [p. 195].

The two Jewish stories occurred to Freud as an association as he was searching for an explanation of his inhibition to visiting Rome. After he overcame the inhibition Freud added in a footnote in 1909: "I discovered long since that it only needs a little courage to fulfill wishes which till then have been regarded as unattainable; and therefore became a constant pilgrim to Rome" (Freud, 1900, p. 194). In spite of remembering two Jewish jokes, Freud did not reach the conclusion in his self-analysis that being a Jew was connected with the prohibition on visiting Rome.

HERO OF THE TALE

The hero of the joke book is unquestionably Heinrich Heine. The first joke Freud subjected to a detailed examination was told by Heine. Gutman's *Concordance* (6 vols., 1984, International Universities Press) shows there are 41 references to Heine in Freud's work.

Heine introduces the delightful figure of the lottery agent and extractor of corns, Hirsch-Hyacinth of Hamburg, who boasts to the poet of his relations with the wealthy Baron Rothschild and finally says: "And, as true as God shall grant me all good things, Doctor, I sat beside Salomon Rothschild and he treated me quite as his equal—quite famillionairely" (p. 16). The neologism is a condensation of familiarly and millionaire.

Freud noticed that, once a joke is expressed in different words, it is not experienced as humorous. The two words *familiarly* and *millionaire* belong to two different universes of discourse. To combine them into one word is an illogical condensation that strikes one as comic. We should note that the Heine joke did not require the interpretation of an analyst. Any logician taking the trouble could have discovered this condensation. The same holds true for the rest of the joke book. To a significant extent, therefore, the joke book remains outside the mainstream of psychoanalysis.

Heinrich Heine was born in 1797 and died in 1856, the year Sigmund Freud was born. Being both German and Jewish, he occupies a middle position in the two traditions. Heine said about himself, "Within me the old lyrical poetry comes to an end, with me modern German lyrics begins" (Ewen, 1948, p. 240).

Ernest Jones (1955) in his biography of Freud reported that, when Freud made a visit to the Père Lachaise cemetery in Paris, he visited only two graves, that of Ludwig Börne and Heine. Börne, it will be recalled, was important to Freud because from him he got the idea of free associations. Freud particularly admired Heine's sarcasm. He often quoted Heine's remarks about philosophers: "With his nightcaps and the tatters of his dressing-gown he patches up the gaps in the structure of the universe" (Freud, 1933, p. 161). The statement was dear to him for he stated it in the introductory lectures (1933) as well as in an earlier letter to Jung on February 25, 1908 (McGuire, 1974).

Noteworthy is the quote from Heine in Freud's paper on narcissism. As to why God created the world, Heine makes God say, "Illness was no doubt the final cause of the whole urge to create. By creating, I could recover; by creating, I became healthy" (Freud, 1914, p. 85). This cita-

tion comes from the last stanza of Heine's "Seven Songs of Creation."
Heine's line is humorous as well as blasphemous. It attributes to God the
insight that a narcissistic state is an illness to be cured by creation.

In "Civilization and Its Discontents" (1930) Freud quoted Heine's
remarks:

> Mine is a most peaceable disposition. My wishes are: a humble cot-
> tage with a thatched roof, but a good bed, good food, the freshest
> milk and butter, flowers before my window, and a few fine trees be-
> fore my door; and if God wants to make my happiness complete, he
> will grant me the joy of seeing some six or seven of my enemies hang-
> ing from those trees [p. 110].

The rapid transition from the modest, idyllic image of a happy child
enjoying his milk to the openly sadistic imagery, also childlike in its freedom from guilt, acts as a shock. The ease with which Heine accepted his
own sadistic wishes acts as a relief from our own superego and gives us
pleasure. It was not an accident that Freud recalled this passage in a book
in which he was working through the need to accept civilization in spite
of the fact that it curbs our sexuality and aggression.

Heine had a profound influence on Freud's sense of humor, as the
following examples from Heine's writings indicate:

> My fellow unbeliever Spinoza [Freud, 1905a, p. 77].
> I have given up the God of Hegel, or rather, the Godlessness of
> Hegel [Ewen, 1948, p. 213].
> The Bible is the portable homeland of the Jewish people [quoted
> by Chasseguet-Smirgel, 1988, p. 210].
> The poet, that overgrown child (Ewen, 1948, p. 221); recalls
> Freud's essay of 1908, "Creative Writers and Daydreaming."
> Everyone knows what whippings are; but no one has yet made
> out what love is [Oring, 1984, p. 27].

Heine is said to have made a blasphemous joke on his deathbed.
When a friendly priest reminded him of God's mercy and assured him
that God would forgive his sins, Heine is said to have replied: "Bien sur
qu'il me pardonnera: c'est son métier" [Of course he'll forgive me: that's
his job] (Freud, 1905a, p. 114). His anecdote reminds us of the punster
joke and gallows humor, where a joke is made even though death is
imminent.

In a humorous vein Freud wrote to Pastor Pfister asking why the
religiously devout had not discovered psychoanalysis. He asked why did
one have to wait for a "Godless Jew." "Godless Jew" is a contradiction.
However, it does not strike us as a joke because it carries with it Freud's

complex sense of Jewish identity. The same idea can be transformed into a joke.[1]

> An atheist Jew sends his child to Trinity School. The child comes back explaining the mysteries of the Trinity—the father, the son, and the Holy Ghost. The father is infuriated. "How many times do I have to tell you that there is only one God and we don't believe in him!"

Anyone familiar with the way Freud spoke about his impending death will note a similarity to the way Heine described his imagined death to Alexander Dumas:

> You may no longer find me in my present apartment, 50 rue d'Amersterdam, and that I may have moved to another lodging, quite unknown to me—and I will not even be able to leave my new address with the porter in case tardy friends like you may ask for me. I have no illusion of my future residence. All I know is that you enter it through a drab and fetid passage, and this entrance displeases me in advance. In addition, my wife weeps whenever I talk of moving [Ewen, 1948, p. 226].

Perhaps more important than what Freud said on humor was the example he set by the humorous style with which he transmitted many of his most important ideas. "When you think of me, think of Rembrandt— a little light and a great deal of darkness."[2]

DREAM WORK AND JOKE WORK

The interest in dreams led Freud to be interested in jokes. The two had much in common. Ricoeur (1970) called the joke book "a brilliant but prudent generalization of the laws of the dream-work" (p. 164).

> In "Jokes and their Relationship to the Unconscious" (1905a), Freud outlines a few precise steps leading to the economic theory of fore-pleasure. What this brilliant and meticulous essay sets before us is not a theory of art as a whole, but the study of a precise phenomenon, a precise pleasurable effect, pinpointed by the discharge of laughter. Within these narrow limits, however, the analysis goes very deep [p. 167].

Grotjahn (1951) noted that both dreams and jokes are often forgotten and both are difficult to recall. However, he also noted a significant

---

[1] I wish to thank Professor Yerushalmi for this joke.
[2] This anecdote was told to me by my teacher Paul Federn.

difference: The forgetting of jokes is usually regretted, but the forgetting of dreams evokes relief. He went to point out that both are forgotten because both require repression. He noted that to hear a joke is a passive experience, and it need not evoke guilt until one attempts to tell it, an active act, and could evoke guilt. He quotes the following joke as an example: A wife says to the husband, "If I die, you must ride to my funeral with my mother." The husband answers, "But that would spoil all the fun." We should not be surprised if a man who wishes to tell this joke forgets it. In psychoanalysis however, even the forgetting of dreams often evokes guilt, because unconsciously the patient knows that this forgetting is in the service of resistance.

In 1905, Freud made the following distinction: "Dreams serve predominantly for the avoidance of unpleasure; jokes for the attainment of pleasure, but all our mental activities converge in these two aims" (p. 180). This sentence was written 5 years after Freud's formulation that wish fulfillment is the central aim of all dreams, and Freud adhered tenaciously to this concept, even in 1933, when in the new introductory lectures, he revised the dream theory. He insisted that, at the very least, dreams aimed at fulfillment of wishes. One can spend a great deal of thought on the difference between wish fulfillment and attainment of pleasure, but the two are not easily separated from one another.

It is difficult to locate the significance of the joke book in Freud's thinking. One gains the impression that Freud himself may have been in the dark about the connection. The joke book follows in the footsteps of Freud's "The Psychopathology of Everyday Life" (1901) when he extended the explanatory range of psychoanalysis beyond the pathological realm towards a new depth psychology. The joke book appeared in 1905 together with the "Three Essays on the Theory of Sexuality" (1905b). Jones (1955) in his biography of Freud reports that the two were written simultaneously. While the latter was one of the most important books ever written by Freud and went through many editions, the joke book remained intact and was only supplemented once in 1927 by Freud's essay on humor (1927b). Strachey, in his preface to the joke book, states that the second edition appeared in 1912, but no further changes were made in it. It seems possible that this is related to the fact that this book lies somewhat apart from the rest of Freud's writings. He himself may have taken this view of it" (Freud, 1905a, p. 6).

Almost a century later we are entitled to say that "The Psychopathology of Everyday Life" (1901) was a permanent success. The term *Freudian slip* entered everyday speech. Freud attempted to deal with jokes by the same technique as parapraxes, but the same success did not crown the joke book.

Among the outstanding characteristics of the joke is that it occurs as if it were involuntary. The person who makes up the joke does not know ahead of time that he or she is going to tell this joke.

> Jokes possess yet another characteristic which fits satisfactorily in to the view of the joke-work which we have derived from dreams. We speak, it is true, of "making" a joke; but we are aware that when we do so our behaviour is different from what it is when we make a judgment or make an objection. A joke has quite outstandingly the characteristic of being a notion that has occurred to us "involuntarily." What happens is not that we know a moment beforehand what joke we are going to make, and that all it then needs is to be clothed in words. We have an indefinable feeling, rather, which I can best compare with an "absence," a sudden release of intellectual tension, and then all at once the joke is there—as a rule ready-clothed in words [Freud, 1905a, p. 167].

Freud's theory in writing the joke book consisted of two parts: First, an economic point of view postulated that humorous pleasure arises in the economy of expenditure of our psychic energy, a rather puzzling statement until we remember that the joke temporarily lifts the burden of repression. Energy is saved when either sexual or aggressive wishes become conscious without mobilizing censorship. In 1905 it was Freud's opinion that repression was itself the cause of neurosis, a statement he would later modify to say that only unsuccessful repression, resulting in the return of the repressed disguised as symptoms, was the cause of neurosis. In 1905 it was, therefore, natural for him to assume that freedom from repression, even of short duration, was experienced as pleasure. The second basic idea of the joke book was that the roots of humor go back to childhood. These two ideas were not well integrated.

By contrast to Freud, the proverbial dull professor looks at his notes and remarks, "At this point in my lecture, I am accustomed to tell the following joke."

Freud (1905a) concludes with memorable lines:

> For the euphoria which we endeavour to reach by these means is nothing other than the mood of a period of life in which we were accustomed to deal with our psychical work in general with a small expenditure of energy—the mood of our childhood, when we were ignorant of the comic, when we were incapable of jokes, and we had no need for humour to make us feel happy in our life [p. 236].

These lines suggest that, seen in a larger perspective, the book takes its place as dealing with a central theme in Freud's work—the difficulty we all have in the transition from the pleasure principle to the reality principle. This change takes place slowly, painfully, and incompletely. Humor helps us to make this transition with less pain and allows us to relinquish the reality principle in favor of the pleasure principle in a way that does not endanger our capacity to test reality.

ON HUMOR

Freud's (1927b) paper on humor is usually cited as a continuation of the book on jokes, and Freud himself made this connection. But the differences between the two are significant. The essay is wider in scope and attempts to capture something more profound. The joke is usually at the expense of someone, while the object of humor is the self. Humor demands a greater capacity for internalization. The essay on humor is based on Freud's discovery of narcissism and the reformulation of the structural point of view that divided the personality into superego, ego and id.

Central to the essay on humor is Freud's comment of a criminal who was being led out to the gallows on Monday who remarked, "Well, the week's beginning nicely" (p. 161). This joke, if it can so be called, belongs to a wide variety of German jokes generally designated as "gallows humor." A variant on the same story is about a criminal, on his way to execution, who asks for a scarf because he does not want to catch a cold. A third variant on the same theme is the French aristocrat who is led to the gallows when a black cat crosses his way. He says: "A man with prejudices would turn back at this point." The third variant is particularly interesting because the man behaves as if he is volunteering for the execution. Similar in spirit is the story of the punster whose puns so annoyed the king that he ordered his execution. In the last moment the king offered to pardon the punster if he promised never to make puns. He responded, "No noose is good news" and went cheerfully to the gallows. When pronounced correctly, the pun is funny in its own right, but the devotion to the craft and his willingness to die for it pokes fun at all martyrs.

> Like jokes and the comic, humour has something liberating about it; but it also has something of grandeur and elevation. . . . The grandeur in it clearly lies in the triumph of narcissism, the victorious assertion of the ego's invulnerability. The ego refuses to be distressed by the provocations of reality, to let itself be compelled to suffer (Freud, 1927b, p. 162).

> Humor in such a situation insists that one is above the dangers that the external world can inflict, that even in extremities, one can use the situation to extract some pleasure [p. 163].

> Humor is not resigned; it is rebellious. It signifies not only the triumph of the ego but also of the pleasure principle which is able here to assert itself against the unkindness of the real circumstances [p. 163].

> We obtain a dynamic explanation of the humorous attitude, therefore, if we assume that it consists in the humorist's having withdrawn the psychical accent from his ego and having transposed it on his super-ego. To the super-ego, thus inflated, the ego can appear tiny and all its interests trivial; and, with this new distribution of energy, it may become an easy matter for the super-ego to suppress the ego's possibilities of reacting [p. 164].

Anyone can tell a joke, but some people lack humor. Humor, as Freud discovered in 1927, is a developmental stage that not everyone has reached. In retrospect, we can say that the topographic model cramped Freud's range of ideas and that the structural hypothesis, dividing personality into ego, id, and superego, opened new vistas. The discovery of narcissism also contributed to Freud's capacity to see humor in a different way. What was new in Freud's essay on humor was the realization that humor becomes possible when the superego adopts a benign and loving attitude toward the ego. Conversely, a person is lacking in humor when his superego continuously attacks the ego.

Freud's analysis of humor is complex. In his view the danger of death brings about an increase in narcissism, which triumphs for a moment over adversity. At the same time a shift of cathexis takes place from the ego to a benevolent superego.

APOSTOLIC AND POSTAPOSTOLIC ERAS

On the basis of these two works by Freud, an extensive psychoanalytic literature on jokes and humor has grown, only a part of which I will comment on here. Valuable additions have been made, but strictly speaking, nothing fundamentally new was added. Later on, I will seek to answer the question why the literature on humor never went beyond the limitations set by Freud. Seen from this angle, the analytic literature falls into three groups: studies dealing with the development of a sense of humor in the child; studies dealing with the nature of humor; and finally, those studies dealing with the role of humor within the psychoanalytic process itself.

Not without humor, Arlow called those psychoanalysts who knew Freud face-to-face as "apostles," designating our own era as postapostolic. Among the apostles, three examined the ideas on humor. Theodor Reik, who knew Freud for many years, in 1929 investigated the role of introjection and projection in Jewish jokes. He may have been the first to compare the joke with manic depressive mechanisms. In German in 1935 and in English in 1948, Reik pursued the similarities between jokes and psychoanalytic interpretations. The *Oxford English Dictionary* defines surprise as "an act of being taken unawares," "to come upon the unexpectable," "to astonish by unexpectedness," and finally as "the feeling and mental state akin to astonishment and wonder caused by an unexpected occurrence or circumstances." Surprise in real life is the emotion evoked by an unexpected event. Since we are not in control of our lives, we encounter good and bad surprises. There are, however, many new events, including important events, that do not evoke surprise. Unlike waking life, dreams do not include external events; yet the emotion of surprise is frequently encountered in dreams. Reik was intrigued by the ways in which surprise emerged in dreams and jokes and, subsequently, in psychoanalytic interpretations.

Kohut doubted that the mastery of the ego over the fear of death in gallows humor ever was authentic. Following his general theory of narcissism, he reformulated Freud's idea as follows (1966):

> Humor and cosmic narcissism ... permit us to face death without having to resort to denial, are metapsychologically based not on a decathexis of the self through a frantic hypercathexis of objects but on a decathexis of the narcissistic self through a rearrangement and transformation of the narcissistic libido; and, in contrast of states of extreme object cathexis, the span of the ego is here not narrowed but the ego remains active and deliberate [p. 267].

> The profoundest forms of humor and cosmic narcissism therefore do not present a picture of grandiosity and elation but that of a quiet inner triumph with an admixture of undenied melancholy [p. 268].

In Kohut's view humor plays a role in the progress from information to knowledge and from knowledge to wisdom.

In Reik's (1948) view, surprise is experienced when we are asked to recognize something that we had known long ago but had repressed. The sudden return of the repressed into consciousness evokes the feeling of surprise in dreams. Jokes contain an unconscious path that resembles the repressed impulse or the repressed idea. The joke offers two kinds of pleasure, pleasure relating to the form of the joke and pleasure relating to the enjoyment of sexual or aggressive wishes without punishment by the superego. In every joke there is a momentary feeling of danger, but that feeling, being brief, contributes to the release. A joke cited by Reik (1948) fits well into the era in which it was written, for example: "To err is Truman" (p. 255). The substitution of "Truman" for "human" releases aggression against Truman. The person about to tell a joke, like the analyst about to make an interpretation, is momentarily in danger. The joke may fall flat, exposing the teller, or the interpretation may evoke criticism in the analysand. Reik also cites the anecdote that, when Gustav Mahler was the conductor of the Vienna Opera, a young violinist was recommended to him with the statement that he was very modest. Mahler replied: "What has he done to be modest about?" It is not likely that many readers will find this anecdote humorous. In my interpretation the intercessor for the young man used "modest" as a euphemism for inhibited and Mahler unmasked the euphemism.

Whether an anecdote is funny or not depends on the connotation it evokes in the listener. As an example I will cite a remark by Groucho Marx. He applied to a swimming club, only to be told that Jews would not be accepted. He then asked: "What about my son who is half Jewish. Will he be allowed to enter the pool up to his knees?" The response is clever, and the anti-Semitism of the club is exposed as absurd. However, whether one finds it humorous depends on how seriously one takes anti-Semitism. Freud had commented on such jokes, emphasizing the sudden transposition from one realm to another. As another example, I recall two quips by Churchill against Clement Atlee, his rival in the election from the Labor Party. Churchill called Atlee "a sheep in sheep's clothing." Another time he described him as a "a modest man that has much to be modest about." While there is much to be admired in the injection of humor into a political debate, I am not sure that Atlee and the Labor Party at that time found these quips humorous. The fact that Churchill lost the election in 1946 nevertheless shows that humor, "nonomnivincet."

Ernst Kris (1938), who was personally close to Freud, pointed out that, when a joke is told, the ego dominates the primary processes. It is the overcoming of the fear that gives pleasure. Often, what was once considered dangerous, but is no longer, is now considered humorous. When the ego acquires domination over what was formerly feared, a sense of pleasure ensues. Kris saw the comic as a mechanism of defense. As long as humor was seen as a resistance, humor was seldom discussed in the psychoanalytic situation.

In his Freud lecture *Psychoanalytic Avenues to Art*, Waelder (1965), who also knew Freud personally, pointed out that the ego is the problem-solving agent of the mind. The ego derives satisfaction not only from the solution itself, but from the economy of means and the elegance with which the solution was arrived at. "The beauty seems to lie in the economy of means; a formal quality which, in this case, can itself be seen as satisfying a fantasy, viz., that of the victory of mind over brute force" (p. 46). As an example he cites the beauty of the bullfighter in escaping being gored in the last possible moment (p. 46). "The beauty of a fine chess problem lies in the fact that a rather inconspicuous move, which at first glance seems to be irrelevant to the issue of the game or even to take the player further away from the goal of victory, should turn out to be the very one that secures victory in record time" (p. 47). For the connoisseur formal beauty can become more important than the latent content. When this happens, a shift takes place from "id pleasure" to "ego pleasure" (p. 33). Waelder believes that great paintings speak to us because they also contain a great deal of economy. It would take many words to express what a certain look conveys in a painting by Rembrandt. Because Waelder had a wider understanding of art, he could illustrate better than Freud what was meant by artistic economy.

As to the role of humor, Waelder cited the anecdote of the French aristocrat, who during the French revolution was walking up to the guillotine, stumbled, and remarked: "A superstitious Roman would now have turned back" (p. 58). In Waelder's interpretation the aristocrat pretends he is still free to turn back if he so wishes, but he is not afraid of superstition. Had he actually believed in what he said, he would have been psychotic, but only pretending to believe it, he assumes a position above fate and refuses to accept mentally the destiny he is powerless to avert.

In 1946 Edith Jacobson contributed a paper, "The Child's Laughter," in which she presented the case of a 50-year-old woman suffering from a severe depression (pp. 48–49). When she emerged from her depression, she turned into a different person—charming and brilliant with an excellent sense of humor—and would laugh at other people as well as at herself. Her sense of humor was related to her childhood. When she was about 4 years old, she saw a boy urinate. The sight amused her. Jacobson believed that the amusement was a substitute for erotic stimulation. Jacobson saw the secret of the comic film as a tentative identification with the suffering of the hero, followed by a quick detachment (p. 59). As the danger no longer applies to the observer, he can derive a sense of pleasure from the situation. Jacobsen quotes Nietzsche who said, "to laugh is to enjoy damage with good conscience" (p. 59).

In 1951, under the influence of Ernst Kris, Martha Wolfenstein studied the sense of humor of children. She found that, up to adolescence, children ignore the double meaning of words:

> Why did the moron jump off the Empire State Building?
> Because he wanted to make a smash hit on Broadway.
> There was also the alternative answer: Because he wanted to show that he had guts [p. 337].

Children ignore the double meaning of "hit on Broadway" and "he had guts." To cite another example: "Simple Si, why do you take the bicycle to bed with you?" "So I don't walk in my sleep" (p. 343).

The latent content of the Empire State Building joke refers to falling with connotations of castration and death. The fright of this imagined situation is still vivid to children, because their capacity to master such fears is not wholly established. The original fright is reevoked but quickly moderated by a sense of elation as the child realizes that he can feel excited without being overwhelmed. The latent meaning of the "bicycle in bed" joke refers to nocturnal activities, particularly masturbation. Here too, there is a similar triumph over anxiety.

Wolfenstein observed a difference between a dream and a joke. The dream adheres to the visual imagery, while the joke uses the word to dissolve the image. The substitution of the word for the image mitigates anxiety. She also noted that in poetry the multiple meanings of a word reinforce each other, approximating diffusion of images in dreams and thus intensifying their emotional impact, while the joke works in the opposite direction. This is the reason why lines of poetry are remembered and jokes are quickly forgotten.

In 1955 Phyllis Greenacre published a dual psychoanalytic pathography on Swift and Carroll. *Gulliver's Travels* and the Alice books have in common a rapid change in bodily size. Greenacre observed similar impairment in the body image among some of her analysands. This led her to investigate the childhood of Swift and Carroll. She interpreted their humor as a defiance and attack on reason and saw nonsense as an aggressive attack upon the reality principle.

It is true that nonsense rhymes free us from the restriction of logic, but anyone familiar with the "Jabberwocky" by Lewis Carroll (in *Alice through the Looking Glass*) knows that liberation from logic is only a small aspect of the success of this nonsense rhyme. Students of Carroll know that the first four lines of this verse were written long before the rest of the poem. Carroll himself explained these four lines as a stanza of Anglo-Saxon poetry:

> Twas brilling, and the slithy toves
> Did gyre and gimble in the wabe;
> All mimsy weer the borogoves,
> And the mome raths outgrabe.

To read these lines is to feel a sense of stillness of long duration. It is like the stillness before the storm when we feel that something ominous will happen. The nonsense words convey a feeling of apprehension beyond the power of words. In the second stanza we are confronted with the monster. The rest of the poem describes the battle, the sense of danger, and the eventual victory over the monster. Nonsense rhymes are akin to music. They are rich in connotation but lack denotation. We should keep in mind that, to the preverbal child, all words that adults use appear as nonsense rhythms. They convey a meaning and have connotations of happiness, approval, anger, and criticism long before their denotation is known. Carroll captured that feeling for us. Thus, in development, connotation precedes denotation, but when we learn a foreign language, we learn what words denote, but often miss their connotation. For the same reason we often cite a foreign expression, not because there is no denotative equivalent in our own language, but because the foreign word carries untranslatable connotations.

We remember the Queen's exclamation in *Alice in Wonderland:* "Verdict first, trial later." It is a mockery of the achievement of justice in the Anglo-Saxon world, but on a deeper level the Queen speaks the language of our id, for in the emotional realm, verdict precedes trial. It is only with difficulty that we listen to evidence designed to change our mind about a topic we feel strongly about.

HUMOR IN THE PSYCHOANALYTIC SITUATION

During the Paris Congress in 1957, a significant symposium on variations on psychoanalytic technique took place. The role of jokes in psychoanalysis was one of the subjects discussed. Loewenstein (1958) was of the opinion that the right joke, told at the right moment, may be used instead of an interpretation, provided the patient's sense of humor made him accessible to a particular type of joke. The advantage of the joke lies in its economy. He also quoted Kris as saying that it is impossible to tell a joke to certain patients (p. 208). These are the patients who either lack a sense of humor or do not respond to a particular type of humor. Some patients react to jokes as if the analyst were making fun of them, while others respond to jokes as seduction. Jokes told by patients often express seductive wishes or competition with the analyst. In general Loewenstein admonished that the analyst should not use the same defense mechanisms as the patient. Even more sharply, Rosenfeld (1958), representing the Kleinian point of view, regarded the telling of jokes as an undesirable modification of analytic technique because it circumvents the resistance and is experienced as seductive. Kubie (1971) also emphasized the danger of using humor in psychotherapy.

A new approach is slowly emerging. When the analysand becomes capable of humor, important changes have taken place. Rose (1969) may have been the first psychoanalyst to apply humor to the psychoanalytic situation. The idea was implicit in Freud's essay on humor, but the fear that humor may be in the service of resistance stood in the way of applying Freud's insight to the psychoanalytic situation itself. In a memorable phrase Rose saw art, neurosis, the joke, and the lie as four types of effort by men, banished from paradise, to escape the reality principle. The Fool in Shakespeare's *King Lear* was seen as attempting to penetrate Lear's madness with careful dosages of reality made palatable with wit (p. 927). Sanity, according to Rose, requires a critical mirror, but when reality tolerance is low, the mirror had better be tinted or funny (p. 928).

Lear: Dost thou call me a fool, boy?
Fool: All thy other titles thou have given away [p. 929].

King Lear, by dividing his kingdom, emasculated himself and turned his two daughters into phallic women. The emasculation was displaced upward in the form of losing his mind (p. 930).

In Rose's (1969) view, Shakespeare has taught us that humor can be used as a therapeutic tool. He sees humor as having a double aspect: a kindly side allied with the observant ego and the ironic side strengthening resistances. Humor can also be directed against the archaic elements of the superego. Rose concluded that: "Humor may be used with such patients to help provide a needed protection for ego boundaries and impoverished self-esteem" (p. 937).

Roustang (1987) applied Freud (1927b) and Waelder (1965) on humor to the analytic situation: when an analytic patient can laugh at himself, we are at the beginning of the end of the analysis.

> To laugh at oneself is to take the minimal distance towards oneself which allows us to appraise what we do, think, and say [Roustang, 1987, p. 714].

> If, by chance, laughter at ourselves or with others were turned into laughter at the expense of others, then that laughter would become sarcasm [p. 712].

> There are, for example, tragic circumstances which forbid all laughter, even though the extreme tension produced by tragic vision is liable to trigger crazy fits of laughter. If, by accident, the pallbearers carrying a corpse make some clumsy blunder, even the most bereaved of the entourage might be shaken with uncontrollable laughter [p. 712].

Roustang (1987) concludes with an example where he succeeded in making a paranoid laugh. A paranoid writer believes that, as soon as he will get his work published, the analyst will attack him with his own pen. Roustang commented:

> "You are absolutely right. My heart will leap with joy when I see the first line of yours in print. For you know that I keep a well-sharpened pen ready to cut you to pieces." He burst out laughing and since then, he has never alluded to my words as menacing. I consider him cured [p. 718].

Roustang did not reflect on this episode. I believe that he got the paranoid to laugh because he expressed dramatically what the patient thought, but did not quite dare articulate. For the analysand to know that the

analyst grasps his suspicion and yet acts humorously towards it offers relief and enables him to laugh. I do not, however, believe that this laughter cured the patient.

Chasseguet-Smirgel (1988) opened her essay with a comparison between humor and melancholia. Humor brings with it a feeling of elation. She raised the question whether humor is more than just a manic defense. Citing Kris (1938), she found that humor protects the humorist against the loss of love. She concluded that the humorist was a person trying to be his own loving mother (p. 205) and added the caution that this loving mother has never been truly assimilated into the ego: the approving mother was occasionally glimpsed, but without ever becoming a psychic reality. Splitting within the ego takes place because part of the ego recognizes its helplessness while the other plays at denying it (p. 206). She cited Baudelaire (1855) that in paradise laughter was unknown; laughter and tears are the children of woe; man laughs because "he has lost his paradisical state of completeness"(Chasseguet-Smirgel, 1988, p. 206). Baudelaire's statement, we might say, was a Freudian insight a year before Freud was born. Chasseguet-Smirgel, like Freud, emphasized the relationship between humor and death. "Humor at its most sublime is produced in the face of death" (p. 211). She then cited Freud's own contribution to "gallows humor": when the Gestapo demanded that he sign a statement that he was correctly treated before departure, Freud added, "I can heartily recommend the Gestapo to everyone" (p. 211).

Chasseguet-Smirgel noted that Freud's (1927a) essay on humor was written only a week after his article on fetishism. Both are based on a split within the ego. Citing the man led to the gallows, she found that he resembles the fetishist in that part of his ego denies the execution as if he were only playing at being executed.

Another example where humor represents triumph over adversity is Oscar Wilde's quip, "If this is how Queen Victoria treats her prisoners, she doesn't deserve to have any." The statement reverses the relationship between sovereign and prisoner. Oscar Wilde acts as if he agreed to become prisoner out of his high regard for the queen. Unlike gallows humor anecdotes, this was written by a man who was actually a prisoner at the time when he made this remark.

In a series of papers (1971, 1975, and 1990) and more recently in his book (1996), Poland, like Rose, also found that humor can play an important role in the psychoanalytic situation. "No matter the extent that the patient's humor may serve as an avenue for emotional discharge, just as a dream might; nonetheless the use of humor inevitably implies concern for the effect one has on another" (p. 173). Poland (1996) goes on to speak about the "gift of laughter": "A capacity for sympathetic laughter at oneself and one's place in the world. . . . With such humor there is an acceptance of oneself for what one is, an ease of being amused even if bemused" (p. 174). Poland differentiates between those analysands who never reach the capacity for humor and those whose humor became inhibited by a development of compulsive neurosis or depression. Poland concludes that "mature humor is a reflection of analytic work successfully done" (p. 181).

Poland found that the development of a sense of humor in an analysand was one of the happy outcomes of psychoanalytic work, even though it was an unintended by-product. As an example Poland cited a patient: "All right I will look at reality, but only as a tourist" (p. 180). I found the metaphor "tourist" apt, because I myself often say to patients we will not make headway as long as you are a tourist in your own analysis.

Bader (1993) confirmed Poland's observations that humor in treatment can have beneficial results if it increases the patient's sense of safety. He points out that an analyst whose repertoire goes only from flat to matter-of-fact fails to convey to his patient that he is enjoying his work. By so doing, he may repeat a pattern from which the patient suffered as a child, that the parents did not enjoy him. The marked change in the attitude of psychoanalysts toward humor of their own or that of their analysands reflects a change that has taken place in the way psychoanalysts themselves experience their work. It is striking that these new discoveries were implicit in Freud's (1927b) paper on humor.

There is a wonderful moment in Goethe's preamble to *Faust*. God, his angels, and Satan are assembled. The angels praise God. The scene is modeled on Job. The devil apologizes that he cannot join the angels in hymns of praise. Were he to try, he would make God laugh, except that God had long overcome the need to laugh. The gods of Greece could laugh and often did, as, for example, when Vulcan ensnared Venus (his wife) and Arius, the god of war, so that they could not extricate themselves. But the God of the Bible does not laugh. Even Jesus during his earthy sojourn told parables but never laughed. Only we human beings can laugh at ourselves; laughter is at the center of our humanity. We relinquish this capacity at our peril. As therapists, we should make use of this capacity and make sure that it is not lost. In this perspective Freud's work on jokes and humor belongs to the core of psychoanalysis.

REFERENCES

Bader, M. J. (1993), The Analyst's Use of Humor. *Psychoanal. Quart.*, 62:23–51.
Bergmann, M. S. (1976), Moses and the evolution of Freud's Jewish identity. In *Judaism and Psychoanalysis*, ed. M. Ostow. New York: Ktav, 1982, pp. 155–141.

Chasseguet-Smirgel, J. (1988), The triumph of humor. In *Fantasy, Myth and Reality: Essays in Honor of Jacob A. Arlow*, ed. H. Blum. Madison, Ct: International Universities Press, pp. 197–213.

Ewen, F. (1948), *Heinrich Heine, Self-Portrait and Other Prose Writings*. Secaucus, NJ: Citadel Press.

Freud. E. L., ed. (1960), *Letters of Sigmund Freud*. New York: Basic Books.

Freud, S. (1900), The interpretation of dreams. *Standard Edition*, 4 & 5. London: Hogarth Press, 1953.

———— (1901), The psychopathology of everyday life. *Standard Edition*, 6. London: Hogarth Press, 1960.

———— (1905a), Jokes and their relation to the unconscious. *Standard Edition*, 8. London: Hogarth Press, 1960.

———— (1905b), Three essays on the theory of sexuality. *Standard Edition*, 7:130–243. London: Hogarth Press, 1953.

———— (1908), Creative writers and day-dreaming. *Standard Edition*, 9:141–153. London: Hogarth Press, 1959.

———— (1913), Totem and taboo. *Standard Edition*, 13:165–190. London: Hogarth Press, 1955.

———— (1914), On narcissism: An introduction. *Standard Edition*, 14:73–102. London: Hogarth Press, 1957

———— (1927a), Fetishism. *Standard Edition*, 21:152–157. London: Hogarth Press, 1961.

———— (1927b), Humour. *Standard Edition*, 21:159–166. London: Hogarth Press, 1961.

———— (1930), Civilization and its discontents. *Standard Edition*, 21:64–145. London: Hogarth Press, 1961.

———— (1933), New introductory lectures on psycho-analysis. *Standard Edition*, 22:5–182. London: Hogarth Press, 1964.

———— (1939), Moses and monotheism. *Standard Edition*, 23:7–137. London: Hogarth Press, 1964.

Greenacre, P. (1955), *Swift and Carroll: A Psychoanalytic Study of Two Lives*. New York: International Universities Press.

Grotjahn, M. (1951), The inability to remember dreams and jokes. *Psychoanal. Quart.*, 20:284–286.

Jacobson, E. (1946), The child's laughter. *The Psychoanalytic Study of the Child*, 2:39–60. New York: International Universities Press.

Jones, E. (1955), *The Life and Work of Sigmund Freud*, Vol. 2. New York: Basic Books.

Kohut, H. (1966), Forms and transformations of narcissism. *J. Amer. Psychoanal. Assn.*, 14:243–272.

Kris, E. (1938), Ego development and the comic. In *Psychoanalytic Explorations in Art*, New York: International Universities Press, pp. 204–216.

Kubie, L. (1971), The destructive potential of humor in psychotherapy. *Amer. J. Psychiatr.*, 127:861–866.

Loewenstein, R. (1958), Remarks on some variations on psycho-analytic technique. *Internat. J. Psycho-Anal.*, 39:203–210.

Masson, J. M. (1985), *The Complete Letters of Sigmund Freud to Wilhelm Fliess, 1887–1904*. Cambridge: Harvard University Press.

——— (1986), *Sigmund Freud Briefe an Wilhelm Fliess, 1887–1904*. Frankfurt: S. Fisher.

McGuire, W., ed. (1974), *The Freud/Jung Letters: The Correspondence Between Sigmund Freud and C. G. Jung*, trans. by R. Manheim & R. F. C. Hull. Bollingen Series 94. Princeton: Princeton University Press.

Oring, E. (1984), *The Jokes of Sigmund Freud: A Study in Humor and Jewish Identity*. Philadelphia: University of Pennsylvania Press.

Poland, W. S. (1971), The place of humor in psychotherapy. *Amer. J. Psychiatr.*, 128:635–637.

——— (1975), Tact as a psychoanalytic function. *Internat. J. Psycho-Anal.*, 56:155–162.

——— (1990), The gift of laughter on the development of a sense of humor in clinical psychoanalysis. *Psychoanal. Quart.*, 59:197–225.

——— (1996), *Melting the Darkness: The Dyad and Principles of Clinical Practice*. Northvale, NJ: Aronson.

Reik, T. (1929), Zur psychoanalyse des jüdischen witzes. *Imago*, 15:63–88.

——— (1935), *Der Uberraschte Psychologe*. Leiden, Holland: A. W. Sijthoff's Uitgeversmaatschappij, N.V.

——— (1948), *Listening with the Third Ear*. New York: Farrar, Straus.

Ricoeur, P. (1970), *Freud and Philosophy: An Essay on Interpretation*. New Haven, CT: Yale University Press.

Rose, G. (1969), *King Lear* and the use of humor in treatment. *J. Amer. Psychoanal. Assn.*, 17:927–940.

Rosenfeld, H. (1958), Contribution to the discussion on variations in classical technique. *Internat. J. Psychoanal.*, 39:238–239.

Roustang, F. (1987), How do you make a paranoid laugh? *Modern Language Notes,* 67:707–718.

Waelder. R. (1965), *Psychoanalytic Avenues to Art*. New York: International Universities Press.

Wolfenstein. M. (1951), A phase in the development of children's sense of humor. *The Psychoanalytic Study of the Child*, 6:336–350.

2

Humor and Play

JEAN B. SANVILLE

"There is no better play material in the world than words". . .
Lucy Sprague Mitchell, 1948

I think I was asked to do this chapter, not because of expertise on the topic of humor, but because I am a former child therapist whose little patients taught me much about playing, that later proved invaluable in treatment with adults. I was grateful for the invitation because it catapulted me into thinking more deeply and widely about the relationship of playing and humor. Playing is fun, but it does not always include the funny, the laughable, the *ludicrous*. That latter word, however, suggests the inseparable connections of humor with the ludic, with play. Both best thrive when there is a relatively safe ambiance that permits taking certain risks because the possible adverse consequences of one's actions or words are minimized. Therapists who engage in "talking cures" try to create in the clinical setting a safe playground for words, their own and those of the patient. They are also aware that the familial and broader social surround may either facilitate or threaten the necessary sense of freedom, both for their analysands and for themselves.

My explorations include a brief look at the history of humor in the Western world over the last several centuries and at some highlights from Freud's book on wit and humor. Although Freud thought that early play with words was the origin of humor, recent observation and research on infancy suggests earlier beginnings. In several vignettes described by analysts who treat children at different ages and stages, we glimpse some develomental aspects of humor in the oedipal, latency, and adolescent

31

years. Other analysts write of humorous interplay with adult patients, including at times the analyst's initiating this play. The final case story will be of an analysand of my own, a screenwriter of 80, whose long analysis resulted in his being able to adopt a humorous perspective on his own aging and increasing infirmities, and even on the inevitability of ultimate death. For our clinical work we analysts draw on our own humorous perspectives, and they may come in handy as we try to cope with the crisis of our profession in today's world.

A BRIEF HISTORY OF HUMOR

It is fun to play with the very word *humor,* which comes from the Latin word, *humor,* meaning moisture, and with the "there and then," shifts in what humor—or humour, in the British spelling—has denoted over time. It could seem that our topic is fluidity, in contrast to rigidity and stasis, indeed relevant to a central goal of psychoanalysis: eluding repetition compulsions. The latter was, as Freud (1914) suggested, to be accomplished by using the "transference as a playground," (p. 154), but the time may not have been ripe for him to develop that seminal idea. Clearly, we are looking at phenomena most evident when there exists the sense of freedom that accompanies playfulness; that internal sense is more likely to thrive in a congenial surround.

During the Renaissance, in the 16th century, humor came to denote an unbalanced mental condition, even a fixed folly or vice, hence a fit subject for comedy, which was then designed to correct irrational or immoral conduct. Ben Jonson detected two kinds: one, "true humour," in which the quality possesses a person, body and soul, and the other, "adopted humour," in which a person goes out of his way to affect certain modes of dress, speech, and social habits. Affected humors, he said, are simulations or imitations designed to make desired impressions, in accordance with shifts in fashions and cultural values, and characterize those who take pride in singularity—our "narcissistic personalities" perhaps? One of Jonson's critics (Drummond, 1618) labeled him posthumously as "a great lover and praiser of himelf, a contemner and scorner of others" (p. 243). His story is a reminder that humor can sometimes be a sharp weapon in the service of hostile aggression. Jonson's famous comedy *Every Man in His Humour* we might assume to deal with something akin to Winnicott's "true self" (although we could suspect that from Jonson's pen, this version might not necessarily be benign), while the later one, *Every Man Out of His Humour,* could be construed as comments on the "false self."

In the 18th and 19th centuries England claimed a richness of the comic stage, an abundance of individualists, including even madmen, *humorists* who were odd types (Tave, 1962). Humor then was seen not as affectation but as a natural expression of free men. Tave cites "another writer of 1777" who put it, "At length Commerce and her companion, Freedom, ushered into the world their genuine offspring, True Humour" (p. 886). But of course Freedom allowed for some differences of opinion: John Stuart Mill insisted that eccentricity was proportional to genius and originality, while Matthew Arnold argued that it was a sign of degeneration, this raw "doing as one likes" (Tave, 1962, p. 886).

Had psychoanalysts been around at the time, we can well imagine the stories they would tell to interpret the views of each. According to Anschutz (1962), Mill had been reared from infancy almost exclusively by his father, a strict disciplinarian of vigorous intellect, who made himself John's only teacher, strenuously subjecting him to subjects usually reserved for college study, so that he became astonishingly precocious. It is doubtful if he enjoyed anything like the playing that we associate with childhood. But his temperament—his humor?—was such that he seemed not unhappy. Not until age 20, when he became aware that his colleagues in a debating society looked upon him as a curiosity, a "made man," did he begin to have misgivings about the course upon which he had been set. But, afraid to tell his father, he dealt with his doubts in gloomy solitude, in a process akin to self-analysis. And he emerged with wider views of what might constitute human happiness, embracing the importance of social life and friendships previously denegrated by his father, and among those he loved were poets whom his father had condemned as "enemies of truth." He did this without abandoning pursuit of what he held of value in his father's teachings, the systemization of knowledge. But when he found that former ideas no longer held together, he did not drop them but wove them in anew. He could value the eccentricity that once characterized him, while developing new idiosyncratic ways.

Willey (1962) writes that Matthew Arnold was the eldest son of the headmaster of Rugby School, also an earnest man, but one who did not drive his boy to premature accomplishments. Matthew graduated Rugby with only second-class honors. He played with words early, winning a poetry prize while yet at Rugby. When Arnold went to Oxford, he was seen by his classmates to be dandyish, with such an air of ironic detachment—a sophisticated kind of humor in which the intended implication is the opposite of what is said—that they thought him a trifler. But his biographers have tended to interpret his levity as a mask, under which was a hidden ground of thought and austerity that soon surfaced. Had he been in analysis, he and his analyst might have seen in this behavior manifestations of a false self, motivated by some urge to transcend the earnestness of his father. As it was, he later put down such eccentricities, perhaps fearing them as endangering the unity of his true self, ultimately not so different from his father's. He went on to revere his father and to spend much of his life in advocating his father's educational and religious aims.

As we know, Freud (1905) was inclined to think that irony was no longer a joke, but he conceded it to be one of the technical methods of jokes (pp. 73–74). His translators had some trouble with the title of his 1905, "Wit and Its Relation to the Unconscious," since in English "wit" and "witty" have restricted meaning, applying only to the most refined and intellectual kinds of jokes. So they simply rendered "Witz" as "joke" and "Scherz" as "jest," and the reader is on his/her own in playing with the words in the English version.

In the 18th century, *wit* was distinguished from humor; it was a form of intellectual quickness, more upperclass, likely to be sharp and cutting, cleverness without passion or heart, believed to require book learning. Some of us who today consider the ideas of Matte Blanco (1988) would surmise that the thinking underlying such wit contains a minimal proportion of the symmetrical; cool logic with its asymmetrical qualities would prevail. *Humor,* in contrast to wit, was not the flash of an isolated sentence; it was more natural, receiving its strength from the life and relationships of the person. It was a universal gift, more wild, loose, fantastical, and not found in the well-bred, who were seen as repressing their feelings. Unlike wit, humor exhibited generous and benevolent sentiments, commanding fondness and love. Again, we who are toying with Matte Blanco's concepts would guess that this "natural" humor might contain some fairly high proportion of symmetrical thinking, where resemblances between people and ideas might seem greater than their differences.

By the end of the 18th century, humor was found to have intimacy with sympathy and pathos. Don Quixote brought a tear to the eye, as well as a smile to the lips. It was both sublime and ridiculous—a relief from the stresses and sadness of life. In the 19th century the word came to denote anything comic, that which makes us laugh; it was also applied to the ability to perceive and appreciate the comic. There are those who see the 20th century as manifesting an astringency; the emotions of audiences, essential in humor, being subordinated (Tave, 1962). However, wit has been revived with its hard, bright quality, and we witness a fusion of intelligence and feeling to be preserved in great poetry. There would seem to be cultural groups where feelings are still allowed abundant leeway.

It is of some significance that, at the end of this century (1997), a modern day Italian jester who *mixes* linguistic buffoonery with biting left-wing political satire wins the Nobel Prize for literature. Margaret Spillance, in *The Nation* of November 3, 1997, wrote that while Fo and his wife, Rame, had once been stars of Italy's variety shows, some 35 years ago they abandoned that model and began a type of folk theater that the Swedish society praised for its use of humor to open our eyes to the abuses and injustices of society. In a way we might say, in returning to their respective humble roots, they emulated the jesters of the Middle Ages in scourging authority and upholding the dignity of the downtrodden. Fo (1987) has outraged the rich, the religious, and the political right, and many great poets are profoundly dismayed at his being granted the prize. Fo himself is reported to have been as surprised as the rest of the world. He and his wife had been banned from the state-run airwaves for 15 years, so they took their shows to piazzas, tents, and factories. Although they broke with the Communist party in 1970, throughout the following decade they were the target of hate groups at home. Clearly, there are those who are very threatened by the power in the sort of humor and wit portrayed by Fo. In 1980 he and Franca Rame were barred from admission to the United States, but 4 years later were allowed to come to see the production of *Accidental Death* on Broadway. Although he is now 71 and has vision impaired by a recent stroke, Fo has been doing a new satiric comedy set in the Renaissance, *A Devil with Boobs*. His is a special humor that survives even vicious attacks; his playfulness, armed with aggressive energy enlisted in the aim of social betterment, persists even when the ambience is far from safe.

PLAY AND HUMOR: THE EARLY 20TH CENTURY

In the beginning of this century, there was a lot of attention to play, including in intellectual circles. Groos (1896), a professor of philosophy, was fascinated by inherited instinctual patterns, which were necessary in the struggle for life and for the preservation of the species. Instincts, however, do not first appear just when they are most needed; practice and exercise are required. Without play practice, the acts would have to be performed by fully developed inherited mechanisms, in which case animals would have no need to make progress intellectually. Animals, he concluded, do not play because they are young; rather, they have a period of youth in order to play—and human animals have a long such period. Groos (1901) was impressed with the fighting instinct and noted that both children and adults turn their belligerent energies into forms of amusement. Children delight in teasing, and youths and grown-ups are not far behind the children in such jests. They engage in deceptions that give them feelings of intellectual superiority. He notes that we celebrate April Fool's Day, when the civilized world gives itself over to such deceptions. He found more puzzling the question of whether there could be such a thing as the playful exercise of the sexual instinct. Citing Wundt on the characteristics of play, namely enjoyment, repetition, and pretence, he saw these as most evident in art and in poetry. But how could these qualities apply to sex? We speak, he noted, of the "sweet sportiveness of love" and found in that expression an element of truth if we compare sex with eating and drinking; in the latter, the real end, the preservation of life, is always in view, while in sex, the practical results are far removed and the acts themselves so pleasurable! So there could be room for make-believe. Children, susceptible to sexual excitement without yet knowing its meanings, show signs of preferences and favorites among friends and relatives, regardless of same or similar sex. And adults, Groos concluded, engage in special kinds of touching, sometimes, but not always, just as foreplay, but for the pleasure itself.

He wondered whether biological conceptions of play are not deeper than the psychological. Imitative play of the child is rarely conscious, so we cannot be certain it is pleasurable, he affirmed. Although Groos may not have been ready to assume that playing was itself an instinct, one that also would need practice to become fully functional, he seemed on the verge of that when he said that repetition could be considered an indispensable condition of play, since eventually impulsive movements will be performed for the sake of the pleasure gained. The true basis of playing is the feeling of freedom, not the idea that "this is only pretense." Instead, there is a voluntary acceptance of illusion. In any event, that author did find a psychological basis for play: in the exercise of attention, the desire to be an efficient cause, and in imagination. All of those features will enter into humor.

In 1905 Freud wrote "Jokes and Their Relation to the Unconscious." He observed that play appears in children while they are learning to make use of words and to put thoughts together. This play "probably obeys one of the instincts which compel children to practice their capacities" (p. 128), agreeing here with Groos, whom he quotes. In doing so, children experience pleasurable affects in rediscovering the familiar and the similarities between sounds. Since the intensive observation and research of infancy and early childhood was not yet available, Freud assumed that this play with words and thoughts, motivated by certain pleasurable effects of economy, is the first stage of jokes. Then, however, he goes on to say, this play is brought to an end by the strengthening of the critical faculty of reasonableness—except in moments when the child is "overtaken by a playful mood." Once more, there is a hint that, when the thinking of the adult is stuck on the higher levels of logic, playing is in some jeopardy.

So the child looks for ways to avoid the necessity of that mood, which cannot always be evoked on demand. Further development toward jokes is governed by his seeking to avoid criticism and to find a substitute for the mood. The only way of reaching this end is to find certain meaningless combinations of words or the absurd, putting together thoughts that have some meaning. He finds a solution in the *jest,* where it is at least *permissible* to say something in a given way, but where it could be heard in a different way. There is sense in nonsense, and nonsense in sense!

Jokes have a different developmental history, a formation in the *unconscious* (Freud, 1905, p. 168). The mark of that history is the peculiar brevity of jokes, a condensation, as in dreams, localized in the unconscious and absent in the preconscious. But, in contrast with the dream, which Freud saw as a "completely asocial mental product," a joke is "the most social of all mental functions" (p. 179). And perhaps Freud's collection of jokes illustrates that. As Rieff (1959) noted, of the two kinds Freud tells, his Jewish jokes are generally the nonsexual ones, about food, forms of social evasion, or the comedy of marriage (p. 80). And in his "Wit and Its Relation to the Unconscious," in analyzing marriage jokes, Freud observed dryly that monogamous marriage "is not the organization which can satisfy a man's sexuality" (Rieff, 1959, p. 704).

Since the infantile is the source of the unconscious, "the thought which, with the intention of constructing a joke, plunges into the unconscious is merely seeking there for the ancient dwelling-place of its former play with words" (Freud, 1905, p. 170). In a footnote on that same page, Freud observed that many of his patients confirm by a laugh when he has been able to give them a picture of their hidden unconscious, even when the content would not seem to justify this. Later on (1915) he observed, "When a primary process is allowed to take its course in connection with the system *Pcs,* it appears 'comic' and excites laughter" (p. 186). We could wonder whether the pleasure may not be the opening of the door to that former abode, which some of us would suggest to be close to Matte Blanco's symmetrical logic, related to emotion.

Freud (1905) pursued jokes into the realm of the comic, which he declared "arises in the first instance as an unintended discovery derived from human social relations" (p. 189). It is found in movements, forms, actions, and traits of character, and one can make *oneself* comic, as well as making others so. He was inspired by Bergson (1900) who, in writing of laughter, said we could "trace in the games that amused the child the first sketch of the combinations which make the grown man laugh. Above all we too often fail to recognize how much of childishness, so to speak, there still is in most of our joyful emotions" (p. 68 ff.). Freud thought that his very childish nature affords the young child and us pure pleasure but that, since he as yet lacks the comic feeling that arises from observing a difference in energy expenditure that arises in the course of understanding another, it will be some while before he appreciates the comic. Freud

(1905) observed that "it *is* comic when a child who is learning to write follows the movements of his pen with his tongue stuck out" (p. 190), since we adults rarely do that. We note however that the sense of amusement in that scene resides in the observing adult. Only after the child discerns his own superiority—as over someone who falls, while he maintains his own upright position—will he be himself able to perceive the comic.

Humor, Freud thought then, is the most easily satisfied among the species of the comic, completing itself within a single person, another's participation contributing nothing new. It is a means of obtaining pleasure in spite of the distressing affects that interfere; it acts as a substitute for the generation of those affects, putting itself in their place.

Humor is the *highest form of defensive process,* because it "scorns to withdraw the ideational content bearing the distressing affect from conscious attention as repression does" (Freud, 1905, p. 233). He found it conceivable that, once again, something of the infantile could put the means of achieving this at its disposal. Only in early life were there distressing affects at which the adult today would smile—as he now laughs at his present ones. So humor is closer to the comic than to jokes.

Freud (1905) summed up his book with an affirmation of his energy notions: "The pleasure in jokes has seemed to us to arise from an economy in expenditure upon inhibition, the pleasure in the comic from an economy in expenditure upon ideation (upon cathexis) and the pleasure in humour from an economy in expenditure upon feeling" (p. 236). But 20 years later (1927) he was rethinking his old ideas. Whereas he had considered humor only from an economic point of view, he now wanted to look at it in the light of his new structural picture of the mind, and he was beginning to attend to a role for the "other." Humorous process could take place in a single person, while a spectator person takes enjoyment from it, or it could take place between two, the second being the object of humorous contemplation by the other.

An essential element of humor, Freud (1927) now averred, is that "the traumas of the world are no more than occasions for it to gain pleasure" (p. 162). There is something liberating about humor: a "grandeur" that lies in the triumph of narcissism, the victorious assertion of the ego's invulnerability. "The ego refuses to be distressed by the provocations of reality, to let itself be compelled to suffer" (p. 162). Again, Freud evokes childhood, suggesting that an adult humorous person is treating himself like a child and at the same time playing the part of the superior adult toward the child. This concept gained support, he believed, from what had been learned about ego: it harbored within its nucleus the superego, the heir of the parental agency, with which it is sometimes merged and again differentiated. When differentiated, there is a new distribution of energy, the ego tiny, its interests trivial. Humor is then "the contribution made to the comic through the agency of the super-ego" (p. 165). Although humorous pleasure never reaches the intensity of that in the comic or jokes, we regard this lesser intensity as of very high value, liberating and elevating.

Thus we see Freud essentially declaring that humor originates in the play of children and that the role of the other and of the social surround are factors in the unfolding of the playful mode. Although in his early work, as we have noted, he emphasized the psychic economies that are effected in the various types of play, he later wanted to apply his structural ideas. Freud, who often seemed to be guarding his ideas closely against any criticism from the outside, was singularly able to play with his own theories, rendering them more fluid and mutable. In my fantasies, he would be pleased to see where others have taken them since his demise. He had little experience himself with the children to whose playfulness he gave so much credit. But it is not surprising that we find in the work of child analysts and in that of infant researchers influenced by psychoanalytic theories many references to the humor to which playfulness gives birth.

IN THE BEGINNING

If we begin with the beginning, we find ourselves "cracking up" with Chris Bollas (1995), who declares the mother–infant relation one of farce. Now that word is one with which we might play too, for it derives from Latin *farcire*, to stuff, originally meaning to make a dish more palatable by filling it with finely chopped and seasoned fish and meat. As Susan Langer said, most of our language is "faded metaphor"; now we use *farce* to designate rendering something more agreeable by a certain pretense, softening and eluding the "real" situation. Still later, it became a word for a light dramatic composition of satirical or humorous cast and— as Bollas now uses it—designates broad humor on the edge of ridicule.

Bollas plays around with Kleinian concepts, such as that the baby does not know initially that the mother who is full of good milk and good humor (those liquids again) is the same as the one who is out of milk and wicked. He declares the positions of the mother and her infant to be at the heart of what is humorous, citing Dario Fo (1987), "Clowns, like minstrels and 'comics' always deal with the same problem, be it hunger for food, for sex, even for dignity, for identity, for power. The problem they pose is—who's in command, who's the boss?" (p. 172). But the problem behind that, as some of us see it, is the regularity with which the clown's actions end in failures when there is no outside help and his attempts at humorous denial of his predicament.

Bollas (1995) draws analogies to the absurdities of the original human scene, where the one who is infinitely superior in power treats the inferior one as an equal; in fact, the frailties of the latter become themselves endearing. The mother by her own actions and vocalizations demonstrates how amusement at one's plight can generate a special sense, the sense of humor. The author here cites the later Freud, who saw humor as involving the loving superior superego taking pleasure in the ego's meanderings. This later intrapsychic inequality owes its structure, Bollas says, to the imbalance between infant and adult, the stupe and the know-it-all (p. 241). Because the good-enough mother can be amused with her baby, she can get him "to laugh at himself before he knows what the joke is" and lays the ground for his developing a sense of amusement about the human condition.

We may or may not agree with Bollas that "the sense of humor precedes the sense of self," although we may concede that the healthiest sense of self will ensue when the "mirroring" mother has approached her infant with a humorous perspective. We find it intriguing that both the sense of playing and the comic sense come into being far, far earlier than Freud imagined. I have liked to make the point that, if the mother were incapable of make-believe, she would not behave toward her infant *as though* there were a self there; her very pretense is part of what calls it into being. There is no evidence for the *primary autism* that Mahler (1952) once imagined and not much either for *primary narcissism*. Instead, the as-yet immature notions of space result in projecting from inside to outside and taking inside that which was outside.

Some of us have posited a basic *primary illusion* (from *in ludere*, meaning in play) in which there is gentle oscillation between the interests of the nascent self and fleeting felt connection with others, without conflict (Shor and Sanville, 1978). It may, we hypothesized, lay down a model toward which later strivings will aim. And here, I might add, the degree of success in achieving new versions of that may well depend upon the quantities and qualities of playing that lead to a humorous perspective.

The newborn does come magnificently equipped for relating, and the mother is enticed, not only by her infant's "frailties" but by his "amazing" qualities (Hack, 1975) and by her sense of agency in actualizing his potential. Far from being a "stupe," he comes with primary *subjectivity*, the rudiments of individual consciousness and intentionality. He has some ability to communicate this to others and to fit his nascent sense of agency with the subjectivity of others, that is, to engage in *intersubjectivity* (Trevarthen, 1979). There is some evidence of Groos's "biological underpinnings" for that play that involves imitation and that is so essential to certain kinds of later humor. There are a number of studies that attest to an innate, pan-human facial "vocabulary" of emotional signs; the infant's

expressions are remarkably similar to those of adults. They will be refined after visual experience with other faces, because of the baby's capacity
to mimic older children and adults.

The *words* used by the mother to soothe and delight her baby are
"understood" mainly in their phatic qualities, and they quite literally
move him. Films such as those by Hack (1975) show the newborn excit-
edly moving his arms and legs in rhythm to the human voice. Long before they attain definitions in his mind, the baby tries out some of the
mouth and facial and head movements involved in forming words. The
details of these prespeech movements suggest to researchers a specific
mechanism for speech, and imitation then is not just passive incorporation but is a remodeling and integration of components already in spontaneous expression. The good-enough mother is herself *moved* by her
baby's pleasure in communication, and she talks to him in that quiet,
gentle, highly attentive way, with repetition and musical intonation, that
we call "baby talk." Or she may become active and playful herself; teasing; making rhythmical, exaggerated movements of her head, trunk, or
whole body; and may touch her offspring in emphatic ways, all the while
remaining sensitive to his reactions and responses. We could say that the
intersubjectivity of the two participants lays the groundwork for later
symbolic play and for humor.

Current writers who observe and study children note that the view
of human play has changed substantially since Freud's time (Slade and
Wolf, 1994). They take further than did Freud the role of the other and
of the mutual social system in evolving intersubjectivity, for they have
sources of data that were lacking for Freud: the interplay of children
with mothers or with clinicians. While clinicians following Freud were
often looking for how the play themes of the child were *disguises,* many
contemporary therapists see playing itself as therapeutic. Slade writes of
children from disorganized families, whose play manifests a quality of
incoherence that precludes meaningful translation. Such children are not
hiding what they can't tolerate; they live in an emotionally chaotic universe that precludes or limits symbolization. Slade uses language, not to
"interpret," but to name objects and toys and to create a "spirit of the
scene." She aims at enabling her little patients to achieve that sense of
being effective, in control, which is one of Groos's basic elements of play.

By contrast, there are 2-year-olds (particularly little girls) who, emerging from beginnings in baby–parent pretending, evolve dramatic role play,
in which they both act and direct (First, 1994). Drawing on the *cross-
identifications* established between infant and mother, the child initiates
an interaction beginning with her announcing, "I'm leaving and you cry."
In that phase, there is reversal of *activity.* Next, the daughter pretends to
be a creature somewhat *like* herself and cues the mother to be somewhat

like herself. In phase three, there is a reversal of *roles,* with the child playing a character who is mother, and mother instructed to play she is the child. Clearly there are develomental leaps when the child can imagine what it might be like to be Mother and can imagine that Mother can imagine what it might be like to be the child. Missing and independence become playable. And we are witnessing the unfolding of that capacity that Freud claimed for the humorous person; this little girl can treat herself like a child and can also play the part of the superior mother with her daughter.

CHILDREN IN PSYCHOANALYTIC TREATMENT

There are children who cannot play or whose attempts at playing when we first see them are via repetitive bodily movements or perhaps body products. This was most particularly the plight of one severely autistic little girl who was brought to me when she was two-and-a-half (Sanville, 1991). She had no words at all until the end of her first year of treatment, and—significantly—that word was *bubble,* since I had introduced her to a bubble pipe. Until then she had been "stuck" with taking mouthfuls of water and spouting wherever and on whatever, so mine had been an attempt to extend her oral pleasures into slightly more socially agreeable channels. She had thus begun what we analysts like to call "sublimation," and had extended her own pleasure possibilities. Over the 10-year period that I saw her, Katie showed ever-increasing capacity for symbolic play and for asserting her own wishes and preferences. While speech was initially confined to subjects suggested by our playroom activities, one of the first things I heard about from the "outside world" was, "I saw a clown at the circus." But, if she grasped the humor involved, of that I did not hear. Unlike the clown, who generally has to cope with his own failures by humorous means, Katie's felt failures—and there were many— were generally dealt with by hysterical tears and by throwing her whole body around. Smiles were infrequent and laughter almost nonexistent.

At the age of 8, there was a spate of bedtime behavior that mother found "dismaying." After prayers were said and her mother had tucked her in, Katie began to laugh and giggle in a silly and uncontrollable way. Her mother first tried to embrace and comfort her, then threatened with a switch, to no avail. Only when her mother burst into tears did Katie stop her giggling, put her arms around her mother's neck, and say, "I love you, Katie" (her way at the time of dealing with pronouns.) And that was the end of the "inane laughter."

Even physically handicapped children seem able to move toward possessing a humorous persepective when they have had excellent mothering. Colonna (1981) wrote about a little boy, his mother's first child, who was born without eyes, and who attended the Hamstead Nursery School for Blind Children. His mother was energetic, provided him opportunities for an active and assertive attitude, showed him rich empathy, and stayed with him when he had to undergo many difficult surgical procedures. Even in his early years, he could know and articulate his own needs; he was curious about the world and showed excellent learning capacities. The school thought he had identified with his mother's visual knowledge. Seen at 26, he manifested a delightful sense of humor and was enjoying his work as a musician, playing in his own band. We could say that he had "true humour," as Johnson had described it, a quality of both his being and doing.

There are children who attempt to make jokes. Mahon (1992) describes a 4-year-old boy who dashes into the office, takes the analyst's chair, and "free associates" to the theft. He beams when the analyst says he's pretending to take over the world, be big, and order people like parents and the analyst around. In his humorous mood, the boy asks if the analyst would like to hear a joke, one that began as a dream. The question: "Why did the chicken steal the bagpipes?" The answer: "Because he wanted to have a perfect house." To Mahon, this didn't sound like a joke. While they were figuring out that the bagpipes were scrotum and phallus, the boy got anxious and had to run to the waiting room to check with his mother. He agreed with the interpretation that he wanted to be sure that his mother loved him even if he played out murderous wishes toward his father. There were more jokes: "I'll steal your chair. I'll take your job." But when the analyst said, "What will I do without my chair and job?" the boy reassured him, "It's only a joke." The joke, however, can't quite contain the hostility, and he knocks Dr. M on the head and then fixes his shoes—that is, "castrates and undoes." He also makes "spells," such as those that could make a door open and close magically. He explains that "spells are like jokes but they don't have words." Mahon observes that a child of this age is relatively new to language and to joking. He tries to represent his conflict in language, "to put a comic face on issues that are not necessarily funny" (p. 323), but makes a poor joke and so resorts to action or magic. Mahon predicts that, when he reaches latency, the conflict will be repressed and his ego will be more in contact with "nonincestuous group life and the heritage of games and jokes" (p. 325). Then it may be easier to joke about the return of the repressed with classmates than it is to talk about the crime and the act of repression itself with your father or analyst. Here, were we to evoke either Freud or Matte Blanco (1988) again, we might say that the unconscious, the symmetrical, may be the majority component of the boy's thinking and that, as he advances further into the language world, the inevitable bi-logic of his thinking will contain more of the asymmetrical, capable of being represented in language.

Mahon and Battin-Mahon (1983) offer the case of seven-year-old Alex, also preoccupied with who is superior to whom, but who shows greater ability to express his feelings in words. He began his analysis saying, "I get angry for no reason." His analyst tells him that there is always a reason, but one can't always remember. Then the child tells of a memory, at the birthday of his little sister when he was two or three, when he was the only boy present, somehow "second fiddle" to the girls. He assures the analyst that the memory was correct; it was corroborated by a photo in which he was wearing blue. In a later session, he demanded to know why the screwdrivers were out of place. When the analyst said he could not remember, Alex chided, "How come you can remember what I told you happened to me years ago, but not what happened today?" Dr. M took this reprimand in good humor, as a piece of wisdom, becoming conscious of his countertransference tendency to place more emphasis on the past than on current events. He realized that the appearance of the playroom was to Alex evidence of the analyst's attachment to others. So he responded to the scolding by commenting, "Other children have been here. You have feelings about it, and you are not even wearing blue" (p. 469), using the child's own story of his former memory prop to introduce a humorous note, affirming his respect for the child's capacities to size things up accurately, here and now.

Other writers who treat latency-age children do not always find it easy to create the necessary verbal medium of communication. Novick (1983) writes of Louisa, seven and a half years old, born of English-speaking parents, but reared almost completely by au pairs, nannies, and cleaning women who spoke a variety of languages. In the beginning of treatment, Louisa brought in a torrent of material, switching so rapidly from one topic to another that she created considerable confusion in her therapist. Louisa did not want to hear what Novick had to say; she preferred "perfect, effortless, mutual understanding" (p. 485). The author details a 6-week period in which Louisa initiated two verbal modes. The first was "saying the opposite," a sort of game in which for one day Novick would be verbal, and Louisa would scribble wildly, and the next day it would be Louisa's turn to talk and Novick's to write. Some of Louisa's scribblings were, she said, secret messages, such as, "Boo boo you you moo moo cow cow," and the therapist observed that this is the way babies describe things. After a while another game was invented, using foreign languages. The girl would, for example, write in German that she wanted to talk of the book and the lamp. Her therapist would write in French, "Louisa is afraid to talk about her secrets." Louisa could write, "Yes." There were periods when words were dropped in favor of drawings. A turning point in the long treatment was when the patient began the session with a drawing of "pushmepullyou" from Dr. Doolittle, and they could use it to talk of things she both enjoyed and worried about. She gave the therapist a stick of gum, and Novick said, "You've given me some m-u-g." Louisa laughed at her therapist's saying the opposite, and the latter commented that she only gives her therapist something to eat when she's angry (which Louisa was, owing to her therapist's missing a previous session). They then played with drawings, the patient's being first of a whole orange, then halves, and she accepted the suggestion that the halves were Louisa and her mother. Louisa then drew "juice" connecting the two halves. Humor in its original sense, we might say, had entered the scene. This was the last time that the game of "saying the opposite" was played, and the next week was the last use of foreign languages. Their conjoint play with words had rerailed the dialogue (Spitz, 1963).

Even children who by latency age are already on the way to a narcissistic disorder can sometimes respond to humorous interventions. Beren (1992) writes of Jane, whose reality testing and judgment were compromised in the service of maintaining a grandiose self. So there was initially little playfulness between them, with either toys or words. Jane showed total disregard for the rules of the game of checkers, insisting her way was right, Beren's wrong. Her manner of playing was so controlling that Beren found herself confused, confined to be used only as an extension, suffering a sense of no play space for herself. She looked for those occasional moments when Jane was more amenable to hearing from her, and she describes one amusing intervention, when she told her patient, "Jane, you know that the only reason I am saying this is because it's my job. That's what therapists are supposed to do, to talk about the things nobody wants to talk about . . . If I didn't do that, I would be out of a job." This often got a big smile, and Jane could allow her then to say she knew Jane hated it because her mother was always telling her how she thought Jane felt, and it made Jane angry. "You bet!" Jane agreed. On another occasion Beren, "tongue in cheek," told her patient that she had bad news for her: her beloved uncle had taught her to play checkers the wrong way. This mild mockery brought a smile and Jane's inquiry about how to play. This child seemed to "get" the meaning thus obliquely conveyed. If Beren was willing to pretend with her that someone else had been ignorant, rather than she, she would be willing to learn. The therapist's use of metonym, "substitute naming," permitted the process to flow.

An adolescent girl of 13, Emma began her treatment with terrors of separating, and she manifested frequent lapses into silence (Levinson, 1984). In the third month, she broke one of her silences with a laugh, thinking of a play she had written about a godmother who turned into a witch, and the prince whom she was to help went to an inn and got

drunk. Levinson asked her whether the inn bore a resemblance to the
Hampstead Clinic. Emma laughed and said that her therapist was being
silly. On another silent occasion, Levinson asked her whether she was
showing her, as she tries to show her mother, that she does not want her
privacy intruded upon. Emma whispered that she had been baking and
that her mother kept putting the ingredients into the mixing bowl for her.
Levinson said, "You don't want me to put my thoughts into your mixing
bowl," thus metaphorically using her patient's account. This adolescent
did gradually laugh more, and on one occasion manifested some rare
humor, reporting how on an excursion with her mother, the latter had
never stopped talking, teaching her all the time, and how she, Emma,
had hardly realized it—she had "turned off," we assume. She and her
therapist also engaged in some humor together, as when, after a trip with
her father, Emma said, "Perhaps it would be easier for me not to live in a
house at all." Her therapist countered with, "If Mother were also on the
road, the two of you would be stuck together," thus lightly recognizing
with her that she is not yet ready for solitary travel. Emma grinned. And
we could surmise that a grin (which my dictionary defines as "to set the
teeth together and open the lips, to show teeth, as in laughter, scorn or
pain") signifies some capacity for ambivalence and ambiguity.

It is evident that child therapists, who have no difficulty finding a
place for playing, also include in their writings stories about their patients' humorous leanings. But it is not exactly a featured subject in psychoanalytic literature that deals with the treatment of adults. One can
search many indexes without finding a single reference to humor. One
reason might be its close connection with play, which—in spite of
Winnicott and the British Independents—until quite recently was thought
by many analysts who treat adults not to be a sufficiently serious topic
for their consideration. Another clue is that some prominent analysts
have declared that humor in the analyst is a likely defense against anxiety, a form of self-display and exhibitionism and a disturbance of the
analyst's *incognito* (Kubie, 1971). There is, I think, reason to hope that,
with the current emphasis on intersubjectivity, play and humor, even in
the analyst, may not continue to be neglected topics in the literature on
treatment of adults.

There is a nonanalyst who has impressed many of us with daring
titles to books that are serious indeed. Oliver Sacks (1985), in *The Man
Who Mistook His Wife for a Hat,* seems able, even in confronting the
tragic, to take a humorous perspective, an invaluable attribute for pro-
fessionals who would minister to those suffering from deprivations,
whether organic or psychosocial. His stance by no means diminishes his
empathy. In his story of Jose, a 21-year-old, "autist artist," said by the
attendants in the institution where he lived to be "an idiot," Sacks could

find a "sense of humor" in the man's drawings, which, although done with near-obsessive accuracy, yet showed curious elaborations and variations that Sacks appreciated as "droll." Jose had had a high fever at the age of 8, followed by frequent seizures, and was admitted to the hospital after an eruption of epileptic violence. Thus his was a case of "secondary autism," with some residual memory—perhaps, Sacks speculated, of the years before his illness when his father frequently took him sketching. Now he was totally without words. He could draw a fish or a flower with accuracy, yet also include a personification as in a dream or a joke. Sacks could appreciate that words are not the only playthings, even of adults. In reading the case, one sees how humor could appear to be solitary, as Freud had declared, but still could not have been available to Jose had he not had a playing relationship with his father in early childhood. There was "basic trust" in his transference to Sacks, who must have seemed to him a caring father-person.

ADULTS IN PSYCHOANALYTIC TREATMENT

I was reminded of Milner's (1955) account of her long treatment with Susan, in which this analyst was ever attentive to the "reparative aspect" of the many drawings done during the 9 months when the patient was in an extremely regressed state. Milner could, like Sacks, see humor in her analysand's images, such as her mocking submission of the devil in one figure, drawn beside what looked like a fetal dragon or a winged tadpole, with a halo! The analyst speculated that the latter might be a symbol for the manic phase of her patient's creative swing and that the little devil's pretense of humility could be seen as a healthful beginning of recognizing what was a split in the ego. Milner also found humor in a figure of a duck with a hat, but then came to see that the hat and beak together created dangerous-looking crocodile jaws. So the fun could have a defensive quality in this woman with her conflicting wishes: to communicate and to retreat into a world of nonencounter.

Long ago, there were those who pondered the problem of the relationship between two forms of thought organization: humor and schizophrenic thinking. Bleuler (1911) wrote of a patient who spoke with him about the eyes all people have and how one can see too much. The patient informed him that in Burghoelzli there were four kinds: "patients, inmates, attendants—and then those who aren't here at all" (p. 590). Bleuler found humor in the distinction between patient and inmate and in the inclusion of those "who aren't here at all." He posited that the humor resided in the contrast between the air of imparting information and the "facts" conveyed and in the unexpectedness of the facts.

We observe that examples such as those offered by Milner and Bleuler cannot lead to laughter in the other because the patients are not themselves manifesting a sense of humor. A sense of humor would be, in Winnicott's (1971a) terms, evidence of freedom, the opposite of the rigidity of defenses that characterize illness. It is the ally of the therapist, who gets a sense of elbow room for maneuvering. And Winnicott, like Sacks and Milner, possessed a keenness for perceiving the humor amid the heaviness of a case. In the final chapter of his *Therapeutic Consultations in Child Psychiatry* (1971b), he gives us an account of an interview with a mother who, at the age of 3, had been removed from her mother and sent to a religious orphanage. This woman had a profound conviction of her "badness," and she gave him many reasons for this. Once, while working in a nursery, she had nearly strangled a child. She had always sexualized relationships, hugging children to get sexual feelings in herself. She stole. But Winnicott was impressed that she gave "quite naturally, in an unsophisticated way, the relationship between stealing and both deprivation and hope" (p. 341). And she told him one story that showed a *sense of fun:* "Once, on a bus, the conductor inquired of "Auntie" (who was a Nun), "Are all these your kids?" Auntie was flustered and said, 'Yes, but they have all got different fathers' " (p. 338). Winnicott experienced that as "like an oasis in the desert," and sadly observed that the woman quickly returned to the desert. He had no illusions of "curing," but the result of the hour was that she was able to turn her own daughter Anna over to social service to be placed in a "suitable school." We note that it was the woman's capacity for using words in a minimally defensive way that allowed the hour to go as it did, and she did not evoke in Winnicott the judgmental. He was affectively attuned to her and entertained positive feelings toward this woman who had suffered most unfortunate early beginnings.

But there are patients with whom attunement can be such that the analyst finds himself in danger of *acting* together with the patient, in ways symmetrical with his. Rayner (1992) described such predicaments, in the periods of an analysis when his male analysand's bodily behaviors and preverbal rhythms and tones seemed to prevail over the verbal, so that interpretations are for some while premature. His solution was both playful and humorous: he began to write brief doggerels, portraying dialogues with the patient. These often had an angry, critical, even punitive note to them. They enabled him to stay in touch with his "fusions" and to keep them from being pathological by allowing this form of expression to himself, rather than interaction in the sessions. He could maintain *transitionality,* could bear the waiting that we must sometimes do before the moment is ripe for constructively sharing with patients what we may be seeing and feeling. And he avoided the "showing off" of which Kubie warned.

There are those on the current scene who at times handle provocations instead by "dyadic enactments." Gedo (1994) has reported becoming increasingly irritated with one patient to the extent that he began to respond in an angry tone of voice, compared the patient to his crazy mother, and finally called him a "shithead," so wedded to obstinacy that he could not allow anyone to save his life. It was, he said, a *mise-en-scène* on the analytic stage, words not carrying the principal import, not conveying the speaker's true meaning. It was analogous to the patient's unreasonable arguments, and the patient knew that it should not be construed literally, that many of his analyst's communications were metonymic. The patient's response was that he wept, thanked the analyst for "going beyond the boundaries of analytic duty," and realized that he had himself been arguing out of pure sadism. Gedo has come to feel a greater freedom, employing all the resources of rhetoric. But a requisite, he declares, is to accustom patients to our not intending all that we say to be taken literally, that we may communicate in a manner conveying emotion without being affectively aroused. Some of us readers thought he *was* describing affective arousal but sufficiently "contained" that it could come off successfully, as it did. An interesting suggestion is made by Gedo—that miscarriage of communication can be a regression or a "communicative apraxia," in which case we have to enable the patient to acquire the missing skills. As long as the patient lacks a sense of humor, he will react with hurt feelings to the very fact that the analyst is less than fully "serious."

Other analytic writers describe resorting to humor to counter the deadening stereotypy in sessions with patients in whom humor is missing. Montgomery's (1989) "Lucy" was forever bearing witness to herself as pathological and saw the world as strictly divided between the sick and the healthy. One day, in a spooky voice, with dangerous inflections, she reported self-destructive thoughts. When her therapist responded in similar tones with, "Sounds pretty creepy," the patient laughed. On another occasion, Lucy called, paralyzed with anxiety, and Montgomery scolded her. In the following hour the patient was angry at her therapist for being angry at her for an anxiety attack. Montgomery told her, "I was not angry that you had an attack, I was angry that you believed in it!" (p. 362). In that pair, the joke and the tease became a way of creating space, "softening the chronic transference" by playing with it. This therapist saw herself communicating implicitly, "I am not the person you expect and neither are you—maybe you have confused us with somebody else" (p. 361). If these were dyadic enactments, à la Gedo, they did have therapeutic results, for the case ended well. One feels, in reading the story, that the therapist's "hostility" was harnessed to empathy so that a sense of mutuality was engendered.

PLAY AND HUMOR TOWARD THE END OF LIFE

Joan Erikson (1988), in extending her husband's work on the last stage of life, writes that "empathy counteracts entropy" and that one of the great virtues of playfulness and humor is that they permit us an awareness of opposites and contradictions. She declares, "Old age is a good time for laughter," and that if we can see even ourselves as funny, it "eases living in close proximity to ourselves" (p. 108).

A patient of mine whose work had involved play with words and images is now in his eighth decade and confronted with the frustration that his former interesting life as a writer and director in film is no longer available to him. Over the years of analysis, he has come to manifest a type of humor that Kohut (1971) saw as a sign of "truly internalized attitudes." Self psychologists would have diagnosed him prior to treatment as a "narcissistic personality" and would view his current capacity for *genuine humor* as a sign of "transformation of archaic narcissistic cathexis," especially since it goes with a strengthening of values and ideals that were not originally his. Before his analysis, William had a reputation for being "the world's angriest man." He was by no means devoid of humor, but it was of a sort that leaned toward that jocularity and sarcasm that Kohut (1966) would have seen as defensive; those who worked with him often saw it as offensive. One of the consequences of his analysis was that, after many not very serious affairs with women, William fell in love and married a woman quite unlike the others, who had been beautiful but not up to him intellectually. This one had a career of her own, and although in the early stages of their togetherness, he found himself accused by her of acting as "director," they both worked and played their story out. He credits the relationship with enabling him to be a better person and has a sense also of enriching her. Family life became for the first time important and included his restoration of a previously somewhat short-changed relationship with his own son.

Currently, he is suffering many experiences in both outer and inner worlds that could be wounds to self-esteem: the rejection of his scripts by studios that once clamored for them and the development of Parkinson's disease, which not only makes for limitations in movement but for difficulty in speaking. The "loss of voice" is both metaphorical and actual. But, in Ben Jonson's words (Tave, 1962, p. 886), a humorous quality has come to possess him "body and soul." Sometimes it is manifested in reflecting about qualities that used to characterize him, such as stinginess. One day recently, he told me that he had given $50 to a charity, and he was amused that he almost did not tell me because, "You might think it was not enough!" A very affluent person, no charities were ever on his gift list in earlier years. He was not altogether wrong in anticipating my reaction, especially since the cause was research on Parkinson's disease. And so I responded with some wry humor, "We might both wonder that you don't fight the enemy more fiercely." He has recently given his yacht to an organization that uses it to teach sailing to underprivileged young-sters. So I heard his account of the current picayune donation as an invitation to us both to look with some amusement at evidences of "left-over" tightness.

In another session, after describing pleasure in taking their maid down to the government offices to get her citizenship, he told of some tensions at home. His wife had a houseguest, Betty, who left the lights on in her suite. William asked Betty if he might turn them off (and in this vignette are humorous admissions of not wanting the electric bill to be a matter of no concern). William's wife, Leah, was tense when she heard his query of her friend, called him aside, and accused him of being rude. He protested, saying Betty is herself a controlling person (something of which Leah has complained about him!). She agreed. He likes Betty, es-pecially her "upfrontness," not being easily offended. She told William that her son had moved to Hawaii to get away from what he experienced as her controlling. William commented, "*You*, controlling!?" as though in disbelief, and she could herself be amused at his irony. Once upon a time, his humor would have been more crude, and he would not have been so discerning about how the other might take it.

A woman with whom he once had a torrid affair now has cancer and is terminally ill. He has felt compassion for her and called her. But, he laughed, he could not tell her that she was the turning point in his life: the first woman who herself demanded to be in control! We had seen this at the time as his comic "experiment" in reversing roles to discover what it might feel like to be the underdog. Later in this session, he inquired whether I had ever seen tango dancing. There, he told me, the man is the one in control. But in samba, the male and female are equal. "So you have learned to samba!" I observed. Yes, he laughed, and went on to speak of his very rewarding relationship with Leah. There is much evidence that both have grown because of their "dance together."

William speaks frequently of death and of how he resents its ulti-mate inevitability. "I used to think I'd like to die, shot by a jealous lover." But in truth his sexual prowess is diminishing. He confessed in one ses-sion that he had tried masturbating and thinking of me. "I thought I had to tell you—that even you could not make me come!" We could laugh together—at his resurrecting a long-ago fantasy, at his feeling of having to tell me, and at how it could not work any more, and even at both of us being at the mercy of the ravages of age in the eighth decade of life.

PSYCHOANALYSIS AT THE MILENNIUM

Psychoanalysis, nearing the close of its tenth decade of life, has itself been suffering deeply a loss of the prestige it once so abundantly enjoyed. Whereas once upon a time, my old teacher, John Murray, declared that what psychoanalysis was building was comparable to construction of the cathedral at Chartres, we contemporary analysts might offer a more modest analogy—that instead we have built our own churches. And the members of each denomination have tended to make strong claims to ultimate truths.

There have always been those who accused Freud of having fixed ideas and of not easily accepting those who disagreed with him. Some of us readily forgave that, seeing it as a consequence of his not encountering an atmosphere of safety for his evolutionary ideas aimed at understanding the human psyche. Although he consciously longed for his theories to be accepted by the scientific establishment, that wish threw him into considerable conflict. In his February 1, 1900, letter to Fleiss, he humorously declared that he was "nothing but by temperament a conquistador—an adventurer if you want to translate the word—with the curiosity, the boldness, and the tenacity that belongs to that type of being" (Masson, 1985). We could say he knew his "true humor" was that of a poet, his "adopted humor" and admission of need for approval from the powers-that-be. He was one of those intellectuals that Huizinga (1944) called "free-ranging players of the mind" (pp. 7–8). Three decades later Albert Einstein (1934) was to write that the painter, the poet, the philosopher, and the scientist each attempts to construct an intelligible picture of the world. And each finds that logic alone will not do it; the task also requires intuition based on "intellectual love" (p. 3).

To be a free-ranging player of the mind involves a capacity to oscillate—to generate hypotheses out of specific clinical experiences and then to submit them to testing by further observation and research, often conducted by other than ourselves. Assuming a humorous perspective, we acknowledge that we analysts are ourselves often falling into the very fixities of thinking that we try to help others to overcome. In our attempts to free people from cultural norms and standards that we see as leading to constrictions, we mistakenly think that we too can be free from the judgments of the social surround. Our true humor has inclined us toward the literary, the narrative, and those who criticize us as nonscientific use words against us that are "downputting." Can we, like Freud, take a lightly jocular attitude about ourselves and work and play toward rerailing the dialogue with intellectuals of more "scientific" humors? If so, we may even learn a new game that could be fun.

REFERENCES

Anschutz, R. P. (1962), John Stuart Mill. *Encyclopaedia Britannica*, 13:490–494.

Beren, P. (1992), Narcissistic disorders in children. *The Psychoanalytic Study of the Child*, 47:265–278. New Haven, CT: Yale University Press.

Bergson, H. (1900), *Laughter: An Essay on the Meaning of the Comic*. Philadelphia: Richard West, 1921.

Bleuler, E. (1911), The basic symptoms of schizophrenia. In: *Organization and Pathology of Thought*, ed. G. Rapaport. New York: Columbia University Press, 1951, pp. 581–641.

Bollas, C. (1995), *Cracking Up: The Work of Unconscious Experience*. New York: Hill & Wang.

Colonna, A. B. (1981), Success through their own efforts. *The Psychoanalytic Study of the Child*. New Haven, CT: Yale University Press. pp. 33–44.

Drummond, W. (1618), A postscript to his *Conversations of Ben Jonson with William Drummond*. Cited by A. W. Ward (1962), Ben Johnson, *Encyclopaedia Britannica*, Vol. 13.

Einstein, A. (1934), *Essays in Science*. New York: Philosophical Library.

Erikson, J. (1988), *Wisdom and the Senses: The Way of Creativity*. New York: Norton.

First, E. (1994), The leaving game, or I'll play you and you play me: The emergence of dramatic role play in 2-year-olds. In: *Children at Play: Clinical and Developmental Aproaches to Meaning and Representation*, ed. A. Slade & D. P. Wolf. New York: Oxford University Press, pp. 111–132.

Fo, D. (1987), *The Tricks of the Trade*. New York: Routledge.

Freud, S. (1905), Jokes and their relation to the unconscious. *Standard Edition*, 8:9–236. London: Hogarth Press, 1960.

——— (1915), The unconscious. *Standard Edition*, 14:166–215. London: Hogarth Press, 1957.

——— (1927), Humour. *Standard Edition*, 21:159–166. London: Hogarth Press, 1961.

——— (1914), Remembering, repeating, and working through. *Standard Edition*, 12:143–156. London: Hogarth Press, 1958.

Groos, K. (1896), The play of animals. In: *Play: Its Role in Development and Evolution*, ed. J. S. Bruner, A. Jolly, & K. Sylva. New York: Basic Books, 1976, pp. 65–67.

——— (1901), The play of man: Teasing and love play. In: *Play: Its Role in Development and Evolution*, ed. J. S. Bruner, A. Jolly, & K. Sylva. New York: Basic Books, 1976, pp. 68–83.

Gedo, J. (1994), Analytic interventions: The question of form. In: *The Spectrum of Psychoanalysis: Essays in Honor of Martin S. Bergmann*, ed. A. K. Richards & A. D. Richards. Madison, CT: International Universities Press, pp. 111–127.

Hack, M. (1975), *The amazing newborn*. Film made at Case Western Reserve.

Huizinga, J. (1944), *Homo Ludens: A Study of the Play Element in Culture*. Boston: Beacon Press, 1955.

Kohut, H. (1966), Forms and transformations of narcissism. In: *The Search for the Self, Vol. l,* ed. P. H. Ornstein. New York: International Universities Press. pp. 427–460.

——— (1971), *The Analysis of the Self.* New York: International Universities Press.

Kubie, L. (1971), The destructive potential of humor in psychotherapy. In: *The Use of Humor in Psychotherapy,* ed. H. S. Strean. Northvale, NJ: Aronson.

Levinson, L. (1984), Witches—Bad and good: Maternal psychopathology as a developmental interference. *The Psychoanalytic Study of the Child,* 39:371–392. New Haven, CT: Yale University Press.

Mahler, M. (1952), On child psychosis and schizophrenia: Autistic and symbiotic infantile psychoses. *The Psychoanalytic Study of the Child,* 7:286–305. New York: International Universities Press.

Mahon, E. J. (1992), The function of humor in a four-year-old. *The Psychoanaltyic Study of the Child,* 47:321–328. New Haven, CT: Yale University Press.

——— & Battin-Mahon, D. (1983), The fate of screen memories. *The Psychoanalytic Study of the Child,* 38:459–479. New Haven, CT: Yale University Press.

Masson, J., trans. & ed. (1985), *The Complete Letters of Sigmund Freud to Wilhelm Fleiss.* Cambridge, MA: The Belnap Press of Harvard University Press.

Matte-Blanco, I. (1988), *Thinking, Feeling, and Being.* London: Routledge & Kegan Paul.

Milner, M. (1955), The communication of primary sensual experience. In: *The Suppressed Madness of Sane Men.* London: Tavistock, 1987, pp. 114–167.

Mitchell, L. (1948), *The Here and Now Story Book.* New York: Dutton.

Montgomery, J. D. (1989), Chronic patienthood as an iatrogenic false self. In: *The Facilitating Environment: Clinical Applications of Winnicott's Theory,* ed. M. G. Fromm & B. L. Smith. Madison, CT: International Universities Press, pp. 345–364.

Novick, K. K. (1983), Modes of communication in the analysis of a latency child. *The Psychoanalytic Study of the Child,* 38:481–500. New Haven, CT: Yale Univeristy Press.

Rayner, E. (1992), Matching, attunement and the psychoanalytic dialogue. *Internat. J. Psycho-Anal.,* 73:39–54.

Rieff, P. (1959), *Freud: The Mind of the Moralist.* New York: Viking.

Sacks, O. (1985), *The Man Who Mistook His Wife for a Hat.* New York: Summit Books.

Sanville, J. (1991), *The Playground of Psychoanalytic Therapy.* Hillsdale, NJ: The Analytic Press.

Shor, J. & Sanville, J. (1978), *Illusion in Loving.* New York: International Universities Press, 1979.

Slade, A. & Wolf, D.P. (1994), *Children at Play: Clinical and Developmental Approaches to Meaning and Representation.* New York: Oxford University Press.

Spitz, R. (1963), *Dialogues from Infancy,* ed. R. N. Emde. New York: International Universities Press.

Spillance, M. (1997), The 1997 Nobel Prize. *The Nation,* 265:5A(2).

Tave, S. M. (1962), Humour. *The Encyclopaedia Britannica,* 11:886–887. Chicago: William Benton.

Trevarthen, C. (1979), Communication and cooperation in early infancy: A description of primary intersubjectivitiy. In: *Before Speech,* ed. M. Bullowa. Cambridge, UK: Cambridge University Press, pp. 321–348.

Ward, A. W. (1962), Ben Johnson. *Encyclopaedia Britannica,* 13:141–145. London: William Barton.

Willey, B. (1962), Matthew Arnold. *Encyclopaedia Britannica,* 2:422–424b. London: William Barton.

3
=

Cracks: On Castration, Death, and Laughter

Barnaby B. Barratt

> "I'll tell you something you can't do."
> "What?"
> "Tickle a gnat's arse with a telegraph pole!"
> (At this, never-failing yells of laughter.)
> Orwell, 1931, p. 89

In this chapter, I discuss one aspect of *Humor and Psyche*, the phenomenon of the *crack*, as it pertains to our intimations of ultimacy and ways in which human reasoning is forever condemned to the conditions of penultimacy, alienation, and estrangement. Later I shall take as my "text" this epigraph, a "crack" reported by Orwell along with the laughter that accompanies its repeated performance. My hope is to point toward a "dimension" of the psyche that, following Bataille, we might think of as the "inner experience" of laughter (or, at least, of a certain mode of laughter) and to suggest that it is a dimension to which Freud's theorizing alludes, yet perhaps leaves, to a "postmodern" psychoanalysis to elaborate more fully.

Starting with Freud, let us note the interesting observation, made in the Editor's Preface to the *Standard Edition* translation of *Der Witz und seine Beziehung zum Unbewussten*, that after its 1905 publication this book on jokes remained unaltered apart from a few minor additions to the second edition of 1912—whereas by contrast, Freud subsequently revised and substantially expanded most of his other major works of the

1900 to 1905 period. Indeed, Freud seems to have had mixed opinions about the value of the book's contributions: in a letter of 1910 he refers to its conclusions as if they were authoritative, but then in the 1916–1917 "Introductory Lectures," he writes about the work as if it were merely a distraction, and his 1925 "Autobiographical Study" mentions the book somewhat deprecatorily. Despite his own enjoyment of jokes, Freud did not revisit the topic theoretically until the 1927 paper, "Humour," which comprises a rethinking of the issues in terms of the recently formulated structural-functional model. And there, it seems, the matter rested.

Part of what interests me about this intellectual history is that, whereas his 1923 to 1926 work on the tripartite model of mental functioning prompts Freud to reconsider the issues of comedy, there is, as far as I am aware, little or no effort to rethink the topic in relation to his 1920 notion of *Todestreibe*. Perhaps this omission results from the fact that Freud himself is, in the trajectories of his theorizing, so intensely ambiguous and ambivalent—some might say *resistive*—toward ideas about the "locus" of death in the genesis of our "mental space." For example, the "Interpretation of Dreams" (1900) and many of the early writings can be read as reiterating an intimation of the ineffable inherency of eroticism and death: their common carnality that contributes to both their terror and their magic. In this sense, I believe it can be argued that "death" forms a recurrent subtext to Freud's theorizing about sexuality, embodiment, and the repetitiousness of representation as the fundaments of mental life. By 1920, the notion of death is explictly theorized in the seminal study of repetition, "Beyond the Pleasure Principle." However, as is well known, Freud then appears to set aside his concept of "death instincts," instead elaborating a structural-functional model, the very coordinates of which, one might argue, almost seem designed as a denial of the inherency of something unstructured, unstructurable, unknown, and unknowable, something "deathlike" in the formation of our psychic realities.

Many psychoanalysts will not share my interest here, since many are inclined to dismiss the notion of "death instincts" as an ill-conceived and irrelevant lapse from "science" to metaphysical speculation: a misbegotten concept illuminating only the pessimistic proclivities of Freud's personal beliefs or reflecting ubiquitously obscure and morose trends in European philosophizing. However, there is an interesting counterargument suggesting that North American theorizing since Freud, despite its scientistic pretensions, has developed out of an ideological imperative to deny the inherency of something "deathlike" in the formative conditions of mental life. Consider here this culture's two major contributions to psychoanalysis: the expansion of structural-functional theorizing and the initiatives of self psychology. There are many possible criticisms of the former despite its utility as a descriptive account of psy-chotherapeutic procedures—I have expressed both my appreciation and my criticism of this model elsewhere (Barratt, 1984). Here I will merely mention the way in which structural-functional psychoanalysis ideologi-cally reduces repetition compulsion to the organized ego's imperialistic motives toward mastery, treating the latter as if such motives to domi-nate, conquer, possess, or control were merely "natural." This reduction results, I believe, in some serious, yet frequently overlooked, theoretical problems, not least of which is a distortive oversimplification of the con-ditions and curative momentum of consciousness. Focusing its account of the psyche around the failures of the world of "selfobjects" to sustain the integrated elaboration of an organized self, the psychoanalysis of self psychology then extends this ideological reduction of the repetitive char-acter of mental life by seeming to erase the conditions of contradictori-ness (and conflict) necessary to the formation of a representational world, and thus its theorizing grossly attenuates the significance of the dynamic unconscious (cf. Barratt, 1991).

Against the precepts of structural-functional and self-psychological theorizing, there are divergent trends in psychoanalysis since Freud that are not so dismissive of his notion of *Todestreibe*. Indeed, there are theo-retical trends that in various ways hold this notion central to our com-prehension of the clinical encounter as an endeavor to intervene on the repetitiveness of psychic reality. For example, Kleinian psychoanalysis interprets "death instincts" rather specifically in terms of its emphasis on the innate destructiveness of psychic life—a somewhat more intention-alistic notion than that of the universal imperative to return to inorganicity (cf. Gillespie, 1971). And Lacanian psychoanalysis, as is by now well known, offers a more complexly philosophical interpretation associated with its theorizing about the curative possibilities of the "symbolic real-ization" of the "Real"—an interpretation about which I have expressed both my appreciation and my criticism elsewhere (Barratt, 1984, 1993). Yet despite these varied currents of thinking about the "death instincts," I am not aware of any substantive attempt to retheorize the topic of jokes in relation to this notion—even though the general issues of humor have inspired many volumes of nonpsychoanalytic publication in the years since 1905. However, the psychoanalytic literature is now so vast—in-cluding clinical and nonclinical contributions, spanning four major lan-guages and housed in dozens of journals with articles difficult to access because our systems of indexing and referencing remain inadequately developed—that I must ask the reader's indulgence and assistance if the arguments sketched in these brief notes run along paths already traversed elsewhere without my knowledge.

It is not my specific purpose here to rehabilitate the notion of "death instincts" as such, not least because it is quite unclear what this notion portends. Yet this preliminary study of "cracks" subtends my general interest in a reconsideration of the "dimensions" of absencing, destroying, annihilating, "death," and kinesis in the formativity of the psyche (Barratt, 1993). The "crack" seems suited to such a reconsideration to the extent that it is critically different from the narratological conventionality of other forms of joke. It does not involve an elaborated storyline like a comic anecdote, jest, or prank; it is significantly unlike most witticisms, puns, or *bon mots*, yet it has an edge that stretches the imaginative playfulness of whimsy to its limit—thus raising questions about the conditions of limitation. I shall argue here that the crack discloses such a condition of limit, intimating what is "within yet beyond," concealing what it is itself revealing. I am aware that the idea of a "meaning" *within yet beyond* human discourse is, at this juncture, enigmatic and extraordinary, but I hope to show that it is crucial to our appreciation of the crack.

Following Bollas's 1995 book, *Cracking Up*, perhaps it is not irrelevant to be mindful of some of the many other connotations of this term.

> *Crack:* a sudden, sharp or breaking sound; to break something into fissure or partial fracture; a rogue, conversationalist, liar or prostitute; breaking of the voice; a cracked brain; that which is of superiority or excellence; to eulogize; to puzzle out or discuss; to break open; to snap or split asunder; to come to pieces or break down; to break anything so that the parts remain in contact but do not cohere; to render of unsound mind; to move with a stroke or jerk; to be preeminent or first-class; the vaginal opening from whence we came; a substance that, when smoked, offers temporarily the delusions of ecstatic transcendence.

The crudity of the crack reported by Orwell both designates and fails to designate a psychic "space" so deftly opened and closed over by *Der Witz und seine Beziehung zum Unbewussten*—there are serious problems with the allegory of "mental space," but I will continue to use the term for simplicity. Orwell's (1931) account of his adventures picking hops in southern England conjures the image of his young, uneducated coworker repeating the "joke" tirelessly, laughing uproariously and perhaps dementedly at each retelling of its wit, and leaving Orwell bemused by the seemingly endless force, the sheer entrancement, of its verbalized imagery.

Significantly, the "joke" begins in the voice of authority—*I'll tell you something you can't do*—an authority that either promises to name something that we lack, an incapacity yet to be designated, or threatens to name something prohibited us and that then requires us to petition the authority to have our insufficiency told to us. The imperative is profoundly compelling—*What?* we have to know what we lack; we long to know what is prohibited us. *Tickle a gnat's arse with a telegraph pole!*

Here begins something that is surely enigmatic and extraordinary. At first, we encounter a "joke" of the absurd. An absurdity of purpose: perhaps the alleviation of a gnat's putative itch or the stimulation of a gnat's erogenous zones. An absurdity of proportion: the instrument is hugely inappropriate to the designated task, yet we readily suspend belief, moving imaginatively to the surreal position in which we are concerned with a gnat's discomforts (caring for the relief of an insect that normally causes us discomfort) or in which we are interested in a gnat's sensual arousal (pleasuring an insect that normally causes us pain). However, the "joke" of absurd proportions quickly gives way to something else. For here is no simple tale of shelling peanuts with sledgehammers, no mere fantasy of using atomic bombs as firecrackers. The specifically anal aspect of the crack now asserts itself. And if it is an *arse* that is being tickled, we are surely not far from sodomous possibilities (cf. Phillips, 1993). The buggering of a gnat is at issue here, so I argue. But by what or whom is the sodomy to occur? The pole is so enormous, the hole is so small, that I believe the allusion is to the mythematics of *father's penis* by which we all wish and fear penetration. By extrapolation, these mythematics of *father's penis* point to the function of the phallus in all human discourse, the phallus by which we are all, as discursive subjects, constituted castrate (I will return to these ideas shortly). Perhaps we are enticed to fantasize ourselves as *he* who wields this gigantic telegraph pole in which case we are abruptly brought face-to-face with the terrible inevitability that our love for the object, our intent to heal its itch or "tickle its fancy" will utterly destroy it. But finally, we are surely confronted with ourselves as gnats contemplating sodomy by a dildo of gargantuan significance. It is a sodomy that is *desired*, both wished and feared, and such "desire" will be the death of us: the hapless subject destroyed, annihilated, obliterated beyond its wildest imaginations.

The crack thus takes us to an abyss: the "joke" precipitating our horror. It is the abyss that at once both defines the inevitability of psychic limit and threatens the psyche with whatever is "within yet beyond" its limited existence. In this sense, the crack is the cognitive-affective corollary of "total" orgasm, the momentum of a temporality caught between anguish and ecstasy. It is a moment of transgression in which is glimpsed this impossible abyss, something unspeakable that contains and pervades all that can be spoken (Bataille, 1954; Kristeva 1974, 1977, 1980; Tyler, 1987), the abyss in which "meaning" is found in something that, descriptively speaking, is irrevocably *nonsense* (Lecercle, 1985). Perhaps this is the Lacanian "Real"—the unrepresentable that impacts the possibilities of representation at their very limit (cf. Lacan, 1966, and the later *séminaires*). Note that, in an almost Kleinian sense, the joke—so to speak—"symbolizes" itself, yet brings the subject articulating it to the brink of a chaotic desymbolization (cf. Klein, 1930; Lorenzer, 1970a, b).

Notice also how the crack does not "work" if retold in the proper forms of narrative: "Once upon a time, there was a gnat that wanted to have its arse tickled by a telegraph pole." Rather, the narratological imperative that structures mental life, constituting the "I-ness" of the subject as a moment that "is-now" within the presentness of a representational world that appears ordered according to a regimented temporality that inscribes a beginning, a middle, and an end, is fractured in the moment of the crack (Barratt, 1993, pp. 116–133). It is a moment that depends on the suppression or suspension of the elaborations of discursive activity—a moment of "time out of time" in which both totality and transcendence are abandoned, thus disclosing an "impossible depth of things" that cannot be designated by the maneuvers of logic and rhetoric. Yet significantly, the crack only "works" because it has effectively passed the subject *through* the realms of cognitive-affective narration and *through* a momentum of "pure" eroticism to a point of utter horror. In sum, to understand the significance of the crack, I believe we must acknowledge its capacity to lead the subject of its discourse to that which is unsurpassably *nonunderstandable*—like the "spot in every dream at which it is unplumbable" . . . "the dream's navel, the spot where it reaches down into the unknown" (Freud, 1900, p. 525).

To comprehend this "inner experience" of the crack, we must also grasp the laughter that accompanies it, and here we are most indebted to the writings of Bataille (1933, 1954). Laughter is a nonproductive expenditure of energy, thus breaking with any notion of mental life that restricts its purview to those functions that are lawfully structured according to principles of economy and adaptation. As a nonproductive "expenditure," the laughter at the crack has its corollaries with the acts of eroticism, sacrifice, sacred gibberish or meditational chant, and poetic effusion. The laughter evades categorical reason and the narratological imperative. It is a mode of discourse that breaks discourse as if slipping "beyond" the law and order of logic and rhetoric. The laughter of the crack, like Derrida's (1972) *pharmakon* is the fulmination of all the inconsistencies and improprieties of thought and feeling. It "work-plays" on a nonidenticality that allows itself to be turned against itself: it is impossible to know that one inevitably kills that which one most loves, and it is impossible to want one's ownmost destruction.

The laughter of the crack, what Kristeva (1974, 1977) calls *le rire apocalyptique* or *déchirant*, is thus a moment of "truthfulness-in-practice." In its self-induced horror, the speaker is both agent and victim, moving and being moved by an "effervescence of passion" in which subject and object are swept away "without end" and "for no reason" (Kristeva, 1980). The subject who speaks the crack, who bursts into laughter at it, has momentarily lost itself in an excess of expenditure—lost as if in a labyrinth caught between the solidarity of community or "sense" and the nonsensicality of death. It is a labyrinth in which Ariadne's thread is always already broken, there being "no way out"—and in which "experience" is always already "otherwise" (Derrida, 1967, 1974; Sollers, 1968; Hollier, 1974; Levinas, 1974). The crack is thus a psychic "space" constellated with laughter that opens a dark abyss before the discursive subject, a laughter in which the subject is momentarily "here" no longer— indeed, "neither here nor there." Yet, for all its self-absencing, this is a moment of the subject's "truthfulness-in-practice" for, in its exorbitance, the subject who speaks the crack and bursts into laughter empties the contents of all that appears secure and known into the abyss of nonknowledge. It thus "realizes" itself, bringing itself, so to speak, face-to-face with each individual's ownmost wound, the wound of castration and death.

Following Freud, Bataille (1954) wrote that there are only two "certainties" in life: that I am insufficient and that I will die. As I appreciate psychoanalysis, its project is both to comprehend how our psychic realities work and play around these two "certainties" and to intervene upon the repetition compulsion by which the subject hopelessly attempts to ascertain itself against the terror and the magic of these two inevitabilities. Today, the psychoanalytic community can be divided between those whose theories seem to subordinate "castration" (insufficiency) to "death" (annihilation or destruction) and those whose theories seem to subordinate "death" to "castration." So I would like to conclude these brief notes on the crack with a consideration of what might be philosophically and clinically at issue in this "dispute."

It will not be forgotten that, a few years after his apparently brief experiment with the notion of the "death instinct," Freud (1926) wrote that "nothing resembling death can ever have been experienced" (p. 130) by the subject, and so "the fear of death should be regarded as analogous to the fear of castration" (p. 130). This can, and has been, read as suggesting that the thinking and speaking subject, the ego, *understands* castration but not death—and thus its anxieties about death are derivatively articulated on the basis of the pervasively structuring influence of castration anxiety. But however one reads such pronouncements, it is at least evident that the psychoanalytic significance of "death" (as well as the repetitiousness that generates mental life) cannot be discussed without examination of the notions of *castration* (as well as the phallus of which the castrate is deprived) and of *understanding* as the characteristic operation of all the representational activity that comprises the fabric of our psychic realities.

The division of the psychoanalytic community that I just mentioned can now be given a more refined definition. There are those whose theories of psychic reality specify a thinking and speaking subject, ego or self, as an entity that exists—so to speak—"precastratedly" and that, confronting fantasies of its castration, structures its operations in response to this threatening possibility. And there are those whose theories of psychic reality specify the emergence of a thinking and speaking subject only through its actual castration. Herein, I believe, lies the significance of the rather peculiar controversy over the "primacy" of castration versus "death" in the genesis of the psyche.

To *understand* death—that is, to apprehend it conceptually or to represent it—may indeed, as Freud indicates, be an impossibility. But this does not imply that "death"—as the inherency of something unstructured, unstructurable, unknown, and unknowable—does not enter into every conceptualization or representation. That it cannot be understood does not imply that something "deathlike" is not entailed in the formation of every instance of the structuring and functioning of our psychic realities. Wood (1989), explicating Derrida's philosophy on the temporalities of signification, writes that "death does not befall a preexisting 'I,' rather a relation to death constitutes the 'I' " (p. 131). Thus, while our capacity to represent "death" even as an event time-tagged in the "future" may be negligible, "death" may be at issue in the formation of each and every *re-presentation* that articulates the *I* of thinking, speaking, and acting in the present of the *now* and the *is*. This is, I believe, of vital importance to our comprehension not only of the significance of the inner experience of cracks, but also of the meaning of "castration" as it pertains to every aspect of psychic reality.

The argument here may be summarized as follows (the references are to the more extensive arguments in my 1993 book). The psychic reality, in which we live and in which the "I" of human discourse is constituted, is composed of modes of signification. Whether one describes the mind in terms of representations, thoughts, feelings, actions, percepts, or concepts, these are all modes of signification, or *signs* of one sort or another. The positing of any sign involves an act of establishment, "I is I" or *Da!* and the meaning of the sign depends on its relation to other signs, its temporal connectedness with other acts of establishment (pp. 48–68). However, the identities posited by this network of signification, the presencing of a sign in the moment of its articulation, appear to repress their contingencies: the dependency of the *Da!* not only on the *Fort!* but also on the difference between them, the dependency of the moment of presencing on the moment of absencing, and so on. The identitarianism of sign systems thus operates by "forgetting" or repressing the contingency of every connection between signs on a "third term," the difference or in Derrida's term *différance* between them (pp. 85–88). The system that encodes the identitarian exchange of signs (*"this* means *that,"* x is *y, a* is not *ā,* and so forth), including all categorical reason constructing the self and the world from multiple hierarchies of binary opposites (inner/outer, me/not-me, male/female, good/bad) and from all the maneuvers of logic and rhetoric, thus operates by "building over," foreclosing, excluding, or repressing its ineffable contingency on something unstructured, unstructurable, unknown, and unknowable, "within yet beyond," inherent yet unarticulable and without formulation—absencing, kinesis, contradictoriness, *différance,* and "death" (pp. 98–111, 116–133).

The subject that is implicated in every exchange of signs, the "I" of consciousness, appears as if it were the author of signs although it is actually authored by the sign system as a temporal moment, *now,* and as the copula, *is,* of the significatory network (*a* is not *ā* is *b,* and so on) with its regimented temporality of repetitious *re-presentation* (pp. 68–82, 88–98, 116–133). "In and of itself" (although there can be no such thing), the "I" is empty and only appears active and unifying to the extent that it is remaindered at every moment in which signs are articulated (Kolakowski, 1988). Thus, only in its Cartesian delusions of grandeur does the "I" create meaning; the insight that psychoanalysis instigated is that the "I" of consciousness is not the subject that produces a system of meaning but rather is produced by it from "elsewhere." However, such a system "must have an author," a central, organizing principle that ensures its coherence and continuity, its law and order. This is the principle of the phallus, which Lacan called "the signifier of signifiers," a function essential to the organization of identitarian thinking and speaking (pp. 102–111); the phallus may be the supreme myth, like the myth of the godhead, but it is a "myth" that we cannot think or speak without if we are to "make sense." The aspect of these ideas that we must grasp here is that the phallus seems to be the abstract locus from which all meanings are generated, the point that secures the "now" and the "is," thus ensuring the narratological imperative of human discourse and its temporality (past/present/future). It is not the father's penis, although ubiquitously confused as such, and, perhaps most importantly, the "I" is not the phallus except in its pretensions: in this respect, the subject of all human discourse is always already castrated, impotent, and absencing.

If reality appears as a seamless significatory system manifesting "all that is the case" with lawfulness and order, then the momentum of the crack and the laughter *apocalyptique* that accompanies it brings the subject to a cut, rent, or tear in the system (Taylor, 1990). Like an encounter with the Lacanian "Real," the moment of the crack is a horror and a magic, anguish and ecstasy, in which the "I" realizes, but can never articulate, the wherefore of its own insufficiency: the impossibility of the phallus and the ubiquity of death "within and beyond" the phallogocentric system of meaning. There is no way out of the contradictoriness that forms our mind, whether in its moments of alienation or of estrangement. But in the inner experience of the crack, the subject is at the abyss in which "I no longer see in me anything but cracks, impotence, useless agitation" (Bataille, 1954, p. 33). The "negative capability" of the crack, its opening to an "infinite space," is thus that, in the crack, one ceases to be desirous of sufficiency; one merely wishes, to paraphrase the words of Psalm 38, "to be refreshed before one dies." Since the subject is inevitably insufficient, castration and death are inseparable and ubiquitous in every human endeavor, for the "I" of discourse is always already born of a "deathlike" kinesis within our system of representations. As the poet says, "There is a crack in everything, that's how the light gets in" (Cohen, 1992).

REFERENCES

Barratt, B. B. (1984), *Psychic Reality and Psychoanalytic Knowing*. Hillsdale, NJ: The Analytic Press.

———— (1991), Semiotics and its "Other": Notes on the psychoanalytic unconscious. In: *Semiotic Perspectives on Clinical Theory and Practice: Medicine, Neuropsychiatry and Psychoanalysis*, ed. B. E. Litowitz & P. S. Epstein. Berlin, Germany: Mouton de Gruyter, pp.127–156.

———— (1993), *Psychoanalysis and the Postmodern Impulse: Knowing and Being Since Freud's Psychology*. Baltimore, MD: Johns Hopkins University Press.

Bataille, G. (1933), Sacrifices. In: *Visions of Excess—Selected Writings, 1927–1939*, ed. and trans. A. Stoekl. Minneapolis: University of Minnesota Press, 1985, pp. 130–136.

———— (1954), *Inner Experience*, trans. L. A. Boldt. Albany, NY: SUNY Press, 1988.

Bollas, C. (1995), *Cracking Up: The Work of Unconscious Experience*. New York, NY: Hill & Wang.

Cohen, L. (1992), Anthem. In: *The Future*. New York, NY: Columbia CDs and Tapes.

Derrida, J. (1967), *Writing and Difference*, trans. A. Bass. Chicago: University of Chicago Press, 1978.

———— (1972), *Dissemination*, trans. B. Johnson. Chicago, IL: University of Chicago Press, 1981.

Freud, S. (1900), The interpretation of dreams. *Standard Edition*, 4 & 5:1–625. London: Hogarth Press, 1953.

———— (1926), Inhibitions, symptoms and anxiety. *Standard Edition*, 20:87–175. London: Hogarth Press, 1959.

Gillispie, W. H. (1971), Aggression and instinct theory. In: *Life, Sex and Death:*

Selected Writings of William H. Gillispie, ed. M. D. A. Sinason. London, UK: Routledge, pp. 162–169.

Hollier, D. (1974), *La Prise de la Concorde*. Paris: Gallimard.

Klein, M. (1930), The importance of symbol-formation in the development of the ego. In: *Love, Guilt and Reparation, and Other Works, 1921–1945 (The Writing of Melanie Klein, Volume 2)*. London, UK: Hogarth Press, 1975, pp. 219–232.

Kolakowski, L. (1988), *Metaphysical Horror*. New York: Basil Blackwell.

Kristeva, J. (1974), *La Révolution du Langage Poétique*. Paris: Seuil.

——— (1977), *Polylogue*. Paris: Seuil.

——— (1980), *Pouvoirs de l'Horreur*. Paris: Seuil.

Lacan, J. (1966), *Écrits*. Paris: Seuil. [Partially translated as *Écrits: A Selection* by A. Sheridan. London, UK: Tavistock, 1977]

Lecercle, J.-J. (1985), *Philosophy through the Looking-Glass: Language, Nonsense, Desire*. La Salle, IL: Open Court.

Levinas, E. (1974), *Otherwise Than Being or Beyond Essence*, trans. A. Lingis. The Hague, Netherlands: Martinus Nijhoff.

Lorenzer, A. (1970a), *Kritik des psychoanalytischen Symbolbegriffs*. Frankfurt-am-Main, Germany: Suhrkamp Verlag.

——— (1970b), *Sprachzerstörung und Rekonstruktion*. Frankfurt-am-Main, Germany: Suhrkamp Verlag.

Orwell, G. (1931), Hop-picking. In: *The Collected Essays, Journalism and Letters of George Orwell, Volume 1: An Age Like This*. London, UK: Penguin Books, 1970, pp. 75–97.

Phillips, A. (1993), *On Kissing, Tickling, and Being Bored: Psychoanalytic Essays on the Unexamined Life*. Cambridge, MA: Harvard University Press.

Sollers, P. (1968), *L'Écriture et l'Expérience des Limites*. Paris: Gallimard.

Taylor, M. C. (1990), *Tears*. Albany, NY: SUNY Press.

Tyler, S. A. (1987), *The Unspeakable: Discourse, Dialogue, and Rhetoric in the Postmodern World*. Madison: University of Wisconsin Press.

Wood, D. C. (1989), *The Deconstruction of Time*. Atlantic Highlands, NJ: Humanities Press International.

4

Humor and Its Relationship
To the Unconscious

JAMES S. GROTSTEIN

The idea of a relationship between humor and mental life had long ago been explored by Freud (1905a, 1927), first in terms of the relationship between jokes and the unconscious and, later, in the psychology of humor generally. When psychoanalysts and psychotherapists since Freud think of humor, they think of four major aspects: (a) the legitimacy of humor in technique; (b) humor as a defense against the seriousness of analytic discourse; (c) humor as a philosophical stance that maturely perspectifies the otherwise all-too-serious aspects of life; and (d) a curious capacity of unconscious mental life.

To these I would add: (e) the unconscious as a significant "subject" in its own right that is capable of enormous aesthetic sophistication, one of whose manifestations is its capacity to generate humor; (f) the phenomenon of puns, which, among other uses, constitute a major system of bridges between the primary process of mythic mental life and the more familiar secondary process of our "realistically" logical lives; and (g) the capacity to be humorous and/or appreciate humor, which extends from anal sadism and the manic defense of the paranoid-schizoid position, where mocking and sarcasm predominate—to the depressive position where humor represents a broader, forgiving, and more philosophical point of view, one which appreciates the humor in paradoxes and ambiguities.

Additionally, I should like to mention: (h) the phenomenon of the *prosody of humor,* by which I mean a style or manner of humor on the part of the therapist that approximates the demeanor of an accepting parent—where the manner of receptivity to the patient, while remaining appropriately serious and attentive and not dismissive—nevertheless adds a "light touch," so as to say, "I know it is hard for you to tolerate this situation, but it is part of life; it is endurable. One day you will be able to laugh at it. After all, isn't humor tragedy plus time?"

I must issue a caveat at this time, however. There are some forms of humor that have no place in technique. These include mocking, sarcasm, ridicule, and the narration of "dirty" jokes. Additionally, I believe that "the jury is still out" on the issue of whether or not the therapist should laugh when the patient tells him a joke, particularly when it is apparent that it serves as a resistance. When it is not a resistance, however, it is a very human experience to share the spontaneous surprise and joy of humor with the patient as a chance testimony to the spontaneity of a shared intimate moment.

BACKGROUND

Freud (1905a) first introduced us to the mirthful side of ourselves with his early work on jokes, which he believed owed their success in achieving their humorous result to being able to bypass the censorship of the unconscious and thereby allow otherwise undesirable and repressed instinctual drives to appear in consciousness. The humor, mirth, or laughter with which we respond to jokes owes its origin, consequently, to this circumspect release of otherwise repressed elements. In this regard jokes can consequently be thought of as an alternative mode of instinctual drive expression and can represent an aesthetic partnership between the functions of primary and secondary processes (Freud, 1911).

Yet the capacity to tell jokes—and to appreciate the humor and truth embedded in them—calls attention to yet another aspect of joke telling and, more particularly, of the nature of the relationship between humor and the unconscious. The unconscious, with the help of primary as well as secondary processes, is a joke teller and humor and pun purveyor! It is well known that Freud wrote his first major work on humor, "Jokes and the Relation to the Unconscious," in 1905 at the same time that he was writing his seminal "Three Contributions to a Theory of Sexuality" (1905b). It was also only five years after he first published "The Interpretation of Dreams" (1900). It is obvious, therefore, that Freud thought that jokes were analogous in many ways to dreams and were revelatory of unconscious mental processes but, because of their nature, allow for a detour or a bypass of censorship because of the very fact of not being taken seriously. In his work on jokes, Freud believed that the purpose of joke telling was either (a) hostile or aggressive or (b) obscene or exposing.

Freud believed that, in a joke, a thought in the preconscious is submitted to unconscious revision, which allows for a partial transient and involuntary release of the repressed.

Baker (1993) draws attention to Freud's belief that the analysis of jokes and the technique of their production closely resembles the transformations that occur in dreams. Baker states:

> Freud's volume includes the analysis of a wide variety of jokes and his observation that the technique of their production bears a close resemblance to the transformations that occur in dreams and certain of the mechanisms described in "The Psychopathology of Everyday Life" (1901): which includes condensation, substitute-formation, displacement, indirect representation, reversal into opposites, failures in pursuit of logical thought, neologisms, fusion into unity, absurdity, etc. The point is that production such as jokes are seen by Freud as emanating from the unconscious. Humor, on the other hand, is seen as a defense against the disagreeable; thus the energy that would otherwise produce pain, in humor results in pleasure. [Baker, 1993, p. 951].

Baker also reminds us that Freud said that for humor only one person is necessary whereas for comicality two persons are necessary and for a joke three are necessary (the teller, the person against whom it is directed, and the listener) (p. 951). Baker (1993) states that Freud (1927) valued humor because "humor is the highest expression of the adaptive mechanisms because it succeeds in restraining the compulsion to make a choice between suffering and denial" (p. 166).

When Freud (1927), after a long hiatus, returned to his studies on the comedic dimension of unconscious mental life, he examined the subject of humor and added the insight that the expression of humor represents a veritable "conspiracy" (my word) between the unconscious superego and the ego in which the former seems paradoxically to relent in its otherwise critical attitude toward the latter in a desire to reassure the ego. Freud (1927) stated that, his earlier work on jokes and the relation to the unconscious, he considered humor only from the economic point of view. There his object was to discover the source of the pleasure obtained from humor.

Freud lists some of the characteristics of humor. He states:

> Like jokes and the comic, humor has something liberating about it; but it also has something of grandeur and elevation, which is lacking in the other two ways of obtaining pleasure from intellectual activity. The grandeur in it clearly lies in the triumph of narcissism, the victorious assertion of the ego's invulnerability. The ego refuses to be

distressed by the provocations of reality, to let itself be compelled to suffer. It insists that it cannot be affected by the traumas of the external world [p. 162].

Later he states:

Humor is not resigned; it is rebellious. . . . the rejection of the claims of reality and the putting through of the pleasure principle—bring humor nearer to the regressive or reactionary processes which engage our attention so extensively in psychopathology. It fending off of the possibility of suffering places is among the great series of methods which the human mind has constructed in order to evade the compulsion to suffer. . . . Thanks to this connection, humor possesses a dignity which is wholly lacking, for instance, in jokes, for jokes either serve simply to obtain a yield of pleasure or place the yield of pleasure that has been obtained in the service of aggression [p. 163].

Freud also points out that in humor the superego paradoxically seems to be a reassuring agency on the side of the ego. Freud seems to suggest that a splitting of the ego takes place where one aspect identifies with a benign superego treating its other ego self as a child. Humor thus is the other side of feeling sorry for oneself.

Christie (1994) discusses the question of the reasonable maturity of one's having a sense of humor. He states:

I am referring here to a certain quality of humor, and questioning whether it can be a generated influence in human communication, facilitating increments of insight and personal growth. If so, it should be contrasted with other forms of so-called humor that can be drawn into the service of manic defense, or into providing slightly modified avenues for destructive impulses such as in obscenity and sarcasm [p. 479].

Strean (1994) is a proponent of the positive aspects of humor in psychotherapy. Strean (1993) points out:

For many individuals, including myself, the act of telling and listening to jokes has many similarities to making love, and the laughter that can erupt can be likened to an orgasm. Further, mutual laughter between two confreres as they exchange jokes can be similar to a mutual orgasm [p. xiii].

Christie (1994) states that humor in its most reasonable aspects represents the ability to tolerate ambivalent feelings toward the object, the capacity to "tolerate antithetical ideas, images, or concepts simultaneously" (p. 480). In other words, humor reflects the capacity for integration of opposites. In discussing the essential nature of humor, Christie believes that having a sense of humor suggests a broader view of the self, a binocular vision, so to speak. Christie, in citing the work of Russell (1991) and Lyam Hudson (cited in Russell, 1991), states: "In the Cambridge research study quoted by Russell (1991) Lyam Hudson found that the following qualities characterize highly creative children—curiosity, flexibility of thinking, a capacity to redefine problems, aesthetic appreciation, tolerance of ambiguity, and a capacity for humor" (p. 481). Christie goes on to say that play and healthy humor provide an essential medium for the mother in her role as organizer of the child's early movements toward ego integration. In other words, humor has a role in the humanization of the primitive superego. Winnicott (1971), according to Christie, places humor in the category of playing. Searles (1965), according to Christie, believes that humor is one of the great avenues by which disillusionment is sublimated in human development.

Warren Poland (1990) takes a positive approach to the whole subject of humor. He believes that it is important to be able to laugh at oneself, that humor represents a sublimation or a neutralization of instinctual drive derivatives. Further, he believes that humor follows a line of development from childhood onward. He quotes Freud as stating that humor represents the triumph of narcissism. One of the purposes of joke telling, he states, is to be able to hold an audience enthralled—that is, the need to impact others. It caters, as Freud has pointed out, to the exhibitionistic instinct within us. Poland points out, "The capacity for humor linked to wisdom about the world is available in varying degrees to all of us, and one of the special delights of clinical analysis is seeing the liberation and development of such humor in the course of a patient's analytic work" (p. 197). Poland links emotional development and maturity with increased capability at laughing at oneself and at the world at large. From the psychotherapeutic vantage point, jokes are of importance in terms of their availing themselves of double meanings—a play on words, so to speak. Poland (1990) refers to the "gift of laughter" and refers to the "relatively mature capacity to acknowledge urges and frustrations, hopes and disappointments, with the humor in which bitterness is tamed but not denied" (p. 199). Almost all jokes deride or demean someone or some commonly held idea. Some jokes are more like riddles or have a riddle-like quality. According to Strean (1993, 1994), there are several different kinds of jokes: some have double meanings; others are riddles; still others deride the use of certain language; they include slips of the tongue, incongruities, grandiosities, denial, mockery, and surprise. He also points out that jokes and the emergence of a sense of humor, which represents an ego strength, parallel psychosexual development and the development of mature object relationships.

The first aspect of humor begins with the infant's earliest smile (Spitz, 1959) during the oral stage and represents the infant's response to the mother's own benignly humorous disposition. In the anal-sadistic stage, there is pleasure in controlling others and also later in telling dirty, smutty jokes with anal references. On the more positive side, jokes that relate to riddles and play on words represent a certain kind of benign anal mastery. In his concept of the developmental line of humorous states, Poland (1990) said:

> The line of development is determined by constitutional drive pressures and by maturing capacity to appreciate otherness, finiteness, and the limits of reality. The adult gift of laughter . . . refers to the relatively mature capacity to acknowledge urges and frustrations, hopes and disappointments with a humor in which bitterness is tamed but not denied [p. 485].

Strean (1993) points out that:

> Just as mature sexual encounter recapitulates psychosexual development, so does a mature exchange of jokes. A fulfilling sexual encounter is usually initiated by words and kisses (oral), accumulations of tensions (anal), and consummation in penetration (genital). When the teller and listener are together in the sensually loving, the mutual laughter that evolves from a joke can be similar to mutual orgasm. In telling and listening to a joke, words (oral) lead to tensions (anal), which result in laughter (genital).

Kubie (1971) has been often cited for his negative view of the use of humor in analysis. Other analysts and therapists believe that humor can be discretely used as an intervention strategy (Olson, 1990; Malamud, 1994; Prerost, 1994; Poland, 1994; Saul and Saul, 1994). Another aspect of humor that is very important is the use of the "king's *fool*" archetype. The fool in real life is oftentimes a child who has made himself the laughingstock of his family by clowning around and behaving in such a way that he is in danger of not being taken seriously. He may help to relieve Mother's depression or Father's rage by sacrificing himself, oftentimes as the designated patient within the family. It is a way of bypassing challenge, castration anxiety, rivalry, and so on. The fool is also related to the concept of the clown or the jester. In this role one can see a certain aspect of martyrdom. On the other hand, there is his aggressive and often sadistic counterpart, the jester or comedian, who uses others as the foil of his rapier wit irony, paradox, satire, parody, and sometimes outright hostility.

Mahon (1992) believes, following Arieti (1967), that humor is a result of the secondary revision that may be needed in order to displace the meaning a little further from its oedipal core. He calls this "tertiary process." Mahon, citing Chukovsky (1925), states that humor can appear as early as age 2 in children. He also emphasizes the importance of double entendres in humor.

Pasquali (1987) raises the question of the propriety of humor in psychoanalysis.

Ernest Jones (1912), in discussing a humorless patient, stated:

> I feel disposed to attribute this lack of humour in part to the strong repression of the exhibitionistic impulse which is known to be of fundamental importance in this connection. . . . As is generally recognized, humour is one of the chief means of self-defense against the slings and arrows of an unfriendly world [p. 373–374].

DISCUSSION

In this contribution I should like to discuss humor from a variety of perspectives. Humor plays a varied but important role in the daily life of virtually every individual, whether it occurs as jokes or as a characterological, philosophical way of relating to life's hardships.

The experience of humor begins early. Most mothers and fathers lovingly "jolly" their infants and children on occasions that may be frustrating for the latter. The parent's demonstration of humor in those instances may constitute a posturing model whereby they show the infant that everything is going to be all right. It has a cosmic reassurance motivation, "All's right with the world, and you'll be O.K." Humor takes on a darker and more sinister cast during the anal-withholding and anal-sadistic stages, best expressed by the concept of the manic defense against the dependency feelings belonging to the depressive position. When the toddler regresses from the threshold of the depressive position and falls back to the paranoid-schizoid position where he may employ the defensive techniques of triumph, contempt, and control, he may sarcastically laugh at others for whom he has contempt. It is only with attainment of the depressive position that humor begins to acquire its human, cosmic, merciful, and philosophical characteristics.

In analysis many opportunities for the emergence of humor occur, either on the part of the patient or the analyst. Most often, humor seems to emerge unexpectedly in the form of puns or double entendres. That they may appear unexpectedly does not mean that their appearance is accidental. Puns and double entendres are generated by a sophisticated "Other" of unconscious mental life. This last point was brought to my attention by, among many sources, the contributions of Lacan (1966), who revolutionized the rereading of Freud and, in line with this rereading, revalorized the importance of the unconscious. In his criticism of ego psychology, particularly of the American school, he believed that Freud had treated the unconscious more respectfully in his earlier work—before 1923, when he formulated his structural theory of the psychic apparatus and launched the field of ego psychology ("classical" psychoanalysis) in place of id analysis ("orthodox" psychoanalysis).

In particular, Lacan felt that Freud's earlier concept of the unconscious was one in which it appeared to be a more sophisticated system than he pictured it later. For instance, the unconscious that generated dreams and jokes revealed its capacity for sophisticated langauge operations and was seemingly at odds with his later picture of it as the seat of a "seething cauldron." The sad irony may now become clear that Freud, the discoverer of unconscious mental life, may have ultimately undervalued perhaps his most immortal discovery!

It was Lacan (1966) who formulated the concept that "the unconscious was structured like a language" and constituted "the discourse of the Other." While not ignoring the fact that Lacan's picture of the unconscious more resembles Freud's description of the *preconscious* (which, unlike the unconscious, utilizes *negation*) than it does of his picture of the *unconscious*, he nevertheless reveals an important idea about unconscious mental life—that the unconscious is socially, linguistically, and semiotically structured and is, as Chomsky (1957, 1968) was also to state, characterized by the capacity for transformational generative syntax—that is, it has the inherent ability to generate the rules and structure of language, to which I would add the alternative, "language" of puns and jokes. It was Lacan, more than any other analyst, I believe, who emphasized the importance of puns and associated their occurrence with revelations of unconscious thinking.

He harangued against the American School of Ego Psychology for its privileging of the ego over the id and lamented that, after 1923, when Freud initiated this fateful and fatal shift, the id became imperceptibly depreciated, demonized as a "seething cauldron," and relegated to the position of the apologetic ego's shameful sibling and scapegoat, one that must be hidden in the metaphoric basement as its "primitive" counterpart—Jacob's Esau, so to speak. Lacan believed that, in early Freud, in which he had emphasized the construction of dreams, jokes, and slips of the tongue, one could discern the effects of a lofty (hardly "primitive") intelligence at work. In other words, Lacan believes—and I agree—that the unconscious has suffered from a seemingly inadvertent, perfunctory dismissal as anything but a veritable power source of "nuclear energy" or the profaned and quarantined storage bin of the shameful archive of our mistreatment at the hands of our otherwise "loved ones."

In brief, the unconscious has a sophistication of high order, one that has not been sufficiently appreciated. Its capacity to dream a dream narrative cannot be simply dismissed as being caused by the mechanism of the dream work of primary process. In other contributions I detail the provenance of orthodox and classical psychoanalytic conceptions in the 19th-century notion of the "second self" or "alter ego." Freud (1923) "borrowed" the term *id* from the works of Nietzsche (1883) and Groddeck (1923) but failed to convey *their* understanding of the term as "the other." In other words, Freud failed to convey that the unconscious, which had been well known in the 19th century, was a "second self," or an "alter ego."

In respect to the study of the phenomenon of humor, the impact of my formulation is such that the unconscious has been insufficiently appreciated as being a clever jokester and sophisticated humorist! In other words, the "intelligence" that seems to underwrite unconscious humor has uncanny wisdom and an unusual sense of perspective about one's ontological position in the world. It reveals and revels in *absurdity.*

Bion (1963) postulated the concepts of alpha function and container/contained as basic mental functions. Alpha function is his idiosyncratic term to designate the integrated and harmoniously complementary activities of what Freud (1911) termed the primary and secondary processes. Whereas the two were believed by Freud and are still believed by his followers to be in conflict, Bion believes that they normally work hand-in-hand with one another. Humor, for example, may be initiated in the unconscious and emerge in consciousness in the form of a pun, but this pun represents the results, not so much of a *compromise formation* as it does the complementary creativeness and expressive communicationality of both systems working together for the epistemological enterprise of analysis. An example comes to mind. A deeply dependent female patient reported a dream to me after a vacation. In this dream she had gone on a buying spree and then had a manicure. I was alerted to her mania by the buying spree association and then called her attention to her "manic cure" of her dependent self in my absence by taking herself away from a sober and mournful state of mind and into a grandiose one.

SOME NOTES ON THE DEVELOPMENTAL ASPECTS OF HUMOR

In all probability a capacity to be purposely humorous or to develop a sense of humor comes about only after the toddler has achieved, not only verbal capacity, but also those aspects of the depressive position (separation/individuation) when (s)he has achieved the capacity for *intersubjectivity* (Trevarthen, 1980, 1983, 1987, 1988, 1991; Stern, 1985) and of sense of mindedness in oneself as well as in the other (Fonagy,

1991, 1995). Another factor would be the infant/toddler's capacity to comprehend paradoxical thinking, a faculty that depends on his/her ability to employ symbolism and also to be able to harbor two incompatible points of view, upon which the ironic contrasts of humor rely. This latter capacity relates to the child's development of a "dual-track," stereoscopic capacity. Thus, the capacity for humor, which also borrows from the infant's capacity for illusion, also demonstrates his/her capacity to play—with thoughts (Winnicott, 1971).

HUMOR IN THERAPY AND ANALYSIS

I believe that jokes, humor, and puns on the part of the analysand occupy a position of complementarity with a humorous dimension in the analyst. In the latter case the analyst may sometimes tell a joke in order to illustrate an interpretation, as Poland (1990) and Strean (1993, 1994) have pointed out. His or her manner may also be humorous as a posturing statement of interpretatively diminishing the analysand's anxieties. Even as I state this I realize that this analytic stance can be interpreted by many as being collusive and constitutive of a parameter because of its being seen as a reassurance rather than as an interpretation. Seriousness, sobriety, abstention, and neutrality have long been considered to be the sine qua non of analytic demeanor for very understandable reasons.

Yet in more recent times contributors from the schools of self psychology and intersubjectivity seem to challenge this seemingly sterile and depriving stance. Lindon (1994), for instance, argues in favor of the concept of provisions, by which he means that the analyst, while avoiding the application of outright collusive parameters, *should* provide a welcoming atmosphere to the patient. What I am getting at here is that the ongoing, moment-to-moment behavior of the analyst, the prosody of his speech, the lightness or heaviness of his manner, his gestural friendliness or coldness, and more, constitute a subject that is rarely discussed. I am suggesting that an important aspect of his demeanor with the patient may have to do with his capacity to show a light touch—discreetly—when a light touch may be called for and to be able to be humorous—discreetly—without trivializing the seriousness of the analytic moment.

I believe that what I am suggesting has more than a shade of difference from improper analysis and more resembles the attitude professed by Winnicott (1971) in his concept of "playing." Let me present an example. A patient who has suffered from colic in her infancy and from chronic anxiety in her adult life reported in one session that she was troubled by her sexual feelings toward a married colleague. After dealing with the oedipal transference implications of the statement, I also stated the following: "Your *colicky* infant self seems to be frightened of being *frolicky*!" Upon hearing this, the patient burst into laughter and began examining what a stranglehold the colicky self had long imposed on her sensual self.

What I am emphasizing here is that aspect of the "posture of technique" in which it is the therapist's humorous demeanor, when humor may be appropriate, that oftentimes allows the patient finally to understand the conflicting paradoxes in his or her thinking and behavior. On one particular occasion, an analysand appeared somewhat late for her session, stating that she had become so caught up in the O.J. Simpson trial that she lost sight of the time. I replied, "You are telling me on another level that it is a trial for you to come here." It was only when she burst out laughing that I realized that I had punned.

I recall in another case that my humorous response to a patient's dream had been important in the understanding of it. This particular patient was an airline stewardess who frequently made transatlantic flights to Europe and the Near East. On this one occasion she proffered a very lengthy dream, one that took about a half hour or more to report. In this dream she and her lover were motoring through the mountains of Spain's Sierra Madre mountain range. The balmy weather suddenly changed into a heavy, relentless downpour of rain. She and her lover became soaked and looked for a place of shelter. The dream reporting went on and on, and I remember becoming bored and sleepy. Finally, I found myself jestfully saying, "But the rain in Spain stays mainly in the plains!" The patient was dumb struck and then revealed that she had recently been contacted by a former lover with whom she had seen the musical, *My Fair Lady*. This man was felt by her to be something of a Pygmalion/ Professor Higgins to her, and she had been pining for him for years. The rain in the mountains of Spain represented her grief over his loss. The reversal of the location of the rain in the mountains from the plains represented her wish to reverse her fate of having lost him.

There are times, as Freud (1900, 1905a) has shown, when a patient's dreams manifestly reveal jokes and puns. I recall a dream that was presented to me by a patient on her second day of treatment. In this dream she had entered a pharmacy in order to purchase vitamins. The pharmacist informed her that she could not purchase vitamins without a doctor's prescription. She was surprised and uttered, "What do you mean I need a doctor's prescription? You don't need a prescription for vitamins!" The pharmacist thereupon stated, "Oh, yes you do! Remember, this is a dream!" The meaning of the dream immediately became clear. No sooner had she committed herself to undergoing analysis when a resistant self emerged, who employed the manic defense against the authority of the analyst and of the dependent self that desired the analysis. As it turned out, this conflict seemed to have underscored much of the course of the analysis thereafter.

On another occasion, a patient reported a dream that took place in an open market where "a wizened old man was selling fish." I now no longer recall the other details of the manifest dream, but after processing the patient's associations, I recall that I had been puzzled by that particular detail—until I detected the pun in "*sell*-ing *fish*!" It was only then that I realized that the patient had projected her own feelings of *selfishness* into me and was therby being critical of me.

Another example is the following: When a patient reported a dream to a colleague on the day following the latter's lengthy vacation in which an automobile "brake shop" figured, it was not hard for the therapist to comprehend that the patient needed "repairs on his autonomy" and in particular needed to be able to fix his capacity to deal with the therapist's "breaks."

One of the most natural, but humorous, analytic occasions of humor for me was the experience with a young, ingenuous housewife who had been reared on a farm in the Midwest. In one particular session she presented a dream in which a sinister and decrepit old man was trying to seduce her. Following her revealing her associations, I interpreted to her, "It is you who wishes to seduce me as you once wanted to seduce your father." She forthrightly replied, "Poppycock!" It was only when she heard my muffled laughter that she began to realize the significance of what she had uttered.

Another patient, a 39-year-old unmarried woman who wanted children but who had no boyfriend or steady lover, found herself pregnant after a "one-night stand." After consulting an obstetrican, she reported to me, "I'm pregnant with twins and there are no two ways about it!" It was only when I began to laugh that she became aware of her slip. We analyzed it and came up with the obvious conclusion that she was both pleased and sorry to be pregnant and was frightened about being "doubly pregnant" because of all the added responsibilities that would be entailed.

Yet another patient, one who was sad about having to interrupt her analysis for external reasons, mentioned to me upon entering the consultation room, "I couldn't remember if you wore glasses." I assumed that she really did know that I always had but that she had experienced a "conversion amnesia." I responded, "You don't want to look at the fact that I soon will no longer be seeing you." She became tearful.

The very capacity to generate puns and humor can attest either to a deceptively disingenuous, cynical, contemptuous, or even arrogant side of either the analysand or the analyst, on the one hand, or constitute either's capacity for eminent humanness, demonstrating a transcendence over the grimness and tragedy of reality. The comedienne Carol Burnett (personal communication) once stated, "Comedy is tragedy plus time!" From this perspective, the ability to place one's predicaments in a humorous perspective attests to the subject's having achieved the grace of the depressive position. This achievement suggests, in turn, that the subject is no longer trapped in the "labyrinth" of the first dimension of psychic space (absolute "either/or"). The subject can now see things in perspective (third dimension), that is, from different points of view and therefore demonstrates their access to a dual-track capacity. Alternatives now exist for him. The subject has become worldly enough to take life in his stride and has acquired enough confidence in himself to know that he can adjust to most of life's demands.

Sometimes the patient may employ a humorous, but telling, mode of relaying a transference message. I recall the borderline patient whose clothing provided powerful analytic statements. On one occasion following my vacation, this patient wore a T-shirt with the following on its front: "God is back from lunch." The deeper the analysis of the statement was not merely that I had returned from my "selfish" vacation. It had more the feel that, when I was gone, she felt deserted even by God, so convinced was she that there was no fairness in the world. "God's being 'back from vacation'" meant to her that she had come to develop faith in herself and in the analysis and had transcended her despair.

In a sarcastic moment of negative transference, a patient who, knowing that I was Kleinian in my orientation, on hearing an interpretation from me about his "manic defense" against his feelings of vulnerability, followed by my saying that he was trying to defy the laws of mental gravity, stated, "There is no gravity. The Earth sucks!" Embedded in that joke was a complexity of associations that he felt helplessly overwhelmed by the peremptoriness of his infantile "sucking" self that the analysis had "forced" him to become aware of. Later, in the same hour, he stated, "Don't ask me, I just work here!" This statement, followed the sucking theme, testified both to his sense of helplessness in terms of his needy self and the transference evocation of it, on one hand, and, on the other, to his impassively bitter protest about it.

Sometimes humor may be used analytically as a shorthand parable to replace what would otherwise be a much longer interpretation. I recall an instance of that with a male patient who had just met a beautiful colleague at a convention who seemed to be taken with him. He had found fault with her. Rather than giving him the "long form" interpretation, I related the contents of an old "Peanuts®" cartoon. In the first box of the cartoon, Linus is telling another little boy, "A pretty girl moved in down the street." In the second box he continues, "I didn't know what to say to her." In the third box he stated, "So I hit her." The patient roared with laughter and then, in that eased atmosphere, was able to accept the fact of his defensive hatred of women and the fear behind the defense— of his envy of them because he admired them and needed them so much.

Just before finishing writing this very contribution, I happened to be discussing the theme of this chapter with a colleague. He thereupon informed me that his own training analyst frequently tells him jokes. At first, he resented it and complained about it, but then he began to realize that his very Jewish analyst was an inveterate storyteller, and that was his best vehicle for conveying meaningful interpretations to his patients. My colleague's final verdict about his analyst's technique was, "It works!"

Sometimes humor is useful in discussion with colleagues. I remember an incident in which I was trying to convince Daniel Stern that he was wrong in deferring the time at which infants can experience phantasies until the time of verbalization (approximately 14 months). He knew that I represented the Kleinian point of view, that is, that infants are separate from the beginning and that they experience conscious and unconscious phantasies virtually from the start. I was intimidated, however, by his outstanding background in research, but at the same time I harbored the belief that his research was too narrowly focused. I thereupon told him the following "Tale of Chelm," as originally written by Sholem Aleichem:

> A traveling salesman approached a village at twilight on the heels of a heavy rain. As soon as he entered the village, he came upon another traveling salesman who was feverishly digging in the mud. The arriving salesman asked the anxious man what had happened, whereupon the latter informed him that he had lost some of his merchandise in the mud. The newcomer decided to help and joined him in digging in the mud. After many fruitless hours of digging, the newly arrived salesman asked the hapless salesman, "Are you sure you lost your merchandise here? We've been digging for hours and haven't found anything." The other then said, "No, I lost them up the street, but there was no street light up there."

Daniel Stern immediately got the point and graciously acknowledged that, unlike the videotape and other instruments that are used in infant research, there are as yet no "phantasy-scopes" for the detection of *un*conscious, let alone conscious, phantasies in the infant's mind.

There is another joke I frequently tell when speaking to the subject of "projective identification." Interestingly, non-Kleinian psychoanalysts and therapists seem to have a harder time initially in understanding it:

> Two female ostriches were walking together down a beach when they suddenly realized that two male ostriches are rapidly approaching them. One of the female ostriches anxiously reports the sight of the approach-

ing males to the other and says, "Those two males are hitting on us! Let's hide!" Whereupon, they hide their heads in the sand. No sooner do they hide their heads than one of the pursuing male ostriches says to his companion, "Where did they go?"

Perhaps the most bittersweet, yet poignant, episode of humor is in the following example:

> A 29-year-old single female who was born and raised in another country had already related in detail a history of privation. Her father abandoned her mother early in the mother's pregnancy with her. Mother then abandoned her to her own bitter, psychotic mother, who then raised her. Her life thereafter was full of bitterness. Anger characterized her disposition. Although quite beautiful by most standards, she always considered herself ugly. She understandably had considerable difficulty in intimate relationships. On the other hand, she always loved animals and currently has two dogs and three cats, to whom she is quite devoted. During one session she related how, on the previous evening, she had seen a documentary on Hitler and was surprised to learn that he too was an animal lover and had created many laws for the protection of animals. The patient then confided, "I've got a buddy!"

SUMMARY

Humor consitutes an affect and an interpersonal technique of relating that poses interesting, as well as important, issues for psychoanalytic and psychotherapeutic technique. Purists eschew its use, whereas more liberal therapists seem to condone it, either as an obligatory, but respected, accidental, but meaningful, occurrence in the therapy or as a viable and respectable technical intervention in its own right. The history of its use in psychoanalysis and of the attitudes about it were discussed. In this contribution I have tried to demonstrate that humor constitutes a philosophical and critical (in the objective and/or subjective sense) statement about life in general and important objects in the patient's life in particular, namely the analyst or therapist. It can be used by the patient to augment his emotional expressiveness and can be used or misused by the analyst either in countertransference enactments or in serious and appropriate technical interventions.

Humor in the course of an analysis, particularly in the form of puns, often reflect the "genius" of the unconscious in allowing an otherwise carefully guarded and repressed association to surface. It can accurately be stated, I believe, that analytic puns "read" the unconscious. Puns therefore may reflect an alternative aspect of the epistemological workings of the unconscious.

Humor seems to be a supraordinate phenomenon that represents an integration between the primary and secondary processes. It can often become a skilled negotiator between each and allows for a philosophical solution to hardships, conflict, frustration, and other forms of suffering. It is an allowable manic defense. On the other hand, humor has an ontological dimension that can originate aside from mental pain. It oftentimes emerges as a poetically compressed verdict on reality or even a celebration of life itself. Humor's capacity to be humorous depends on our ability to shift perspectives, to be able to decenter ourselves from a fixed, cyclopean point of view, in order to be able to see things differently. If we really stop to think about it, the curative benefits from psychoanalysis and psychotherapy derive largely from introducing alternate and compelling perspectives about their own fixed views about their problems.

The role of humor in analysis is complex. The most favorable use of humor is the occasion in which it is not being used as a technique but, rather, when it spontaneously springs up improvisationally in either the analysand or the analyst. That form of humor known as puns comes closer to resonating with the unconscious. It is possible that in any given therapy or analysis most of the puns remain unnoticed by either participant. It is as if double entendres abound looking for an audience to appreciate them—too often in vain.

REFERENCES

Arieti, S. (1967), *The Intrapsychic Self*. New York: Basic Books.

Bader, M. J. (1993), The analyst's use of humor. *Psychoanal. Quart.*, 62:23–51.

Baker, R. (1993), Some reflections on humour in psychoanalysis. *Internat. J. Psycho-Anal.*, 74:951–960.

Bion, W. R. (1963), *Elements of Psycho-Analysis*. New York: Basic Books.

Chomsky, N. (1957), *Syntactic Structures*. The Hague: Mouton.

——— (1968), *Language and the Mind*. New York: Harcourt, Brace & World.

Christie, G. L. (1994), Some psychoanalytic aspects of humour. *Internat. J. Psycho-Anal.*, 75:479–489.

Chucovsky, K. I. (1925), *From Two to Five*, ed. and trans. M. Morton. Berkeley: University of California Press.

Fonagy, P. (1991), Thinking about thinking: Some developmental and theoretical considerations in the psychotherapy of a borderline patient. *Internat. J. Psycho-Anal.*, 72:639–656.

——— (1995), Playing with reality: The development of psychic reality and its malfunction in borderline patients. *Internat. J. Psycho-Anal.*, 76:39–44.

Freud, S. (1900), The interpretation of dreams. *Standard Edition,* 5:339–630. London: Hogarth Press, 1953.

—— (1901), The psychopathology of everyday life. *Standard Edition,* 6:1–290. London: Hogarth Press, 1960.

—— (1905a), Jokes and their relation to the unconscious. *Standard Edition,* 8:9–236. London: Hogarth Press, 1960.

—— (1905b), Three essays on the theory of sexuality. *Standard Edition,* 7:130–243. London: Hogarth Press, 1953.

—— (1911), Formulations of the two principles of mental functioning. *Standard Edition,* 12:218–226. London: Hogarth Press, 1958.

—— (1923), The ego and the id. *Standard Edition,* 19:12–66. London: Hogarth Press, 1961.

—— (1927), Humor. *Standard Edition,* 21:159–166. London: Hogarth Press, 1961.

Groddeck, G. W. (1923), *The Book of the It.* New York: Mentor Books.

Jones, E. (1912), Analytic study of a case of obsessional neurosis. In: *Papers on Psycho-Analysis* (2nd ed.). London: Balliere, Tindall & Cox, 1918.

Klein, M. (1960), *Narrative of a Child Analysis.* New York: Basic Books.

Kubie, L. S. (1971), The destructive potential of humor in psychotherapy. *Amer. J. Psychother.,* 127:861–866.

Lacan, J. (1966a), *Écrits.* Paris: Seuil. Republished: *Écrits: 1949–1960,* trans. A. Sheridan. New York: Norton, 1977.

Lindon, J. (1994), Gratifications and provisions in psychoanalysis: Should we get rid of "the rule of abstinence?" *Psychoanal. Dial.,* 4:549–582.

Mahon, E. J. (1992), The function of humor in a four-year-old. *The Psychoanalytic Study of the Child,* 47:321–328. New Haven, CT: Yale University Press.

Malamud, D. I. (1994), The laughing game: An exercise for sharpening awareness of self-responsibility. In: *The Use of Humor in Psychotherapy,* ed. H. Strean. Northvale, NJ: Aronson, pp. 149–156.

Nietzsche, F. (1883), *Thus Spoke Zarathustra,* trans. R. J. Hollingdale. London: Penguin, 1961.

Olson, H. A. (1994), The use of humor in psychotherapy. In: *The Use of Humor in Psychotherapy,* ed. H. Strean. Northvale, NJ: Aronson, pp. 195–198.

Pasquali, G. (1987), Some notes on humour in psychoanalysis. *Internat. Rev. Psycho-Anal.,* 14:231–236.

Poland, W. S. (1990), The gift of laughter: On the development of a sense of humor in clinical analysis. *Psychoanal. Quart.,* 59:197–225.

Prerost, F. J. (1994), Humor as an intervening strategy. In: *The Use of Humor in Psychotherapy,* ed. H. Strean. Northvale, NJ: Aronson, pp. 139–148.

Russell, E. (1991), The excited child. *Austral. J. Psychother.,* 10:166–179.

Saul, S. & Saul, S. R. (1994), The application of joy in group psychotherapy for the elderly. In: *The Use of Humor in Psychotherapy,* ed. H. Strean. Northvale, NJ: Aronson, pp. 157–166.

Searles, H. (1965), *Collected Papers on Schizophrenia and Related Subjects.* New York: International Universities Press.

Spitz, R. (1959), *A Genetic Field Theory of Ego Formation: Its Implications for Pathology.* New York: International Universities Press.

Stern, D. N. (1985), *The Interpersonal World of the Infant: A View from Psychoanalysis and Developmental Psychology.* New York: Basic Books.

Strean, H. (1993), *Jokes and Their Purpose and Meaning.* Northvale, NJ: Aronson.

—— ed. (1994), *The Use of Humor in Psychotherapy.* Northvale, NJ: Aronson.

Trevarthen, C. (1980), The foundations of intersubjectivity: Development of interpersonal and cooperative understanding in infants. In: *The Social Foundations of Language and Thought. Essays in Honor of J. S. Bruner,* ed. D. Olson. New York: Norton, pp. 316–342.

—— (1983), Development of the cerebral mechanisms of language. In: *Neuropsychology of Language, Reading, and Spellilng,* ed. U. Kirk. New York: Academic Press, pp. 45–80.

—— (1987), Sharing making sense. Intersubjectivity and the making of an infant's meaning. In: *Language Topics: Essays in Honor of Michael Halliday, Vol. 1,* ed. R. Steele & T. Threadgold. Amsterdam and Philadelphia: John Benjamins, pp. 177–199.

—— (1988), Universal cooperative motives: How infants begin to know langauge and skills of culture. In: *Ethnographic Perspectives on Cognitive Development,* ed. G. Jahoda & I. Lewis. London: Croon Helm, pp. 37–90.

—— (1991), The other in the infant's mind. Paper presented at "The Psychic Life of the Infant: Origins of Human Identity." Conference sponsored by the University of Massachusetts at Amherst, June 29.

Winnicott, D. W. (1971), *Playing and Reality.* New York: Basic Books.

PART II

Therapeutic Process

5

Humor, the Transitional Space, and the Therapeutic Process

PETER L. GIOVACCHINI

Psychoanalysis has been enveloped by an aura of seriousness. Around 40 years ago, I noted when attending professional meetings that the atmosphere was funereal. Bearded psychoanalysts smoking huge cigars would make profound judgments with such solemnity that it appeared that the future of civilization was at stake. Arguments could become acrimonious, and heaven help the heretic who threatened the supremacy of Freud's pronouncements.

I wondered whether some of these eminent psychoanalysts lacked a sense of humor, which may have been reflected in a lack of imagination and forceful dogmatic assertions, usually punctuated with a foreign accent. Somehow, many of my generation mistook some of these peculiarities for greatness, which in many instances concealed a sadistic orientation.

I am discussing humor by discussing the opposite. I am not going to explore the elements of humor and its dynamics. Certainly, it often has a hostile intent and is frequently a method of controlling raw sadistic impulses and raises them up to a pleasurable, aesthetic level (Freud, 1905). I find it noteworthy that the lack of humor also concerns sadism, but without the mitigating effects of comic and playful constructions. It is interesting that the lack of humor is sometimes mistaken for humor and cleverness.

I remember being interviewed when I was applying for matriculation at the Chicago Institute for Psychoanalysis by a senior, seemingly dedicated, but humorless analyst. He asked me to sit down, and for about a minute we sat in silence. My anxiety built up as I sat in a dark, depressing room with a small window. Finally, he spoke and asked me a question. He asked me to tell him my name. I thought this was strange because he had my application blank in front of him, but then I conjectured that maybe he wanted to hear how I pronounced it, because it is often mispronounced. I poised myself for the next question, which came after another minute of silence. A minute under those circumstances seemed as if it were an eternity. He asked where I lived. I answered his question, but again, if he had wanted to know the answer, all he had to do was look at my application on his desk. I did not know how to elaborate on his questions or free associate to them. I reasoned that maybe he was building up to something, that this was part of some byzantine strategy. After several minutes, he stood up, shook my hand, and dismissed me.

My peers were, of course, anxious to hear about my interview. When I told them, they were puzzled but concluded that this analyst was subtle and shrewd and had made me submit to some type of stress interview. I agreed about the stress, but I could not, in any way, understand the purpose of this silent inquisition without the exchange of any relevant information.

I felt that I had absorbed some of the humorless, depressed atmosphere of that office and carried it with me for about two weeks. My spirits were lightened, however, when I received a letter announcing that I had been accepted for matriculation. I was still puzzled, not knowing what had happened, but I was willing to forget about the whole episode because the outcome was good.

About two years later, I had to face another administrative hurdle that once again required being interviewed. As the fates would have it, this analyst was once again assigned to interview me. I did not feel a great amount of trepidation, because at the advanced level of my training, no one, so far as I know, had ever been rejected. I also expected that, being closer to being a colleague, he might be more sociable and pleasant and, perhaps, even talkative.

I was partially correct. He was a little more talkative in that he added a sentence to our discourse that he had not included in our first interview. Otherwise, the interview was an exact replica of the first. This time, I was even more puzzled when he asked my name, since I had been at several parties that he had attended and had introduced him to my wife, and on one occasion, someone had introduced me to him. In this second interview, before dismissing me, he enigmatically said: "Psychoanalysis is a serious business." To this day, I do not know whether this was a rebuke. I certainly had not felt frivolous in his dour presence, or perhaps he was sharing a bit of wisdom with me. In any case, as I had anticipated, I was again accepted.

I give these examples because I believe that psychoanalysts are particularly prone to the "Emperor's new clothes" phenomenon, a situation in which one attributes significance and importance to some event or phrase, but in fact there is nothing there.

Many analysts have narcissistic problems that lead to unconscious, but profound, feelings of inadequacy. There may be accompanying problems in their capacity to understand and assimilate subtle and difficult theoretical issues. To compensate for their shortcomings and to bolster their narcissism, they construct theories in a ponderous, pedantic, but serious fashion to cover up their lack of substance. I am not referring to any particular system, but I suggest that the reader pick up a prestigious psychoanalytic journal, open it at random, and pick out a sentence. Chances are that, after the sentence is parsed and then put in simpler words, it will make no sense.

As has often been noted, many of these older generation psychoanalysts were depressed and among them was an unusually large number of suicides. These were driven, humorless men. Many of them would have considered a light-hearted approach to psychoanalytic concepts blasphemous, and anything that deviated from Freud would be labeled as capricious and irresponsible.

It is interesting, however, that Freud, although he frequently demonstrated that he was depressed, especially in his letters to Fliess (Bonaparte, Freud, and Kris, 1954), nevertheless had a keen sense of humor. He enjoyed jokes and was capable of turning witty phrases. He gathered a depressed group of followers around him, but many did not have his sense of humor, as was true of my interviewer who had been in Freud's group as a young analyst.

HUMOR AND THE TRANSITIONAL SPACE

Without attempting a precise definition, humor can be viewed as a human attribute that involves a mode of perceiving and an attitude and outlook about relations between the internal world of the psyche and the external milieu. It contains both primary and secondary process elements as does creativity (Giovacchini, 1960), and it is related to creativity. Certainly, wit, as Freud (1905) refers to it, is a creative accomplishment, and a good joke is recognized by its appreciative audience, a quality that Kris (1952) found to be indispensible for creative activity.

Play is associated with humor, humor always having a playful quality.

Winnicott (1953) conceptualized a transitional space as an area in which play and illusion develops. I have conceptualized the creation of this transitional space as a developmental stage (Giovacchini, 1996).

This transitional stage represents a watershed in which the child moves into the external world and simultaneously moves it into himself. Perceptions and judgments about inner and outer reality stem from inner stimuli, impulses, and needs rather than from external sources and impingements, According to Winnicott, this is the area of illusion and omnipotence as well as creativity.

When the child has progressed to this stage, he has made considerable progress on the road to establishing object relationships and the recognition of an external world separate from the self. This is an in-between stage between the inside and outside and contains elements of both.

Winnicott (1953) believed that, because of optimal mothering the child believes he is the source of his own nurture. The baby feels hungry and then is fed. *It is as if a need creates its own gratification* and there is no recognition of the mother as mother. Winnicott referred to this belief of self-sufficiency as omnipotence, but it is doubtful that infants could sustain such a complex phenomenon as omnipotence. Rather, they feel secure in that their needs will be met, and at such a young age (around six months), there is not much of a concept about the source of nurture.

Because of maturational forces, infants begin to make more discrete and accurate discriminations between inside and outside. Finally, the illusion of being the source of their own nurture, most likely a *primal illusion,* gives way to the recognition of the mother as the font of gratification. However, under optimal circumstances, the illusion is not shattered. Instead, the child plays with it. These children can relinquish it, but they can bring it back by playing with it. Instead of omnipotence, as Winnicott postulated, they develop the capacity to play and can maintain equilibrium and mastery through play and the deliberate creation of gratifying fantasies.

Play later in life is an extension of the primal illusion of self-sufficiency and complete autonomy. Within the context of play, these beliefs are maintained, but at the same time dependent feelings and vulnerability coexist. It is the pretended denial of such feelings and their satirical or caricatured exaggeration that constitute humor.

The child, during the transitional phase, is simultaneously living in two worlds through the use of humor. Humor is the product that permits harmony between reality and illusion as it introduces a viewpoint that can make potentially grave situations appear not only nonthreatening but amusing. I have often stated that the task of psychoanalytic treatment is to convert grim reality into playful fantasy, and this occurs in the transitional zone. Often, this conversion is accompanied by humor, a by-product of this transformation. Putting this process in the form of a sequential progression, grim reality changes into playful fantasy, and this produces humor.

In structural terms, the act of entering or creating the transitional zone also generates humor, which in a positive feedback fashion, contributes to detoxifying reality as it is replaced by playful fantasies. This introduces an observational perspective in which patient and analyst examine the patient–analyst relationship and if, on occasion, there is some light-hearted banter in their dialogues, it is in the interest of therapeutic resolution.

Ogden (1994) has written of the analytic third that emphasizes the interaction between patient and analyst, which becomes the essence of therapeutic scrutiny. Rather than the analytic third being operative in the treatment process, I believe that it is more appropriate to think in terms of four persons. At one level, the patient and analyst are interacting with each other in a transference–countertransference context. At another level, the patient and therapist are standing together on an observational platform looking at the interaction going on below them. If the relationship on the platform is cordial and accompanied by good humor, that interaction is cooperative and collaborative, and even the most savage and primitive feelings can be discussed and experienced with a relative degree of comfort.

DEVELOPMENT OF HUMOR AND PSYCHOPATHOLOGY

Humor is a developmental achievement and is a component of the establishment of object relationships. It is both a mode of relating and an adaptive technique. Freud (1905) distinguished between wit and humor, the former being a type of manipulation in which hostile feelings are mitigated. Humor may also deal with destructive impulses, but as just discussed, it is more concerned with feelings of vulnerability and their mastery and is the outcome of transitional relatedness.

The transitional space is a structural entity that represents a developmental achievement. It contracts and expands as it moves back and forth from the inner world of the psyche and external reality. The intermingling of fairly primitive interior psychic processes with secondary process perceptions and judgments of external reality occurs in both the production of humor and creativity. As the psyche focuses on primitive layers, this might be considered to be a regression, but this would be a regression in the service of the ego as Kris (1950) described some time ago. He was describing the operations of the ego during creative activity, but I believe something similar occurs with the production of humor, which, as stated, is similar to creativity.

At a clinical level, humorless patients are usually hard to work with and tedious. I find myself, whenever possible, giving them early morning sessions so I am still fresh and energetic and can look forward to the rest of the day, because they can be difficult to deal with and exhausting. In part, this is because of the fact they are not particularly psychologically minded. Their thinking tends to be concrete and mechanistic, and this makes it difficult to construct an observational platform on which the patient and therapist can stand. For the most part, such patients are schizoid and narcissistically constricted. They have a paucity of object relationships, lack the capacity for symbolization, and are devoid of imagination.

Their prognoses often depend on their capacity to develop humor and to advance to a state of object relatedness that is compatible with the formation of humor. With some patients, even severely disturbed patients, there are occasional episodes when they, in spite of their misery and suffering, can poke fun at themselves or simultaneously view and evaluate a catastrophe in the external world as horrible but also as having a funny or ironic twist. Sometimes, this type of humor is black or gothic.

Besides being a positive ingredient for the establishment of a therapeutic relationship, humor can also be a barometer that indicates the degree of ego integration. As with other psychic processes it can lead to developmental advances, or it can regressively degrade as the outcome of psychic disintegration.

For example, a usually good-humored, middle-aged salesman suffered a tragic loss when his wife was killed in an automobile collision when he was driving. He suffered considerable grief, but in a clumsy attempt to console himself, he said, "It could have been worse; at least I had collision insurance." His therapist did not find this remark funny. In fact, he was offended by the crudeness of the statement, a failed attempt to make the best out of a bad situation.

It is interesting how the analytic attitude can dispel untoward reactions to a totally misfired humor. When this analyst told a colleague about this interchange, the colleague who had some emotional distance from the situation responded that he felt compassion for the patient. He sensed the underlying misery the patient felt that he was covering up with such a crass comment. What had the semblance of humor had misfired because the patient was overcome by his loss, something that he wanted to make light of. The pent-up hostility that was precipitated by the accident burst through to the surface; his attempt to contain it with a humorous twist failed. Some hostile narcissists might have found something funny in what was essentially sadistic; but the analyst's colleague's reaction was concerned with the patient's decompensation that was manifested in a weak defensive response that did not succeed in comforting him. The analyst's colleague was trying to explain the patient's misguided humor in psychodynamic terms.

Humor or lack of humor are characterological traits that, as mentioned, determine how persons adapt to the external world as well as how, as patients, they will progress in a therapeutic context. There seems to be a direct correlation between the degree of psychopathology and the lack of humor. I believe this generalization, though there are notable exceptions, is more valid than the equation that the more severe the psychopathology the less capacity to effectively function. Some very disturbed patients, from a characterological viewpoint, can be eminently successful, at least financially.

HUMOR AND THE CREATIVE PERSONALITY

I have postulated that creative accomplishment belongs to higher levels of psychic integration and represents efficient and progressively unique modes of functioning, a contrast to the inadequate adaptations of severe psychopathology (Giovacchini, 1960, 1974, 1993). Although there have been stereotypes of scientists and artists as serious and dedicated humorless persons who condemn frivolity, the really great scientists and artists are often playful, witty, and humorous.

Some of their fun-loving activities may get out of bounds. For example, the Nobel prize winning physicist Richard Feynman was a very colorful, witty, but mischievous character (see Feynman 1989a, 1989b; Gleich, 1992). He was given considerable latitude because of his immense talents and his seminal contributions that were involved in the success of the Manhattan project. Dr. Feynman had a penchant for safe cracking, which at times was useful when someone had mislaid a combination, but apparently, from what was rumored, he would take classified documents out of the safe, which the F.B.I. would recover because they knew he was the culprit, but they let these incidents pass as harmless pranks. He loved to hear and tell jokes and had considerable fun playing the bongo drums.

On the other hand, he was dedicated and extremely serious about his work. He could also feel deeply and make sensitive humanistic evaluations. His loyalty to his dying first wife demonstrated what a decent and loving human being he was. He was a popular teacher because he was fun to listen to and uninhibitedly informative, quite in contrast to many teachers who do not want to share what they know, probably because they have so few inner resources that they cannot give any part of themselves to their students. Feynman, a truly creative person, was the antithesis of these mediocre, but fairly numerous teachers; he was totally open and giving.

The creative scientist has an extensive reservoir of self-esteem; and he can give to others because he does not fear their surpassing him or their envious retaliation. Often, he does not take himself seriously, but he is deeply involved with his work. He has projected his inner world into the reality he is changing or making accretions to it in the form of the creative product. One might say, as he is moving into reality, he is bringing himself, that is, his mind, on the journey and shaping certain segments of the external milieu according to his unique viewpoints.

Creative activity, as the therapeutic process, occurs within the confines of the transitional space. There is an interplay between fantasy and reality, a transitional space activity. Perhaps the transitional space of the creative scientist is more elaborate than ordinary. It can stretch further into the outer world but also push deeper into the psyche. It is quite expansive, especially during the inspirational phase of creativity (see Kris, 1952).

As I have repeatedly stated, creativity and psychopathology often coexist, but they are not etiologically connected. In fact, psychopathology interferes with the unfolding of the creative process. In terms of character structure, in certain forms of psychopathology, there is greater access to primitive structure and primary process thinking, and these qualities are favorable to creative accomplishment if kept under ego control. This control is sometimes lost, and then we have a mad scientist. His madness, however, is not part of his creativity, but of a character constellation that, with the addition of ego control and the transitional space, is favorable for creative endeavor. Humor is an additional and essential ingredient.

CLINICAL MATERIAL

The following patient illustrates the significance of the holding environment, essentially internalized as a transitional space, for the therapeutic process, with humor as a binding force. A scientist in his middle twenties had become increasingly paranoid for about a year before he started therapy. He had been urged by a university psychiatrist to seek professional help, but initially, the patient resisted this suggestion. He was practically coerced into treatment, because it was implied that he was at risk of losing his position at this university.

The patient, in general, was extremely angry, and he expressed his indignation and resentment at being forced into treatment because he was not the one who needed therapy. His immediate superior was deranged and not him.

His superior had been recently appointed. Prior to his promotion, the patient had a similar position to him in the hierarchy. He believed that he was the favorite of the chief of the laboratory and expected that he would get the promotion. He was furious when he did not. Furthermore, he was certain that his rival had stolen his ideas and was getting the credit and adulation that he deserved. These feelings kept increasing in intensity and caused his peers and friends to believe that he was paranoid.

He was the oldest of six children, three brothers and two sisters in a blue-collar family. Both his parents were quite aggressive and would frequently beat the children for allegedly misbehaving.

His next younger brother was a better than average athlete, and his father admired him, whereas the patient's academic accomplishments meant nothing to him. This was a physically, action-oriented family with a propensity for violence. Intellectual achievement or scholarship was scorned.

His male siblings were known as the "tough group" of the neighborhood, and they considered their brother a "sissy" and effeminate. The patient became very angry when they teased him for being different from them and the family. The patient's resentment increased when they were favored over him and held in higher esteem, especially by the father who was an alcoholic and physically abusive.

In school, he was the favorite of the science faculty. They found him brilliant and charming, with a captivating sense of humor. In addition to encouraging him in his scientific pursuits, they had frequent social contacts with him that included going to concerts and plays and having dinner at their homes. This caused resentment in some of his fellow students who, in the academic area, were envious of his favored status.

The patient was living in two worlds: the blue collar physically oriented world of his family and the genteel, gentle world of the arts and sciences. He preferred the latter, and in his mind, he lorded it over and felt superior to the blue-collar working class.

He had some women friends who were his confidantes, and in turn, they confided in him. His sexual orientation was homosexual, something he tried to keep hidden, but from what I could gather, most people knew he was gay, but at this liberally minded university, even at that time several decades ago, it did not particularly matter. He idealized several upper-middle-class men but was afraid to approach them sexually. Instead, he had affairs with blue-collar men whom he found physically attractive but morally and intellectually inferior. In spite of his obvious bigotry, he was pleasant and affable.

During his opening sessions with me, he revealed that he was ambivalent about seeing me. He would have preferred a WASP therapist, but I had an advantage of being a gentile. Having an Italian name placed me in the blue-collar category. However, I had a reputation as an analyst who had treated several prominent scientists, and this impressed him.

I was curious about my warming up to a patient who was a hypocrite and a snob. To me, this was an interesting countertransference response. It was even more interesting because it persisted even when he was being cantankerous and paranoid.

For many months, he focused on how unfairly he had been treated at work and on all the friends who had used and exploited him and had done nothing in return. In college, as well as lower schools, he had been generous in helping less intellectually endowed fellow students. He was particularly vehement about having his ideas stolen by his immediate superior.

Ordinarily, analysts find this type of patient tedious and sometimes irritating. The paranoid orientation is not easy to bear even when there is some justification for it. I, of course, knew nothing about the actual situation at work, although to my astonishment, many years later, while nostalgically looking through a yearbook, I discovered that the target of his paranoia had, in fact, been a classmate of mine. This is especially amazing in view of what happened in the treatment, which I will soon describe.

During the first six months of treatment, I could explain my lack of retaliatory resentment as the outcome of a good analytic outlook. If therapists can understand why patients have to act and think in the aberrant and sometimes offensive ways they do, then these analysts can remain objective and calm and merely view their behavior and attitudes as interesting material. In view of my patient's background, his bigotry and paranoid reactions could be explained as reactions to the traumatic infantile environment. He needed to reject the blue-collar physical environment of his family because he could not maintain self-esteem in that setting. He could not compete with his stronger but dull, uneducated brother. The only way he could excel was with his mind, but this had no effect on his family since they did not value the intellect. Consequently, the patient had to demean their frame of reference and try to move into another world, that of the gentleman and the scholar. He chose blue-collar lovers to control and ridicule them, to mock his family's macho orientation.

Because he felt cheated by the family, his next brother being the favorite, he repeated this situation in the laboratory. This was a manifestation of the repetition compulsion; he was attempting to resolve his sense of inferiority and defeat by placing himself in a different frame of reference, the more sophisticated world of science, but he again failed and repeated the past trauma of rejection and humiliation. I believe these are the reasons his reaction was so intense.

Looking at his reactions from these perspectives makes them understandable, if not reasonable. From an analytic viewpoint, they are expectable, and analysts do not require that patients be rational. If they could be, they would not be patients. Therapists have to accept the patient's frame of reference and believe what they say, whether or not it is or is not connected to the historical truth (Searles 1961, 1986; Spence 1982; Schafer 1992). I felt that reminding myself that I am a psychoanalyst accounted for my benign response to his ill humor and paranoia.

I believe that my professional attitude played a role in my lack of a disruptive countertransference response, but in my opinion, more was involved. *This highlights again the importance of countertranference, because even the lack of negative responses requires exploration.* In this case, there were other qualities he presented that mitigated the emergence of disruptive countertransference.

His general demeanor, in spite of the grim nature of much of his material, was often expansive and entertaining. There was an engaging quality about him manifested by wit and humor. His observations were keen and poetically expressed as he made interesting connections between what, on the surface, appeared to be disparate elements. Although the content of his material was grim, there was a playful quality about the way he expressed it.

As is true of creative personalities, this patient seemed to have a well-developed transitional space. He was able to operate in this area while engaging in creative activity, as well as with me when he was being effusive and clever.

When he started therapy, he was ambivalent about me. I was not a member of the WASP elite group he had idealized. Because of my ethnic background, he equated me with his family. On the other hand, I had been an undergraduate and graduate student at the same university where he was working, and this elevated me in his eyes. I also had two of his acquaintances in analysis who had positive feelings about me and who had encouraged him to see me. These were not close friends, merely remote acquaintances, but he had considerable respect for them.

Gradually, his ambivalence faded, or rather, the positive side of it strengthened. He found me to be a receptive audience, and eventually, he turned his attention to his thoughts and feelings in the context of unconscious motivation. He granted that he might have made some contributions to the way he felt people had been treating him.

This patient had obviously reached a transitional level of relatedness, and he was capable of highly sophisticated symbolic reasoning. This meant that he had the capacity for psychological mindedness, but he also could regress and decompensate losing all these abilities and deteriorating to a florid psychosis.

After about a year of a fairly comfortable relationship, he started feeling a certain amount of tension when he was coming to a session and during it. This was especially interesting because, in general, he was doing much better, and even the situation with his immediate superior had eased considerably. He felt less suspicious of him and conceded that he had perhaps been somewhat oversensitive.

His tension was related to the strengthening of the intrapsychic focus. I believe we had been successful in constructing a holding environment in which he developed a modicum of trust and security. This allowed him to reach a wider range of feelings, permitting him to access the negative transference, since at this point in treatment, he had restricted himself to a certain degree of idealization of me and the positive transference.

Some of the problems he had been having in the outside world were now being brought into the analysis. For instance, he began to wonder why I was so interested in him. This seemed to be a ludicrous question, since in analysis or any other type of individual psychotherapy, the patient is in the limelight and the center of focus. His inquiry was portentous of ominous events as he regressed to a frank psychosis.

He had also become irritable and started to question the value of the treatment. He felt I was charging too much money for the benefit he was receiving. The playful, pleasant elements of the treatment had totally vanished, and he was sullen, morose, and suspicious of my motives.

His hostile feelings escalated and he attacked me for my "blue-collar" mentality. Apparently he had developed a father transference, but he had almost completely lost the intrapsychic viewpoint. He no longer believed that his psychic orientation had anything to do with his perceptions. His perceptions contained accurate appraisals of reality. Once again, he was looking for the sources of his reactions and feelings in the outer world, a concrete, mechanistic approach. The transitional space no longer existed as he retracted his ego boundaries.

I wondered why we lost the transitional space, and he would not let me analyze the transference. It did not surprise me that a negative father transference had developed. It would be expected in an analysis. What puzzled and dismayed me was the malignant quality of his projections and that, because he was no longer psychologically minded, he would not examine himself to understand why he felt as he did. He lost his trust in the analytic process and in me.

I wondered if I had inadvertently caused his regression by some countertransference quirk or whether some hapstance in the external world had upset his psychic equilibrium. Modell (1963, 1990) emphasized how external traumas become introjected as internalized object relations that are then manifested in the transference, which, in my case, was turning into a psychotic transference because the patient denied it had any intrapsychic elements. He viewed his feelings as being realistically based and not the products of psychological processes.

I continued exploring what I might have unconsciously done to disrupt the treatment. Paranoid ideation develops in many treatment situations, but if the holding environment is sufficiently solid, the treatment will withstand such onslaughts. The fact that it did not made me suspicious of my participation in having stimulated his regression. *I believe that as a general principle, the analyst must look for some untoward countertransference response when the regressive process becomes malignant.* In this case my contribution became apparent when he had a psychotic break.

After a Friday session in which he had been particularly surly and grim, he went to see the chancellor of the university at his home, which was on the campus. He told the chancellor how he had been discriminated against in his department because his colleagues were envious of him and kept stealing his ideas for their aggrandizement. He also stated that the CIA had been following him because they thought he was a communist, and that I also was somehow involved. I imagine that the chancellor was somewhat astonished, since he excused himself and went into another room to call security.

The patient overheard the conversation and bolted out of the room. He was, however, easy to recognize as he ran on an esplanade toward Lake Michigan. As he was running, he shed his clothing bit by bit until he was stark naked. Apparently, he intended to jump into the lake, but two security guards caught him before he could reach it. They took him to a nearby State Hospital.

After he was admitted, he immediately calmed down and told the staff nothing about his paranoid delusions. He stated that he had been overworking and that he had a nervous collapse, but now he had been able to pull himself together. The hospital wanted to keep him for observation, but he persuaded them that he was fine and to release him in the custody of a friend. He also told them how important it was to keep his Monday session with me, so on Sunday evening they discharged him in the care of his friend. In the hospital, he had been in good humor and got along well with the nurses and doctors.

When he arrived at my office, he was tense and anxious. He looked like a cowering animal. He screamed at me not to get near him. He wanted to keep a distance of at least fifteen feet between the two of us. This would have been hard in view of the architecture of my office and the position of the chair and couch.

I replied that I was not concerned that he would hurt me, believing that he was afraid that his destructive impulses would get out of control. He shouted that he was not concerned about hurting me; he was afraid I would attack him. He needed to keep me at a distance because he feared for his life. Nevertheless, he finally lay down on the couch.

What followed was typically paranoid. He talked about his superior gaining his reputation with the ideas he stole from him. He described the chief of the laboratory as favoring this thief, and now he was impugning the chief's integrity as well. Both of them were working with the CIA and were plotting to have the patient arrested as a communist. They would have him put in prison and arrange for three of the guards to rape him. I was in some mysterious way also working with the CIA and his immediate superior.

The role of the past and transference projections were easily understandable. The chief of the laboratory represented the father who favored his brother, and now I also represented both the chief of the laboratory and his immediate superior. He literally believed that I was plotting with them against him like his father and brothers had done in the past. As I mentioned earlier, it was uncanny when I discovered in the yearbook that I actually knew his immediate superior, although he was just a casual acquaintance. At this time of intense paranoia, I was not aware that he had been my classmate.

The introspection and playfulness of the past was replaced by a patient who now was living in a grim reality. The whole world was against him, a feeling that he had had in the midst of his family. Then he found another world, that of academia, to escape the brutality and diminishment he suffered from his father and brothers. Now, the blue-collar world of infancy permeated the contemporary milieu of science and scholarship and coalesced into a delusion that also encompassed our relationship.

The patient, in addition to having me work with his colleagues and the CIA, believed that I was also hired by the mafia. With a name such as mine, this is an occasional feature of some of my patients' delusions, dreams, and fantasies. He said that I was being paid $150,000.00 a year to pick his brains, and he meant this literally, that I was going to ram an icepick through his skull and macerate his cerebrum. This struck me as funny and I chuckled. The patient must have thought I was mad, because he sat up and looked at me with utter amazement. I explained that it was not necessary for the mafia to pay me for what was included in his fee. He replied that I enjoyed persecuting and extracting knowledge from him. I agreed with enthusiasm and added that this was a fascinating experience. Incredulously, he said, "You enjoy picking my brains." I answered "Absolutely, and I have learned a good deal from you." At this point in time, his demeanor suddenly changed. He became as different as night and day. He laughed as it dawned on him that "picking his brains," as a metaphor, had a benign meaning.

He then talked about how he had picked many brains as a student and how he wanted to get inside the heads of famous scientists in order to know everything they knew. His attitude now was in sharp contrast to the grimness at the beginning of the session. He was once again playful and reviewed in detail and in a mischievous fashion the events that led to his hospitalization. He was amazed that he could have been so bold as to accost the chancellor of the university and to have run toward the lake discarding his clothing. He acted as if he were Pecks' bad boy and related to me as an accepting appreciative audience. He took it for granted that I would be amused about his adventures, which, in fact, I was. My reactions also had changed. Before the change of atmosphere in my consultation room, I viewed with trepidation what he did as a malignant and grim psychotic episode and regression. He had intruded the psychotic world he had created into his current reality, and this could have been a self-destructive experience. In my office, what he had done no longer felt oppressive. It almost seemed that what he was telling me was a whimsical fantasy full of ridiculous details about the CIA and picking brains, but now picking brains was not meant literally.

I found it relatively easy to maintain my analytic decorum because his symptoms were so severe. This is another paradox that frequently occurs when treating patients with primitive mental states. My patient displayed obvious distortions of reality testing. I knew that I was not being paid by the mafia or colluding with the CIA and his immediate superior.

The scientist had reached a level of emotional development that was capable of moving in and out of the transitional space, even though his symptoms were frankly psychotic. The fact that he was a creative scientist also pointed to the existence of the transitional space, which is the location of creativity (Winnicott, 1953). He must have been highly creative, because in spite of his antics, his job was never really threatened. There are many instances of brilliant and eccentric scientists who are tolerated because of their creativity.

Again, the function of the analyst was to be with the patient at his own level. In this case this presented some difficulties because he had incorporated me in his delusion and counted me as one of his enemies. By so doing, he discounted me as a therapist and made me part of his psychopathology. Whatever supportive qualities I had were no longer effective and he dropped me as an observing collaborator.

Fortunately, we had had many positive and productive sessions, which demonstrated that he could relate in a psychoanalytic treatment context. When he was the most vehement about my exploitation of him, I reminded myself of our past analytic work. In retrospect, I also find it interesting that in spite of his outlandish behavior beginning on a Friday afternoon and his being hospitalized, he managed not to miss a single session. To me, this demonstrated that he was invested in the treatment and that I could take some risks in the way I related to him, such as laughing at his material.

As mentioned, my laughing was spontaneous and not a deliberate intervention. Still, I must have felt somewhat secure to allow myself such spontaneity, especially in view of his grimness and anger. A witty, light-hearted response could have been out of place and unempathic.

Nevertheless, I knew that I could infuse my good mood into him and bring him back into the transitional space. With other patients having acute psychotic episodes, my response would have been considered as indelicate and demeaning, and instead of leading to the construction of a transitional zone, it would have been drawn quickly into the delusion.

I was aware of how histrionic he could be and of how he would react to some of my statements even if they were outrageous. I would, for example, confront him head-on about some of his attitudes. On several occasions when he referred to someone as a "low life" because of his blue-collar background, I called him a snob. He retorted in an exaggerated fashion with feminine gestures about how could I say such a horrible thing about him, but then he laughed with great amusement. He considered what I had said as melodramatic, and he enjoyed the exaggerated attention I was giving him. As often happens with play activity, our exchanges could take a certain amount of liberty and allow some hyperboles, but he reacted with playful glee for being in the limelight.

He began many sessions with paranoid grimness. Usually he talked about how he had been maltreated at work or how his immediate superior was quizzing him so he could steal his ideas. I might good-humoredly state that I could not blame his colleague. Being in the presence of such a dazzling mind created an insatiable hunger for bright ideas with which he could identify. How could he blame his immediate superior for that? I must emphasize that I was in a good mood and displayed no signs of sarcasm or irony. The patient then jokingly conceded that I had a good point. As long as I used the proper tone, he could be pulled out of his grimness no matter whether I was saying something grandiosely positive or directly confronting him with his unreasonable attitudes.

The session after he was hospitalized was similar to many, but it was much more intense and followed a frank psychotic episode. It proved to be a tour de force, and I had been thoroughly integrated into the transference psychosis. He was able to understand that, by going along with him, I did, indeed, want to pick his brains. We were able to view this, as we created a transitional space, as an enhancing, rather than a destructive, activity.

I emphasize that the treatment of patients such as I have just described can be a very delicate matter. I allowed myself a certain leeway, but I would not generally advocate such a course of action. It is difficult to maintain objectivity while one is the object of paranoid projections. Searles (1959) and Schulze and Kilgalin (1969), among others, have stressed how the patient can drive his madness into the therapist. This has been discussed by many as the outcome of projective identification, which I do not wish to discuss, except that any therapist can become the victim of such a process, a process that is poorly understood, vague, and confusing.

My patient's grandiosity and his occasional failure to maintain it could be viciously destructive. Grandiosity in the creative person, that is, when he is operating at the level of personal relatedness, is not threatening or offensive. It is enhancing. Archimedes said that, if you could give him a spot to stand on, he could move the earth. This is a perfectly acceptable statement in the context of his theory of levers. As long as my patient stayed in the transitional area, his grandiosity was delightful and charming, but outside it, it was devastating.

Before his breakdown, I had had enough experience with him in the transitional area that I could identify with his what I will call creative grandiosity, so that I could withstand it when it became malignant. This was a specific and unique quality of our interaction based, of course, on certain features of my character structure as well as his. In this instance our interaction worked in favor of the treatment, but with other characterological constellations, disruptive countertransference feelings could have led to disaster.

I was able to reconstruct the transitional space when he had a psychotic break. As I was pondering his creative and malignant grandiosity, I realized how my countertransference feelings contributed to his regression and how they were connected to "picking his brains."

Many of our discussions centered around his ideas and other scientific matters. Perhaps I was too involved in the content of our discourse, rather than understanding its significance for his psychic economy. My eagerness and enthusiasm, to some degree, might have been at cross-purposes for the aim of the treatment, I also believe that I was in a mild way competing with him. My grandiosity was clashing with his albeit minimally, and this could have moved us out of the transitional space.

The patient, at some level, might have interpreted my interest as being connected with an intent to steal his work and to surpass him. These attitudes, when moved out of the play area of the transitional area, could easily be represented by paranoid delusions that moved our interaction into what had become grim reality. Later in therapy, we were able to discuss that he had reacted to feelings that I had toward him and his work, but were not perceived by either one of us at that time. He found it amusing that we could have such profound effects on each other. We could move from grim reality to playful fantasy.

SUMMARY AND CONCLUSIONS

In the past, I have espoused two seemingly opposite viewpoints about the conditions of treatment, perhaps another paradox. For years I have stressed that treatment is not a unilateral process. Two persons are involved, and it is the fit between the two that determines whether the patient is treatable by that particular therapist, not the patient's psychopathology alone, as Freud (1912) insisted. My treatment of the scientist seems to be an example of such a fit.

On the other hand, I also believe that, provided the therapist remains in an analytic frame of reference, at least in his thinking if not in his behavior, he will be able to understand various structural configurations and react in a proper therapeutic fashion. He need not have a particular psychic configuration that may be more in resonance with the patient's needs. This means that no special skills or forms of psychopathology are required to work with severely disturbed patients and schizophrenics.

As always, this brings the clinician back to countertransference. In all therapeutic situations, countertransference is as inevitable as transference. The therapeutic task is to maintain a similar analytic attitude toward the countertransference as toward the transference, but there are, nevertheless, certain qualities analysts will find useful to make it easier to establish such an analytic viewpoint. I am referring to the ability to view feelings and events in terms of humorous tolerance, including idiosyncrasies and foibles that may be part of many therapists' personality make-up.

As long as such foibles are not too intense, they may lead to analytic progress although they may temporarily upset the balance of the treatment process. When analysts display such attitudes, as I did when I was becoming overinvolved and perhaps competitive with the patient's accomplishments, they are, undoubtedly, reacting to their own narcissistic needs and grandiosity. Rather than feeling guilty or defensively denying having such reactions, analysts should maintain a viewpoint of self-observation. This means that analysts are looking at countertransference feelings with benevolent tolerance in the same nonjudgmental fashion as they view transference. To condemn or to be rigid about the self is just as poor an analytic attitude as harboring similar feelings toward patients.

Being nonjudgmental toward the self also requires a sense of humor. Human foibles are neither objects of derision nor subjected to superego condemnation or ego-ideal humiliation. Humor enables the analyst to look at himself as an object of interest, which allows him not to take himself too seriously. As stated, this is also an optimal therapeutic perspective as it is directed toward the patient, although therapists take their patients seriously.

Still, analysts do not look at their patients as tragic victims who have been crushed beyond repair. Many patients may have been treated with inhuman cruelty leading to profound feelings of hopelessness and despair. Therapists can feel deeply about their patient's plight, but to be effective clinicians, they must have hope, not be overwhelmed by despair, and maintain cautious optimism. This is a serious but not grim attitude, and its purpose is eventually to construct a transitional space in which humor can play an increasingly significant role.

When countertransference causes therapeutic disruption, as occurred with my patient, this need not necessarily lead to failure as may occur with unmanageable regression. Recognition and a benign appraisal of the therapist's behavior allows the emergence of a sense of freedom that enables the therapist to be somewhat dramatic and to play with metaphors as happened with my "picking" my patient's brain.

The problems my patient and I were experiencing were at similar psychic levels. We were both dealing with narcissistic issues and grandiosity. I conjecture that many analysts have narcissistic and grandiose configurations. What is important for therapeutic purposes is how the analyst reacts to such feelings, how he acknowledges them and otherwise responds. Narcissism and grandiosity are still, for the most part, considered in a pejorative fashion, although much has been written about healthy narcissism.

I imagine that Archimedes may have chuckled when he boasted that, if given a spot to stand on, he could move the world. Einstein and Bohr playfully related to each other in a competitive childish fashion as they constructed brilliant hypothetical experiments in which Einstein tried to undermine some of the fundamental principles of quantum mechanics. String theory, which deals with bubbles and sheets, is impossibly abstract, vastly grandiose in scope, and goes far beyond the fourth dimension, yet it seems to be the result of a playful and quirky imagination.

Grandiose theories are formulated by grandiose persons. Sometimes, grandiosity goes astray and becomes offensive and disruptive, especially in a therapeutic setting. If it is kept in a humorous context, however, it is not necessarily an overcompensatory stance for damaged self-esteem, but simply a state of feeling good about the self; then, it can lead to creative accomplishments and analytic progress.

Humor and creativity are essential ingredients of the analytic interaction.

REFERENCES

Bonaparte, M., Freud, A. & Kris, E. (1954), *The Origins of Psycho-Analysis: Letters to Wilhelm Fliess: Drafts and Notes.* New York: Basic Books.

Feynman, R. (1989a), *Surely You Must Be Joking, Mr. Feynman. Adventures of a Curious Character*. New York: Bantam.

—— (1989b), *What Do You Care What Other People Think?* New York: Norton.

Freud, S. (1905), Jokes and their relation to the unconscious. *Standard Edition*, 8:9–236. London: Hogarth Press, 1960.

—— (1912), Recommendations to physicians practising psycho-analysis. *Standard Edition*, 12:109–120. London: Hogarth Press, 1958.

Giovacchini, P. L. (1960), On scientific creativity. *J. Amer. Psychoanal. Assn.*, 8:407–426.

—— (1974), Characterological factors and the creative personality. *J. Amer. Psychoanal. Assn.*, 19:524–542.

—— (1993), The ego-ideal of a creative scientist. In: *Treating Character Disorders*. Northvale, NJ: Aronson, pp. 444–460.

—— (1996), *Schizophrenia and Primitive Mental States: Structural Collapse and Creativity*. Northvale, NJ: Aronson.

Gleich, J. (1992), *Genius: The Life and Science of Richard Feynman*. New York: Vintage Books.

Kris, E. (1950), On preconscious mental processes. *Psychoanal. Quart.*, 19:540–556.

—— (1952), *Psychoanalytic Explorations in Art*. New York: Basic Books.

Modell, A. (1963), Primitive internalized object relationships. *Internat. J. Psycho-Anal.*, 44:282–292.

—— (1990), *Other Times, Other Realities*, Cambridge, MA: Harvard University Press.

Ogden, T. (1994), *Subjects of Analysis*. Northvale, NJ: Aronson.

Schafer, R. (1992), *Retelling a Life*. New York: Basic Books.

Schulze, R. & Kilgalin, B. (1969), *Case Studies in Schizophrenia*. New York: Basic Books.

Searles, H. F. (1959), The effort to drive the other person crazy. In: *Collected Papers on Schizophrenia and Related Subjects*. New York: International Universities Press, pp. 521–555.

—— (1961), Phases of patient–therapist interaction in the psychotherapy of chronic schizophrenics. In: *Collected Papers on Schizophrenia and Other Subjects*. New York: International Universities Press, pp. 521–559.

—— (1986), *My Work with Borderline Patients*. Northvale, NJ: Aronson.

Spence, D. F. (1982), *Narrative Truth and Historical Truth*, New York: Norton.

Winnicott, D. W. (1953), Transitional objects and transitional phenomena. In: *Playing and Reality*. London: Tavistock, pp. 1–126.

6
=

The Delicate Balance
Between the Use and
Abuse of Humor
in the Psychoanaltyic Setting

Ronald Baker

EARLY THEORETICAL CONCEPTUALIZATIONS

In "Jokes and Their Relation to the Unconscious," Freud (1905) defined a continuum in which humor is regarded as a higher developmental achievement than its "poorer cousins": comicality and jokes. Jokes are seen as emanating from the unconscious, but humor is regarded as *a defense against the disagreeable*; thus, the energy that would otherwise produce pain, in humor results in pleasure. Freud suggested that for humor only one person is necessary; it is very personal and another person's participation adds little or nothing to it. Another person may become aware of it and enjoy it, but it differs from a joke, since a joke requires three persons, the teller, the person against whom it is directed, and the listener.

In a later paper, Freud (1927) placed humor among those methods used by the human mind to fend off suffering, in particular the compulsion to suffer. He perceived humor as possessing "a dignity which is wholly lacking . . . in jokes, for jokes serve simply to obtain a yield of pleasure or place the yield of pleasure . . . in the service of aggression" (p. 163). The implication is that humor is at the healthy end of a developmental line, which begins with play and proceeds through comicality and jokes, with various manifestations, for example, irony, on the way. "Not everyone is capable of the humorous attitude. It is a rare and precious gift" (p. 166).

The controversy over the role of the superego in humor has exercised psychoanalysts since Freud's initial formulation in which he suggested that in humor the superego played a consoling role in relation to the ego. Of this, Strachey (1927) notes, "For the first time we find the superego presented in an amiable mood." Previously the superego is usually seen as "a severe master" (p. 160).

Freud states that in humor the superego repudiates reality and serves an illusion by speaking words of comfort to an intimidated ego, as a lenient and forgiving parent might console a child. By implication, he places the roots of humor in the mother–child dyad, in the permissiveness, in the play, in the area of creativity. "If the superego tries, by means of humour, to console the ego and protect it from suffering, this does not contradict its origin in the parental agency" (p. 166). An internal narcissistic union is thus reactivated in which the ego is divided into an adult part identified with a compassionate superego and a child part, which the adult part benevolently consoles.

Both Jones (1912) and Alexander (1929) support this view in separate clinical descriptions of patients with severe and unforgiving superegos and show how this is associated with a puritanical attitude and absence of humor. When such a forbidding superego is located in the analyst, there is a distinct likelihood that the psychoanalytic process will be distorted. The analyst's pathology, in particular his humorlessness, would thus stand in the way of spontaneous emergence of humor in his patient, and in turn his patient's severe superego will be reinforced through the analyst's unconscious countertransference enactment; for instance, a psychoanalyst singularly lacking a sense of humor and widely recognized as being dour and puritanical was always ready to lay punitive interpretations on his patients. He was totally unable to accept that humor could have an affectionate aspect (based on a benevolent superego) that could be serviceable in analysis and could only see it as the analyst's attack on the patient.

Dooley (1934) and Kris (1936) saw irony as a variety of humor that is mediated by a more primitive and sadistic superego. Dooley believed that humor could only develop when the conflicts of childhood were *not* so severe and the superego development was *not* too strict. Kris regarded gallows humor as irony directed against the self that protects the ego in its offensive against the ego ideal. Freud's (1927) criminal on the way to the gallows saying, "Well, the week's beginning nicely" (p. 161) is seen by Kris as cynical and sarcastic and thus closer to aggression, rather than self-comforting. A full exploration of the complex subject of irony is beyond the scope of this chapter.

Bergler (1937) disputed Freud's view of the benevolent superego, preferring Freud's (1933) later position, that is, "the superego . . . picked out only the parents' *strictness and severity*, their prohibitive and punitive function, whereas their loving care seems not to have been taken over" (p. 62). Bergler saw the superego as being *forced* into an attitude that *resembled* comforting in order to avoid a complete break with the ego, behind which the superego scorns the ego and undertakes aggression against it. Comforting arises only *after* the ego has been punished. He postulates that the superego has set up the ego ideal as the stick with which the ego beats itself. The ego then battles with the ego ideal using various manifestations of humor with which to attack it, for example, megalomanic wit, comedy, sarcasm, clowning, and so on. Humor is thus seen by him as an attacking force by the ego against the ego ideal, in particular those aspects of the death instinct contained in it. Bergler thus sees the humorist as a masochist who bewails his misfortune and enjoys it unconsciously at the same time. Again, like irony, it is apparent that the variety of humor that Bergler refers to is possibly a more primitive form, as suggested in the following anecdote: A deeply upset man consulted Freud because of intractable depression. Following a long consultation Freud explained to him that analysis was a long and arduous treatment which could possibly help. However, it was not an approach that would bring quick relief. He suggested to the man that he might go to the circus, where the great clown Grimaldi was performing, "Nobody who sees Grimaldi could fail to find a smile" he said. The man insisted that this would not succeed. "Why not" asked Freud. "Because" said the man, "I am Grimaldi."

CONTEMPORARY THEORETICAL CONCEPTUALIZATIONS

Eisenbud (1963) placed the origin of humor in the oral phase of psychosexual development, in the infant's relationship with the mother's breast. In a brilliantly observed paper he exposes the link between humor and the nursing situation, and the connection between nursing and smiling. He states, "The transformation of a passively endured oral helplessness into some active form of denial or reversal is . . . one of the more frequent latent situations to be found in humour" (p. 53). He sees humor and the gratuitous laughter it provokes as a perfect gift but also as "a situation par excellence where an important feature of the economic gain

is always the passive listener effortlessly getting something for nothing"
(p. 63), a response that replicates the infant's experience at the breast.

Chasseguet-Smirgel (1988) confirms Freud's view that in humor the
ego is elated whereas in melancholia it is crushed. She stresses Freud's
(1926) notion that "the child's biological situation as a foetus is replaced
for it by a psychical object-relation with its mother" (p. 138), how the
child's need to be loved will accompany him through his entire life, and
how his helplessness guarantees that anxiety will result from separation
from the mother. For Chasseguet-Smirgel the ultimate form of anxiety is
the fear of being punished by the superego and the loss of its love. She
asks whether the humor-producing adult part "represents the paternal
superego or the mother of early childhood who, by the care she gives her
infant, by her caresses, her milk, her love, comes to replace the intrauter-
ine life for the child who has been thrown too soon into the world, impotent and helpless" (p. 204). She concludes that it represents "in their
totality, all the mother's efforts of care and attention, efforts liable to
clothe the naked infant with the narcissism she has forfeited in its favour"
(p. 205). She asserts convincingly that it is the mother and not the oedipal father on whom the superego is founded, and she states, "It is the precocious lack of maternal care that explains the relation between humor and
depression. *The humorist is a person trying to be his own loving mother*" (p.
205). She believes that this loving mother has never been assimilated into
the ego but supposes that "the child has furtively been able to catch a
glimpse of what the 'loving mother' might have been" (p. 205).

Chasseguet-Smirgel makes an important point in relation to depres-
sions that do not lead to introjection of the lost object,

> as if the object had only been a substitute for the insufficiently present
> "loving mother" of childhood, a loving mother who has never been
> introjected and whose disappearance from the exterior world has left
> the subject naked, feeling worthless and useless. This is what happens
> to the humorist when internal and external factors prevent him from
> bringing about the "narcissistic rehearsal" he achieves with humor
> [pp. 207–208].

And so far as Jewish humor is concerned, she notes, "The Jew's surround-
ings have never been equivalent for him of a 'loving' and consoling
mother. . . . He has been a dependent, naked and impotent child, exposed
to every danger. . . . A people without a land is a people without a
mother . . . an infant in a state of helplessness" (pp. 209–210). It is well
known that comedians recounting their failures describe that experience
as "I died." Chasseguet-Smirgel describes this perfectly, that is, the loss
of the audience (mother) has left the subject naked, feeling worthless and
useless.

THE USE AND ABUSE OF HUMOR
IN THE CLINICAL SETTING

Reik (1933) developed Freud's views on wit in his delineation of surprise, namely "surprise presupposes an expectation which has become unconscious" (p. 325). This view became a cornerstone of his theory of psychoanalytic technique. He saw analysis as "essentially a series of confirmations of unconscious expectations" (p. 326). Reik proposed that there is a far reaching psychological affinity between the technique of the analytic method of investigation and the technique of wit. His understanding of the situation was as follows: the first response is one of shock (not necessarily in conscious awareness), which is quickly followed by release of affect (relief in analysis, laughter in wit). He was the first to note the psychological significance of surprise in wit and was convinced that the most important insights in psychoanalysis are of the nature of surprises, for both patient and analyst, provided analysis proceeded without any preconceived purpose or expectation.

The relief following an interpretation that confirms a repressed expectation includes the surprise response. The initial reaction to an interpretation that reveals what is under repression is reinforcement of the repression. This is optimally followed by relief and surprise. Such patients, through their infantile curiosity or experiences, will have already been aware of, and repressed the content of the interpretation, so that it will not be available to them consciously before the analyst presents it to them. Thus, where there has been no curiosity because of intense prohibitions, there will be no surprises. This is why patients who cannot experience surprise; for example, those patients who anticipate all possible interpretations of a situation in advance are less easy to help, since the inhibition of their curiosity is much more fixed. Equally there are people who can never allow themselves to respond spontaneously or with surprise to a joke, including those who know all the punch lines. Both groups have vigorously reinforced their repression barriers, possibly because of narcissistic vulnerability but always at great personal cost.

Two recent contributions to the study of humor in psychoanalysis (Poland 1990; Baker 1993) cited a pair of contrasting humorous anecdotes, which when placed under analytic scrutiny, confirm the importance of the capacity for humor and surprise on the part of the listener/patient. The first is

> the story of two elderly nursing home residents in adjoining wheelchairs. An old woman insisted that she could tell an old man's age despite his scepticism. She challenged him to let her prove her ability. When he finally agreed to let her try, she said she first had to hold his

penis. After fondling it several minutes, she announced that the man was eighty-seven years old. Astonished by her accuracy, he asked how she could tell. "Easy," she answered, "you told me last week" [Poland, 1990, p. 208].

The second is, "A 5 year old boy says to his 4 year old sister, 'I found a contraceptive on the veranda,' to which his sister replies, 'What's a veranda?' " (Baker, 1993, p. 952).

The element of surprise can be readily observed in both stories. The initial fear or shock (surprise) can be seen to be caused by an intensification of inhibition aimed at reinforcing repression, which is then released in the form of laughter. Laughter is dependent on our not having entirely disposed of our repression potential. We laugh at the veranda story because children *should not have reached* the stage of being wise to or excited by sexuality. We laugh at the "old-timers" story because they *should have long passed* that stage. Generational anxieties are implicit in these anecdotes, for example, the difficulty we all have in being able to imagine our parents performing sexual intercourse. In both cases the repression barrier is breached because the displacement away from the parents is either onto the children or the grandparents.

In a similar way the distinguished American comedian Jackie Mason, in his "facts of life" routine says, "My parents were ashamed to tell me. . . . They felt if they didn't tell me I'd never find out. When I found out for myself I COULDN'T BELIEVE IT. I said to myself, MY mother—NEVER—somebody else's mother, I could see it. But my mother is a quiet woman . . . then I took a look at my father. I said to myself—HIM? MAYBE."

Humor and jokes overlap; for instance, one needs to have a sense of humor in order to appreciate a joke. A joke contains an expression of the teller's sense of humor, which may be both revealing and embarrassing. For this reason, *a patient's jokes, like dreams, should always be taken seriously and handled analytically.* Clearly, humor on the part of the analyst is the essential ingredient in the psychoanalytic understanding of the unconscious meaning of jokes, for without it, a joke told by a patient will have as little chance of being understood as would a dream to somebody who regards dreams as insignificant. Moreover, such understanding can facilitate the deepening of an analysis. A psychoanalyst without humor could therefore be regarded as a somewhat handicapped clinician.

Poland (1990) avers that a person must be "enough at peace with himself to keep alive warmth and humor in the face of frustration and pain" (p. 197). He says that "one of the special delights of clinical analysis is seeing the liberation of such humor in the course of a patient's analytic work" (p. 197). He recognizes that sympathetic laughter at oneself and one's limits reflects personal self-regard, a mature awareness of inner conflict and a self-respecting modesty. It has nothing to do with the pathological pursuit of gaining pleasure from pain, consciously or unconsciously. On the contrary, it implies "an acknowledgment and even acceptance of pain and loss without resignation to depressive hopelessness and hatred" (p. 198). According to Poland, for the patient to process and integrate the analyst's humor constructively, the achievement of a mature capacity to recognize conflicts and narcissistic limits in himself is essential. Such an acknowledgment can only be the result of serious and conscientious psychoanalytic work.

Poland and I share the view that a patient's capacity for humor should be regarded positively, rather than seeing it simply as a defense. Thus to deny humor access in an analysis may be to deprive the analysis of a corner of creative and growth-promoting exploration. He and I also believe that the abuse of humor in the psychoanalytic setting can only create unwelcome problems for the analyst and patient, which then have to be resolved.

Here is an example of the abuse of humor:

> A young adult woman in analysis craved a sexual experience, but was unable to make a close relationship with a man. As the summer break approached, she talked of her forthcoming holiday in Spain. She said, "I'd like to have a Spanish course and an art course and a tennis course and . . . (she hesitated)." I suggested, "An intercourse?" She was furious. Too late, I realized how justified she was, but fortunately it was possible to work this out. This was a salutary and memorable experience for me. My intervention was not humor but a joke, and she was the butt. For "an intercourse" to have been a mature manifestation of humor, it would have had to have originated in and been stated by the patient in response to an ironic self-observation. She would then have achieved the ability to sympathetically laugh at a part of herself, as if she were telling herself a joke that she was hearing for the first time and responding to the humor in it.

The psychoanalyst is responsible for ensuring that the thin line between use and abuse in the psychoanalytic situation is not violated. There is no substitute for the analyst's disciplined countertransference monitoring as a means of protecting that boundary. Calef and Weinshel's (1980) notion of the analyst as "the conscience of analysis," that is, "the keeper of the analytic process," is important in this regard. Reflecting on the difficulties of certain analyses, they noted how frequently the dissatisfactions and disappointments in relation to outcome could contribute to conflicts in the psychoanalyst that might seriously influence his analytic work. In studying this they observed the tendency in analysts to react to such disappointments by a giving up of the analytic position in favor of extraanalytic or nonanalytic interventions. In their view, when a psychoanalyst compromises his analytic functions because of such frustrations, even transiently, he no longer serves as the conscience of the analysis.

Sometimes a clinical innovation is presented to psychoanalysts that may represent a departure from what is generally regarded as psychoanalytic orthodoxy. When this is examined carefully, the conclusion may be that the proposed ideas are not psychoanalysis, but psychoanalytic psychotherapy, as was the case of Alexander and French's (1946) delineation of the corrective emotional experience. Many psychoanalysts would, however, regard the analyst's intentional and contrived role-play and transference manipulation in becoming a figure different to the traumatizing parent as a manifestation of countertransference acting out. In everyday analytic practice it is widely regarded as countertransferential for the analyst to provide such gratifications for the patient. Yet most analysts would agree that the provision of safety in the analytic setting is both essential and gratifying for the patient but that it may properly be provided *within the context of strict boundaries* and the proviso that the pregenital gratifications are confined to what is contingent in the setting and that they are ultimately subjected to detailed transference analysis.

The contemporary use of the term *abuse* by the popular press does conjure up overtones of blame. It could thus be argued that the term *abuse* is tendentious and judgmental and that the *softer* term *misuse* is more appropriate in this connection. The *Shorter Oxford English Dictionary*, however, does not distinguish sharply between the two terms. It could equally be proposed that a differentiation between abuse as applied to the psychoanalytic method and abuse as applied to the analyst's assertion of power over the patient would be of value in this connection. In my view this would confuse issues because I am asserting that abuse of the method *is usually* an abuse of the patient. In short, *the abuse of a technique supposedly used in the service of helping a vulnerable other vitiates standards and is tantamount to abuse.*

What then is countertransference acting out or enactment? This is indeed a problem. For very many psychoanalysts, countertransference acting out is what *other* analysts do. It is apparent that it is not an easy criticism for analysts of any orientation to bear, and they understandably resent the charge if it is leveled at them, especially if they are unaware of their countertransference enactments. However, certain "unorthodox" approaches, behaviors, or interventions are strongly rationalized, idealized, and even paraded or vindicated in an exhibitionistic way. Not unusually, a breakthrough in a treatment impasse is ascribed to such an approach, for example, the not uncommon report of the analyst who loses his temper and bawls a patient out, following which there is a clinical improvement. However, sometimes presentations that describe such interventions have a subtle effect on later generations of analysts who feel they have tacit permission to work in a similar way.

In my view, there is no psychoanalytic merit in countertransference enactment or acting out; indeed, it is a serious abuse of the patient and the psychoanalytic setting. When this occurs, the analyst has become a transference object for the patient; that is, he has replicated a traumatizing figure from the patient's past. Moreover, he has departed from the *discipline* of psychoanalysis, he has left the neutral space, and he has breached the principle of abstinence. While it will be agreed that all such responses may arise under pressure or even by invitation of the patient, they remain manifestations of poor technique, and punctilious psychoanalysts strive to obviate these. I do not believe that the "correct" stance should be one in which the analyst's neutrality reflects austerity, detachment, remoteness, or emotionlessness. That would indeed be a parody of psychoanalytic technique and one that could only be unhelpful and antitherapeutic.

The following somewhat tasteless joke captures the essence of that caricature:

> A psychoanalyst is so classical that he will only reflect back to the patient what the patient tells him. The patient becomes more depressed and talks of suicide. The analyst says, "Now you are talking about taking your life." The patient gets off the couch and moves towards the window. The analyst comments, "Now you are going to the window." The patient opens the window and sits on the ledge. The analyst calmly says, "Now you are on the ledge." The patient disappears, and the analyst says, "There you go!"

Virtually all analysts agree that whatever our psychoanalytic orientation, *we should not provide gratifications for our patients.* How then can we harness humor in the service of therapeutic gain and psychoanalytic insight at the same time as protecting the analyst's abstinence and neutrality? In my opinion, the answer is that the humor must approximate an interpretation, in particular a transference interpretation, and as such must always be offered prudently.

There is a distinct danger that the analyst, through the injudicious use of humor, might come to represent the absent or lost comforting mother (a consoling superego) and so provide a corrective and/or gratifying experience. When this occurs, the analyst has left the neutral space, become a transference object, and acted out his countertransference.

Equally a patient's humor, when it distracts the analyst from his task, might be considered an abuse of the setting and here is a brief example:

> A middle-aged patient, who rarely acknowledges his patently obvious depression and whose facade of joviality in the face of distress has been a feature of his analysis, has reached a crisis in which his

characteristic defense is working less well. He tells me he cannot sleep, his business is under threat, his overdraft has been recalled, he is feeling hopeless to the point of wanting to end it all, and his wife is totally lacking in sympathy, indeed she is aggressively critical of him. I say: "You're clearly wanting me to be aware of how deeply depressed and hopeless you are feeling," to which he responds, "You should see me on a bad day." This was characteristic of the skill he developed in social situations of distracting his peers from the concerns they had about him, by evoking humorous responses. It can immediately be seen that were he to succeed in his attempt to hide his depression behind humor, this could provide relief for an analyst who could not cope with his depression, as it did for his parents. The depression is side-stepped and denied while they are busy laughing. If the analyst responds likewise he has become a transference object, and a counter-transference enactment has occurred.

Psychoanalytical provision, which emphasizes neutrality, abstinence, the mirror metaphor, and more is responsible historically for the critical attitude towards the analyst who advocates the use of humor in the technique of psychoanalyzing patients. On the other hand, I would distance myself from a point of view that suggests that humor is *always* a counter-transference enactment when the analyst uses it. This would be like saying that an analyst's use of abstinence is *never* a countertransference enactment. However, I can see no way around my asserting that *this chapter is not aimed at promoting humor as a technical parameter, but it is an attempt to warn against invoking techniques that amount to transference enactments.* I stress this point at a time when there is ever-increasing liberality in relation to the whole problem of enactments, a time of increasing interest in the intersubjectivity between patient and analyst and, not least, a creeping skepticism about the value of neutrality, anonymity, and abstinence.

Although the analyst's humor, used other than sparingly, is inevitably a distraction from the psychoanalytic work and therefore an abuse, there is a place for the use of humor in certain psychoanalytic treatment situations. Here are some examples:

1. A young Jewish lawyer, pathologically attached to a controlling and guilt-inflicting mother who always warned him, "Never marry out or I'll kill myself," was enabled with the help of analysis to properly value a relationship with a Gentile woman whom he loved. He came to a session following his disclosure of his marriage plans to his mother. He was deeply distressed and clearly shaken. "It's no use," he said. "I can't go through with it. My mother says she is going to put her head in the gas oven." He ruminates on this for a few minutes, stressing only his mother's threat of suicide. I say to him gently, "I

have the feeling that you're not going to get rid of her so easily." After an uncomfortable silence, he begins to expand on the vista of his factual and fantasy relationship with his mother, dating back to childhood; his hatred of her, including his new awareness that she needed him even more than he needed her; and particularly the transference implications of this, without my having to torment him with oedipal and death wish interpretations. His subsequent marriage and separation from his mother could be seen as the achievement of an oedipal failure with the help of analysis.

This "humorous" intervention had an enhancing effect on the patient and the analysis. The condensed language of the interpretation and the patient's preconscious and unconscious awareness of its links with his struggle with me in the transference meant that it approximated a transference interpretation. This enabled the "amiable" superego to perform a difficult and complex task. It allowed for permissiveness and curiosity in play and exploration, but it also promoted development, including the provision of boundaries and limits that effectively reduced his infantile omnipotence. He could begin to recognize through the transference that he was not responsible either for his mother's death or the fulfilment of her oedipal needs. Only with that could the child in the adult "achieve" healthy failures preoedipally and oedipally. I would suggest that the use of humor in this way is only effective when the treatment alliance is intact. But this is not simply a retrospective assessment, since in a good analysis the analyst would have recognized this unconsciously, and so it should come *spontaneously* to an analyst to make that sort of intervention. If it has to be contrived or thought about, it is probably too late for it to be of value. Poland (1971) suggests that "integrated, appropriate, spontaneous humor is indicative of a high degree of alliance" (p. 637). Humor fosters and reflects that alliance in much the same way as does a well-timed transference interpretation. Indeed, it is only when the alliance is weakened or vulnerable that such interventions may be experienced by the patient as an attack. Poland cites Racker's (1957) concept of the analyst's "concordant identification" with the patient, a concept close to empathy, as the factor that allows for the validity of partial interpretations made with the inclusion of humor.

2. A university lecturer aged 35, who is married to a domineering woman toward whom he is virtually totally passive and ineffectual and against whom he never asserts himself, struggles in a session as he tries to find the courage to tell me a joke. Finally he begins, "A husband and wife are walking by the seaside when a pigeon flies over and drops a shit on the wife's new hat. In disgust, the wife screams at her husband, 'Don't just stand there, you bloody fool, get some paper,' to

which the husband replies, 'But the bird must be miles away by now.'
As he reels on the couch laughing and also a little embarrassed, I say,
"He was very envious." There follows a puzzled silence for a few
moments. Then the patient anxiously says, "What? What do you mean?
Envious? Of whom?" I reply, "Of the bird." This facilitates much
more effective work on the defenses against his aggression, particularly in relation to his wife, his mother, and in the transference, than
he has been able to face hitherto.

Again, this example takes it effectiveness from the tangential way
that the analyst's comment, "He was very envious," links with unconscious and preconscious repressed feelings and wishes. The patient's initially stunned reaction (which incidentally is shared by psychoanalysts
hearing it for the first time) is caused by its primary process impingement
on the repression barrier. Only with his realization that it is his wish to
be able to deal with his wife like the bird, which cannot be denied now, in
the wake of his laughter at the punchline of the joke, is he able to experience the relief that follows the surprise response. As in the previous example, the potential for this interpretation to be mutative is dependent
on the quality of the treatment alliance.

> 3. A woman in analysis who is training to be a psychotherapist is
> experiencing great difficulties with her supervisor. She cannot get an
> interpretation right, and however well she formulates her interven-
> tions the supervisor remains critical of her. Many sessions are taken
> up with this endless complaint. In particular, the supervisor takes up
> in a pedantic and nit-picking way the minutiae, and there are evident
> parallels between the supervisor, the patient's mother, and the analyst
> as he is perceived in the transference. Over a number of years, this
> patient has bitterly opposed my own interpretations of how she at-
> taches herself in a masochistic way to people who criticize her. It is
> also clear that in her relationship with the supervisor she presents her
> material in such a way as to invite criticism, and the masochistic com-
> ponent is patently there. At the same time I am aware of her opposi-
> tion and rejection of any such interpretation. In the event, the next
> time she began her complaints about the supervisor, I found myself
> approaching the situation differently and saying to her, "I wonder
> why you have to tell her everything." To my surprise, this resulted in
> the patient being able to associate to her masochistic tendencies for
> the first time, acknowledge the role of her relationship with her mother
> in this, and subsequently move toward some resolution of the prob-
> lem.

This is a more complex example because it may seem to contain an
element of enactment on my part. For instance, at first sight it looks as if
I am giving her permission not to tell *me* everything. However, the com-

ment is directed toward the supervisor, whom she holds onto as a transference object. The interpretation calls this attachment into question, and she realizes that there is a case for being a little more circumspect in the way she approaches the supervision. She can then begin to see that the complaints that she fills her analysis with are part and parcel of the same effort to draw me into an enactment in which I too will criticize her. It thus becomes possible for her to begin to see me as other than the transference object that she insists that I am and so the transference distortions can begin to be analyzed.

These examples of the use of humor have much in common with aspects of the later work of Matte Blanco (1989) when he comments on the therapeutic value of certain unusual or even unorthodox technical devices, for example, rhetorical utterances, poetry, jokes, and so on. For instance, Rayner (1995) suggests that it is important "to speak to the patient in the language of the unconscious" (p. 124). He says that "one way of doing this is to use jokes and humor which are in tune with or have a form similar to, an essence of the patient" (p. 124). I am indebted to Eric Rayner (1996, personal communication) for drawing my attention to this when he emphasized Matte Blanco's attachment to the importance of the therapeutic relation at the time and whether the analyst's motive is kind or cruel (I would say affectionate or sadistic) (see also Britton, 1996 below). Thus, in the context of a healthy treatment alliance with patient and analyst in good attunement, it is the limited use of primary process contained in the humorous communication (interpretation) that carries the day and facilitates growth, as in my examples above. Conversely, the complete absence of primary process would make the humorous intervention useless.

Kubie (1971), however, makes a strong case against the use of humor as virtually always having drawbacks. Nevertheless, he is particularly impressive in his warning against the use of bantering or belittling humor; hostile, defensive, or distracting humor; humor that makes it difficult for the patient to believe that the analyst is serious; and especially humor aimed at drawing the patient's attention to the analyst's humorous facility, all of which techniques we would surely agree are countertherapeutic and, as such, are abuses of humor.

In the main, a psychoanalyst listens to, contains, and tries to understand various manifestations of his patient's pain and suffering. Without doubt, *a psychoanalyst's humor would be a clear and undesirable distraction* from the analytic work were it to intrude inconsiderately into a patient's distress. Most, if not all, psychoanalysts would agree that this type of *countertransference enactment* is unacceptable. In particular, its *conscious and/or unconscious seductiveness and hostility towards the patient* is self-evident, yet in the wake of recent developments in psychoanalysis, we cannot ignore that this position is currently challenged.

Despite such warnings, Bader (1993) argued that the *intentional* use of humor, jokes, and banter verging on sarcasm proved helpful in overcoming treatment impasse and promoted improvement in patients *in analysis* whose pathology rendered them refractory to interpretation.

Bader describes his patient John, a 31-year-old man, who came into analysis because he was stuck in an unsatisfactory relationship with a woman of whom he was tremendously critical but too guilty to leave. This was a pattern. The analyst showed him that, in these guilt-laden enmeshments, he ceded power and had anxieties about separation, concerns that he hurt women with his superiority, demands for control, and impulses to reject them. He felt angry that his guilt led him to comply with such women. He denied that these themes were operative in the analysis, and he questioned the veracity of any such transference references by the analyst.

John's mother, a very ambitious woman, was deeply critical of his performance, and he felt trapped under her control, yet burdened by her feelings of inadequacy and victimization. His father had died soon after his birth, and the mother then married a man who worked in her factory. He was a rather maternal person, but he too could not respect John's competence. He was thus seen as a weak and compliant man in relation to the mother and disappointing as a father figure.

John's ambivalence about women was seen as a repetition of the conflictual relationship with his mother. Although his masculinity was endangered by her criticism of him, he could not separate from or condemn her because he feared she could not tolerate his criticism and rejection of her. As the work progressed, the analyst could show John that some of these issues were surfacing in the psychoanalytic relationship. This took the form of John insisting that the analyst give him advice. When the analyst tried to understand his insistence, he would accuse him of one-upping him or pulling rank or blaming him. When the analyst was silent, John excoriated him for hiding behind his inadequacies.

The analyst felt demoralized in his countertransference. The treatment was at an impasse. He was tempted to enact his hostility by playing his "abstinence card," that is, by remaining silent. The patient acknowledged the dominance–submission paradigm and his anxieties about mutuality, closeness, and guilt about separation. He was also aware that his provocations were unfair but was nevertheless trapped in his need to denigrate the analyst.

After some supervisory consultations, the analyst reported that he could begin to understand his countertransference better and could be more compassionate in relation to John and also "internally freer to respond *in violation of* the 'rules of engagement' by which John had coerced us to play" (Bader, 1993, p. 32). He thus began to respond to John "in a more playful way" and "with humor."

> For instance, John might make a comment like, "Did they teach you at school to make interpretations that your patients can't understand or use?!" I would respond, "Do you think I went to school to learn how to do this?" Or else I might retort, "Yes, it was in the same course where they taught me to blame the patient for my mistakes!" John ended one session . . . complaining that he was getting worse . . . with the comment, "Perhaps you could work through your conflicts about this with a consultant or your own therapist before our next session," to which I responded, "If I do, can I raise my fee?" [p. 32].

Yet another example was when John was

> imperiously . . . instructing me in exactly how a comment of mine had been worded poorly . . . He ended it all with the question, "Are you able to follow this?" I [the analyst] responded, "Wait, could you speak more slowly." He replied that he was trying his best but that I was a poor student, . . . and I responded: "But I thought this was just a Sunday drive!" (An allusion to pressure filled Sunday drives that John took with his mother.) [p. 32].

Bader (1993) writes that "my use of humor was . . . both reactive and deliberate" (p. 34). He states that it was efficacious and that John was reassured by it. He further explains that his humor conveyed to John the analyst's acceptance of his (the analyst's) limitations and his ability to defend himself against any expectations to be otherwise. He avers that this work led to progress and collaboration and so the impasse receded.

I see this as a high-risk strategy that is not psychoanalysis, despite the therapeutic result. Moreover, in my view, it gives permission for undisciplined and nonpsychoanalytic interventions, a charter for acting out, no less. Indeed, I am opposed to the use of humor or a humorous attitude as a parameter *aimed at reviving a dying analysis* or an analysis that has reached an *impasse*. Such an intervention would create more difficulties than it would solve, and I am confident that this view is shared by most psychoanalysts. So far as jokes are concerned, I feel still more strongly. Even with those patients who are relatively healthy, on those rare occasions when I have been tempted to illustrate an interpretation or mechanism by means of a joke, I have always regretted it. I am left with the image of my patient in rapt attention as I expose myself in a new role or project myself into what is experienced as a "special" communication. This is invariably followed by feelings of anger, idealization, or disappointment, to which I have been the primary contributor and which in any case I could have done without. Psychoanalytic work is difficult enough as it is without inviting this on oneself.

> Tragi-comic figures, such as the so-called "nebbish" or "Oi Vay" char-
> acter, often present their analysts with tricky countertransference prob-
> lems. They cannot be dealt with humorously without the analyst's
> aggression breaking through, which is abuse. For instance, a patient
> who told me, "I bought a nonstick frying pan, but I couldn't get the
> label off" turned out to have a severe masochistic depressive psycho-
> sis. Socially, people feel attacked by such people and avoid them if
> possible. There is something amusing about them, yes, but not for
> long. They are, however, real-life characters and usually deeply de-
> pressed behind their unfortunate defenses. The use of banter, sarcasm,
> ridicule, or repartee, however well-intentioned, cannot be helpful in
> such situations. For instance, early in his analysis the same patient
> told me, "I can always beat the system. If I want to cheat the Railway
> Service, I simply don't use the return ticket." Here the humor was
> amusing but also concretized; however, the masochism was virtually
> total. I chose not to respond to his invitation to join him in the "joke."
> My interpretative attempts at understanding focused on his evident
> self-punitive tendency. He was not amused. He accused me of being
> without humor. In this particular case the one-way ticket turned out
> to be the train that took his ancestors to Aushwitz, a piece of detail
> that only became apparent and interpretable through disciplined psy-
> choanalysis over many years.

I am particularly wary about the use of humor *in any form* in very disturbed patients, certainly *borderline or psychotic disorders*, notwith-standing the fact that these patients may have access to humor of a most moving and relevant kind. However, the underlying persecutory nature of their inner world is often such that the humor is not of the same order as that which is observed in healthier characters. At the root it is directed against the self, but it may not be tolerated when its source is an external object, especially the analyst.

While a patient's joke may be as revealing as his dream, I am op-posed to Strean's (1993) idea that we might usefully say to our patients, "Tell me whatever comes to your mind—your feelings, thoughts, memo-ries, fantasies, dreams and jokes" (p. 213). That would be an inappropriate departure from basic technique.

DISCUSSION

A good sense of humor would appear to be something of an advantage in contemporary society. I am indebted to Dr. Brendan McCarthy for drawing my attention to the frequency with which this personality asset is sought in advertisements for partners in Lonely Hearts columns. Indeed, the abbreviated form "g.s.o.h." is the rule rather than the exception. It is also widely known that women prefer a good sense of humor to characteristics such as wealth, intelligence, good looks, or the like when it comes to their attraction to partners. McCarthy (1996, personal communication) speculates that the reason why "a good sense of humor" is so highly valued is because it offers the hope that in its presence wrangles and misunderstandings might have a greater chance of being repaired before too much damage is done. This is fully in keeping with my anticipation that the absence of a sense of humor in a psychoanalyst is something of a liability.

In a previous paper (Baker 1993), I proposed that the use of humor in the psychoanalytic situation can only be effective if it is *spontaneous* but also under control to the extent that it is *in the service of deepening the psychoanalytic process*. In this respect it is rather *like a good interpretation,* and its delivery must therefore *meet the unique requirements of the patient* with his own particular defenses. In particular, the *timing must be impeccable.* When it misfires, like with a clumsy interpretation, the patient feels abused, misunderstood, or even attacked. In my view this closely resembles a patient's response to a countertransference enactment.

Valerie Sinason (1994) grasped the essence of this when, writing about the roots of humor in the mother–baby relationship, she stated,

> With very little children or with mothers and babies we experience the beginnings of humor. The peep-bo between mother and babe elicits a smile of pleasure as well as a giggle when the rhythm between the two is working well. Where a mother tickles a baby slightly too much or gives the visual equivalent of a punch line at the wrong time, she is a failed comedienne with devastating results. Perhaps the reason why we find a failed joke or unsuccessful comedian so unbearable is that it takes us back to the feeling of betrayal when mother mistimed. Perhaps too that is why we are grateful to brilliant comic writers/performers . . . because *we can trust we will not be betrayed in the vulnerable act of giving ourselves over to laughter* [p. 24; italics added].

As already indicated, I believe that a humorous comment meeting the clinical criteria for an interpretation and *especially a transference interpretation* can be liberating and productive of progress and change. To be effective, it must emerge in the context of an intact treatment alliance, with the analyst following the material and the transference very closely. But not all interpretations are "good"; indeed some may carry a degree of abuse of the patient, and others are clear countertransference enactments. Thus, the psychoanalyst who has not adequately assessed his patient uses humorous interventions at his peril. Humorous interventions carry serious risks, and it is crucially important that these hazards are known. Many of the more obvious ones have been listed above.

Lowenstein (1958) wrote:

> [T]he right joke, told at the right moment, may be used *instead of* an interpretation when a patient's sense of humour makes him accessible to a particular type of joke. Yet there are many instances when a joke not only falls flat, but may even have the opposite effect. . . . Some persons lack a sense of humour and do not respond to a particular type of humour. Some patients react to jokes as if the analyst were callously making fun of them, others as if it is a veiled seduction. And the analyst had best beware of using this approach with those who themselves like to tell jokes in analysis; either the patient knows the joke already, or it will become a competition between them, or a mutual seduction. . . . The analyst should refrain in analysis from using the same defence as the patient. . . . The analyst's task thus may be employed in weighing the various possible effects on the drives, on the super-ego or on the various parts of the ego, which might result from telling a given joke to a given patient at a given moment in the analysis. *Similar considerations always apply . . . in the choice, the mode, the wording and the timing of interpretations.* [p. 209; italics added].

I regard this view as a sound clinical position.

Eissler (1958) sees jokes as a pseudo-parameters that appears

> at first glance like new technical device, whereas their relevant, dynamic effect is that of an interpretation. . . . The analyst is *forced* to use them in instances where the direct interpretation arouses unacceptable resistances. . . . With the help of pseudo-parameters one may be able to smuggle interpretations in to the pathognomic area with a temporary circumvention of resistances. A frequent device of this kind is the right joke told at the right moment. . . . [A resistant patient] may laughingly accept the meaning in the form of a joke. . . . The joke and its ensuing laughter establishes a community of affect, fostering greater closeness between analyst and patient, or may be taken by the patient as a gift for which he makes return by diminishing his resistance [pp. 224–225; italics added].

Eissler is suggesting that humor or jokes used as a pseudo-parameter may result in more material being elicited, a piece of psychoanalytic work being summarized, a split between two disparate trends of thought being brought together, a potential opening through which a new perspective may be highlighted, and the eliciting and containment of anxieties that could not otherwise be broached.

The weakness in Lowenstein's and Eissler's papers is that they invite us to consider the use of a joke or humor *instead of* an interpretation, in order to get behind defenses or resistances that cannot otherwise be analyzed. *Indeed, they more or less give us permission to do so.* This weakness is something that I find worrying, since they are both aware of the risk factors, especially the seduction potential, yet it is presented as a parameter. Eissler believed that the pseudo-parameter could be analyzed later. Lowenstein was the more cautious. Nevertheless, in both cases the joke or humor seemed studied, contrived, and intentional, which does not meet the criteria for *approximating* an interpretation.

Rosenfeld (1958), contributing to the same discussion, said: "We should think of the use of jokes and similar communications . . . as undesirable modifications of analytic technique which not only circumvent the resistance . . . but introduce new and stimulating factors from the analyst's side and that this must be experienced by the patient as seduction" (p. 238). My inclination is to agree with this rather rigid stance, with the reservation that he does not allow for the humorous intervention that approximates an interpretation.

In agreeing that wit might make interpretations containing bitter truths more palatable, Britton (1996) recently stated that this would depend essentially on the state of mind of the patient, the spirit in which the analyst is offering this and the state of play between them *at that moment.* His stress on that moment reflects his view that it is important that the analyst recognizes that the patient shifts in his psychic position from moment to moment. Britton notes that the patient's capacity for integration is dependent on the size of the gap between the capacity to feel subjectively and the capacity to think objectively. He avers that, when this is so large that there is no meeting place, there can be no sense of humor. He suggests that the gap may be measured by simply comparing what one might say directly to the patient and what one might say about the patient to a colleague. If the gulf is unbridgeable, then deadly seriousness rather than humor is in the ascendant.

Loewald (1960) recognized psychoanalysis as an interactional process but emphasized the need for psychoanalytic neutrality and objectivity in interpreting and reducing the patient's transference distortions as essential. Without this the *new* experience will elude the patient. The situation of holding and containment in the interactional situation is exemplified by the child who feels safe with the mother, the audience who feels safe with the humorist or comedian, and certainly the patient who must feel safe with his analyst if growth and a new experience is to come about. In a similar vein Christie (1994) notes that "a creative (adaptively regressive) state in the mother draws the two individuals [mother and baby] close enough together to allow the emergence and unfolding of a new relationship. Regressive states of this kind are commonly characterised by playfulness and humour" (p. 480).

Enactments militate against this type of development because in such situations the psychoanalyst has become a transference object. Enactments do, however, occur widely in psychoanalytic settings, and in skilled hands they can and should be turned to the patient's therapeutic advantage. However, *this is no reason why we should not continue to see them as rooted in countertransference and/or poor technique* and conscientiously seek to anticipate and prevent them.

We surely must remain mindful of the seductive element in the audience factor of joke telling and listening. Patients do not come to analysis to tell or hear jokes. Nor do they come to be humorously amused: this can be equally seductive and destructive. If a tendency arose whereby the analyst was compelled to be humorous, had to tell a joke, or needed to respond to a joke with another one, as individuals do in social groups, then the analyst will have lost his way. It may be a countertransference acting out or a wish on the analyst's part to gain gratification or even a genuine approach to an impasse, but whatever else it is, it is not analysis. On the other hand, an analyst who ignores a patient's joke has missed what invariably is a significant communication.

Humor as an enactment has no place in psychoanalytic treatment. The psychoanalytic setting is a serious structure. Even in ordinary social relationships, there are many people who prefer not to be told a joke, not to be the passive recipient of humorous interplay. We are all aware of the self-consciousness that can consume us when we face the awesome responsibility of being the "audience" of a joke. In this connection there is also the anxiety that we will not find the joke funny, that we have heard it before, and that we will not be able to laugh. When this is placed in the context of the psychoanalytic setting, the risks are obvious, not to speak of the repercussions. So let us protect our patients from it.

Some analysts believe that humor can usefully cushion a painful interpretation, but this may be experienced as reassurance, with all its attendant problems in the transference. That is not to say that patients do not pick up the fact that an analyst is capable of a humorous attitude or that his demeanor is unfriendly or that he does not smile or laugh, but I have to say that the use of *humor as a contrived communication worries me*.

Finally, we are required as psychoanalysts to know our patients as well and closely as possible, certainly to be aware of their vulnerabilities and careful not to interpret in ways that might damage them. Although it is not possible to legislate in general as to what we can or cannot do, it is probably prudent to advise against invoking humor as a communication in *an analytic situation in which the analyst does not understand the material*, a ubiquitous and certainly not uncommon situation.

REFERENCES:

Alexander, F. (1929), The need for punishment and the death instinct. *Internat. J. Psycho-Anal.,* 10:256–269.

───── & French, T. M. (1946), *Psychoanalytic Psychotherapy.* New York: Ronald.

Bader, M. J. (1993), The analyst's use of humor. *Psychoanal. Quart.,* 62:23–51.

Baker, R. (1993), Some reflections on humor in psychoanalysis. *Internat. J. Psycho-Anal.,* 74:951–960.

Bergler, E. (1937), A clinical contribution to the psychogenesis of humor. *Psychoanal. Rev.,* 24:34.

Britton, R. (1996), *Brit. Psychoanal. Soc. Bull.,* 32:1–3.

Calef, V. & Weinshel, E. (1980), The analyst as the conscience of the analysis. *Internat. Rev. Psycho-Anal.,* 7:279–290.

Chasseguet-Smirgel, J. (1988), The triumph of humor. In: *Fantasy, Myth and Reality: Essays in Honor of Jacob Arlow,* ed. H. Blum, A. Kramer Richards, & A. Richards. Madison, CT: International Universities Press, pp. 197–213.

Christie, G. (1994), Some psychoanalytic aspects of humor. *Internat. J. Psycho-Anal.,* 75:479–489.

Dooley, L. (1934), A note on humour. *Psychoanal. Rev.,* 21:49.

Eisenbud, J. (1963), The oral side of humor. *Psychoanal. Rev.,* 50:57–73.

Eissler, K. R. (1958), Remarks on some variations of psychoanalytic technique. *Internat. J. Psycho-Anal.,* 39:222–229.

Freud, S. (1905), Jokes and their relation to the unconscious. *Standard Edition,* 8:9–236. London: Hogarth Press, 1960.

───── (1926), Inhibitions, symptoms and anxiety. *Standard Edition,* 20:87–175. London: Hogarth Press, 1959.

───── (1927), Humor. *Standard Edition,* 21:159–166. London: Hogarth Press, 1961.

───── (1933), New introductory lectures on psychoanalysis. *Standard Edition,* 22:5–182. London: Hogarth Press, 1964.

Jones, E. (1912), Analytic study of a case of obsessional neurosis. In: *Papers on Psychoanalysis,* 2nd ed. London: Bailliere, Tindall & Cox, 1918, pp. 515–539.

Kris, E. (1936), The psychology of caricature. *Internat. J. Psycho-Anal.,* 17:285–303.

Kubie, L. S. (1971), The destructive potential of humor in psychotherapy. *Amer. J. Psychiat.,* 127:861–866.

Loewald, H. (1960), On the therapeutic action of psychoanalysis. *Internat. J. Psycho-Anal.,* 41:16–33.

Lowenstein, R. (1958), Variations in classical technique. *Internat. J. Psycho-Anal.,* 39:240–242.

Matte Blanco, I. (1989), Bi-logical psychoanalytical technique, a proposal. Unpublished.

Poland, W. S. (1971), The place of humor in psychotherapy. *Amer. J. Psychiat.,* 128:127–129.

——— (1990),. The gift of laughter: On the development of a sense of humor in clinical analysis. *Psychoanal. Quart.*, 59:197–225.

Racker, H. (1957), The meanings and uses of countertransference. *Psychoanal. Quart.*, 26:303–357.

Rayner, E. (1995), *Unconscious Logic: An Introduction to Matte Blanco's Bi-Logic and Its Uses*. London: Routledge.

Reik, T. (1933), New ways in psychoanalytic technique. *Internat. J. Psycho-Anal.*, 14:321–334.

Rosenfeld. H. (1958), Contribution to the discussion on variations of classical technique. *Internat. J. Psycho-Anal.*, 39:238–239.

Sinason, V. (1994), But psychotherapists don't laugh do they? Unpublished.

Strachey, J. (1927), Introduction to Humor. *Standard Edition*, 21:160. London: Hogarth Press, 1961.

Strean, H. (1993), *Jokes: Their Purpose and Meaning*. Northvale, NJ: Aronson.

7

Humor Is a Funny Thing: Dimensions of the Therapeutic Relationship

W. W. MEISSNER, S. J.

Funny is itself a funny word, especially when applied to humor. It can connote something humorous or amusing, like a good joke or an amusing event, but it can also suggest the idea of something peculiar, strange, odd, unusual, or unexpected. Humor, it seems, can be "funny" in both these senses, and humor in both senses can occur in analysis. At times, a communication or interaction may be intended as amusing but turns out to have more of a strange or peculiar connotation than we intended. Freud's (1905) contribution to the understanding of jokes and humor in general made us acutely aware that, like dreams, humor is always overdetermined and reflects multiple levels of meaning and motive.

The purpose of this chapter is to sort out some of the implications of humor and to explore their implementation in the analytic process. The main focus of my discussion will be to examine some of the forms of humor in relation to dimensions of the therapeutic or analytic relationship. My views regarding the analytic relation have been expounded at length elsewhere (Meissner, 1986, 1988, 1991, 1992, 1996a,b). Briefly, I would argue that the therapeutic relation is compounded of three major components—transference (along with corresponding countertransference in the analyst), the real relation, and the therapeutic alliance. These also constitute overlapping and intermingling frameworks for interaction between analyst and analysand. My thrust here is toward assessing the role and function of humor with regard to each of these aspects of the analytic relation and interaction. The meaning and implications of humor are distinctly different in relation to each of these components and have potentially diverse reverberations for the analytic process. I would hope that in this fashion some of the obscurity, uncertainty, and ambiguity surrounding the problem of humor in analysis and therapy can be clarified. Before turning to the analytic situation as such, I would like to explore some of the meanings of the comic and humor, as one form of the comic, and consider issues related to the sense of humor as characteristic of either analyst or analysand.

SPECIES OF THE COMIC

Our guide in exploring the terrain of the comic is, of course, Freud, particularly in his joke book (1905). Freud divided the sphere of the comic into jokes, the comic as such (as distinct from jokes and humor), and finally humor. We can distinguish a comic vision or orientation from comedy itself—the comic vision, as we shall see in a moment, speaks more to one's characteristic orientation to reality and values than to a comic event or situation. Freud tended to view jokes and their extension into the comic and the humorous as manifestations of energic processes, in keeping with his current efforts to base his psychology on principles of psychic energy and discharge. I shall prescind from an energic model, preserving nonetheless an economic perspective.[1]

Joking

I will make no attempt to trace the intricacies of Freud's argument regarding the complexities of joking and the multiplicity of forms of joking and their motivation. But I will focus on interpersonal dimensions of the joking interaction. Jokes are usually told in a social context, whether in individual conversation or a group setting, like a group of friends or even, as for the professional comedian, an audience. From a literary point of view, a joke is a brief narrative usually transmitted orally and whose authorship is anonymous. The intent of the joke is humorous or amusing and typically meant to entertain, although jokes can be put to other uses. Like other forms of brief narrative—parables, fables, fairy or folk tales— jokes can serve to make a point, teach a moral, or convey some other lesson.

---

[1] For a discussion of the distinction between energetics and the economic principle and their relevance for analytic theory, see Meissner (1995a, b, c).

The teller of the joke and his listeners adopt a particular frame of mind adapted to the joke situation, a kind of Winnicottian transitional space in which ordinary realistic and/or logical suppositions are for the moment suspended. We assume a mental set of openness to the absurd, the naive, the illogical, the comic. If Freud was right, this attitude of mind sets the stage for the attuning of ego capacities to the innuendoes of meaning; for softening of superego attitudes to make room for the reprehensible, the immoral, the socially disapproved, or distasteful; and to relax instinctual barriers and controls to allow displacement of instinctual material from the unconscious to the conscious level, however disguised and transformed in the joke. The material of jokes is protean and, for the most part in social contexts, has as its objective to entertain, amuse, give pleasure, but also at times and in certain contexts to instruct, inform, and even admonish. A secondary phenomenon that commonly occurs socially is that the telling of a joke elicits the telling of another joke from someone else in the group. This can have a quality of sharing in the fun and joining in the camaraderie of mutual amusement, but often it is also tinged with elements of competition and rivalry. I am reminded of the old radio show, "Can You Top This," in which the competition was registered by the "Colgate® Laugh Meter."

Freud argued along similar lines that what made jokes funny and stimulated laughter was relaxation of censorship and release of instinctual energies. In this sense, the comic and jokes were closely related. Jokes could approach the comic when they touched on the naive, but the naiveté of the comic was found, while that of the joke was made. The lifting of censorship was accompanied by no more effort than simply listening, but this accounted for only part of the pleasure in the naive. There was a point at which the pleasure can be overridden by indignation or disgust, as in obscene jokes that are excessively crude. To the extent, Freud argued, that internal inhibition is lacking in the comic object, we are better able to avoid the pain of indignation and respond in the spirit of the joke. A degree of empathy and comparison of the object's state of mind with our own allows for the discharge of tension in laughter.[2] Freud concluded that this process was essential to viewing the naive as comic, and to the extent that this process was involved in a joke, it added the comic pleasure to that of the joking.

The Comic

The comic has to do with actions and character traits, probably first physical and later mental characteristics, of human interactions. Ani-

---

[2] For a discussion of physiological aspects of laughter, see Piddington (1963) and Meerloo (1966).

mals and even inanimate objects become comic by reason of personification. One can make others comic, as well as oneself. Making oneself out
as clumsy or stupid can produce a comic effect. The methods Freud listed
were putting one in a comic situation, mimicry, disguise, unmasking,
caricature, parody, and travesty, among others. As Freud noted, "It is
obvious that these techniques can be used to serve hostile and aggressive
purposes. One can make the person comic in order to make him become
contemptible, to deprive him of his claim to dignity and authority"
(p. 189).[3] The pleasure was derived from the implicit comparison between oneself and the exaggerated or ineffectual action of the comic object. One thinks automatically of slapstick comedy, in which the bumbling
and physical abuse offer the possibility for such comparisons.

But there is also an operative presumption, let us say in laughing at
the Three Stooges, as an aspect of the transitional experience we engage
in in joining the audience, that all the abuse, pratfalls, knocking about,
and head banging are without the serious consequences that such behavior would entail in the real world. This presumption, incidentally, is part
of the comic experience that children miss when they imitate the stooges
in play. In the real world such behavior can create injuries. If we laugh at
the stooges, we cannot laugh at the same behavior in children. The sup-
position of make-believe offers us permission to suspend our concerns
and replace them with laughter. When we enact a comic role, the comic
effect in making ourselves look awkward or clumsy is based on the same
comparison. The effect, Freud noted, was not to make oneself ridiculous
or contemptible, but at times even admirable. The feeling of superiority
derived from the comparison does not arise in the observer, if he also
knows that one has only been pretending.

When we act to put others in a comic situation, as in practical jokes
making another look foolish, clumsy, awkward, or stupid, we enact aggression and retreat to a narcissistically superior attitude. Other vehicles
of making comic, such as caricature, mimicry, parody, travesty, or unmasking are usually directed against objects having some claim to authority or respect (Freud, 1905). Freud emphasized the aspect of
degradation of the object common to all these forms of the comic—caricature by emphasizing or exaggerating a single trait, thus distorting the
general impression; parody and travesty "by destroying the unity that
exists between people's characters as we know them and their speeches
and actions, by replacing either the exalted figures or their utterances by
inferior ones" (p. 201); mimicry, which involved elements of caricature,
by reason of comparisons to inanimate autonomisms or mechanisms
(à la Bergson); and unmasking when the comic object has assumed a

---

[3] See Rosen's (1963) discussion of the varieties of caricature and parody in analysis.

dignity or authority by deception so that the pretense or deception is revealed.

The same effects can be conveyed by comic stories—both allow for giving conscious play to unconscious modes of thought, accounting for the comic effect. Freud used the example of the borrowed kettle as an example of comic effect from the play of unconscious modes of thought—the borrower, you remember, denied that he had borrowed the kettle at all, then claimed that it already had a hole in it when he got it, and besides he had given it back undamaged without any hole. The persistence of mutually exclusive thoughts reflects the modality of unconscious thought. The primary line Freud draws between jokes and the comic is that the pleasure of the joke relies on the release of unconscious impulses or motives and their translation to conscious levels (along the lines of the dream model), while comic pleasure pertains more to preconscious expectations and comparisons.

Freud isolated certain conditions for comic pleasure: a cheerful mood in which one is inclined to laugh, an expectation of some comic effect (the special mind-set of being open to comic influence), and the presence of other pleasurable circumstances producing a kind of contagion or fore-pleasure that increased receptivity to the joke or comic event. Unfavorable conditions would include any serious imaginative or intellectual work the person may be engaged in at the moment, the more so the more abstract the content—as Grotjahn (1957) pointed out, laughter tends to disappear as soon as we focus on it and try to understand it—or any conscious focusing of attention on the implicit comparison from which the comic emerged, or if the comic situation gives rise to any strong affect.

Humor

Freud regarded humor as one of the highest psychic achievements, a view echoed by Kohut (1966), who viewed humor as one of the mature transformations of narcissism, and by Vaillant (1977), who ranked it high among adaptive behaviors. The presence of distressing affects acts as a deterrent to comic pleasure, and the individual so affected must be able to ward off the displeasure to experience the comic effect. Humor, however, comes into play as a means of getting pleasure even in the face of distressing affects.[4] It acts as a substitute for those affects by replacing them in *statu nascendi*, as Freud says. The person experiencing the painful affect then would feel humorous pleasure, while an external, uninvolved

---

[4] Millar's (1986) reflections on the connection between humor as such and pleasure conclude to the role of humor in the mastery of self and environment and to the victory of reason and cognition over emotion and unreason.

observer might experience comic pleasure. Freud (1927) gives the example of the criminal being led to the gallows who remarks, "Well, this week's beginning nicely" (p. 161)—an otherwise painful situation is transformed into something humorous.

The varieties of humor seem endless. Humor may be expressed in a joke or some other expression of the comic, in which case its purpose is to get rid of a possible dysphoric affect. Or it may stifle this affect only partially, producing a mixed effect—humor smiling through tears. In any case, humor has a defensive function, which Freud (1905) described in energic terms: "Humour can be regarded as the highest of these defensive processes. It scorns to withdraw the ideational content bearing the distressing affect from conscious attention as repression does, and thus surmounts the automatism of defence. It brings this about by finding a means of withdrawing the energy from the release of unpleasure that is already in preparation and of transforming it, by discharge, into pleasure" (p. 233). This humorous displacement serves to protect the ego by a kind of self-enhancement—"I am too big (too fine) to be distressed by these things"—restoring narcissistic equilibrium and a threatened sense of superiority. Thus humor is more closely related to the comic than to jokes—as Freud (1905) noted, "It shares with the former its psychical localization in the preconscious, whereas jokes, as we have had to suppose, are formed as a compromise between the unconscious and the preconscious" (p. 234).

Freud returned to the subject of humor some years later (1927) in the wake of his formulation of the structural theory. His analysis of humor then replaced the earlier energic considerations. In interpersonal terms, one person can adopt a humorous stance, while a second person, acting as spectator, can enjoy it, or one can take no part in the humorous process but is made the object of humorous observation by someone else. Appealing to the criminal on the gallows, the subject himself enjoyed a degree of humor, while the spectator derived his pleasure second-hand. On other terms, a narrator might describe the behavior of someone in humorous terms while that person displays nothing humorous himself. Freud (1927) summarizes: "To sum up, then, we can say that the humorous attitude—whatever it may consist in—can be directed either towards the subject's own self or towards other people; it is to be assumed that it brings a yield of pleasure to the person who adopts it, and a similar yield of pleasure falls to the share of the non-participating onlooker" (p. 161).

The essence of humor remains that one spares oneself the possibility of painful affect and dismisses the possibility with a jest. Communicating humor requires that humorist and hearer share a certain mental attitude. Humor shares with jokes and the comic a liberating effect, but it also has a quality of elevation or self-enhancement that other ways of obtaining pleasure from intellectual activity lack. Humor entails a triumph of narcissism, a triumphant assertion of the invulnerability of the self. As Freud

(1927) put it, "The ego refuses to be distressed by the provocations of reality, to let itself be compelled to suffer" (p. 162). It thereby connotes an advantage of the pleasure principle over the harshness of reality.

This refusal of victimization and rejection of the necessity to suffer carries with it a sense of self-dignity missing in jokes, since jokes are limited to simply gaining pleasure or putting pleasure at the service of hostility or sadism. In probing this humorous attitude further, Freud (1927) appealed to the child in the adult, that, in adopting the humorous attitude and thus warding off possible suffering, one treats himself on the one hand like a child and on the other plays the role of an adult toward the child. The split in the self is accorded to the superego thus: "We obtain a dynamic explanation of the humorous attitude, therefore, if we assume that it consists in the humorist's having withdrawn the psychical accent from his ego and having transposed it on to his super-ego. To the super-ego, thus inflated, the ego can appear tiny and all its interests trivial; and, with this new distribution of energy, it may become an easy matter for the super-ego to suppress the ego's possibilities of reacting" (p. 164). Thus, the formula for jokes is cast in terms of the revision of a preconscious thought process by the unconscious, as Freud (1927) said, "A preconscious thought is given over for a moment to unconscious revision" (p. 165), that is, a contribution made to the comic by the unconscious.

Humor, on the other hand, becomes a contribution to the comic from the superego. This superego is in a sense a departure from the earlier picture of the severe and punitive superego in "The Ego and the Id" (Freud, 1923); now it is cast in terms of a more benign and protective function, allowing the self a measure of pleasure and protecting it from more severe onslaughts of reality. Freud's (1927) comments are much to the point:

> It is true that humorous pleasure never reaches the intensity of the pleasure in the comic or in jokes, that it never finds vent in hearty laughter. It is also true that, in bringing about the humorous attitude, the super-ego is actually repudiating reality and serving an illusion. But (without rightly knowing why) we regard this less intense pleasure as having a character of very high value; we feel it to be especially liberating and elevating. Moreover, the jest made by humour is not the essential thing. It has only the value of a preliminary. The main thing is the intention which humour carries out, whether it is acting in relation to the self or other people. It means: "Look! here is the world, which seems so dangerous! It is nothing but a game for children—just worth making a jest about!" [p. 166].

We might add that it is this rendition of the superego that the analyst appropriately enacts when he makes use of a joke in analysis—the benign superego Strachey (1934) saw as so central to the therapeutic action of analysis (Meissner, 1991). Freud's humorous perspective found further elaboration in Poland's (1990) description of humor as a character trait:

> [A] capacity for sympathetic laughter at oneself and one's place in the world. Humor of this sort does not imply pleasure in pain but reflects a regard for oneself and one's limits despite pain. With such humor there is an acceptance of oneself for what one is, an ease in being amused even if bemused. This humor exposes a mature capacity to acknowledge inner conflict and yet accepts oneself with that knowledge, even when it is the knowledge of one's narcissistic limits. Such humor, often linked to an appreciation of irony, requires a self-respecting modesty based on underlying self strength and simultaneous recognition of and regard for others [p. 198].

On these terms, a mature sense of humor almost approaches an analytic ideal.

SENSE OF HUMOR

The sense of humor is part of the mental equipment that both analyst and analysand bring to the analytic encounter. The sense of humor is always unique to the individual—some people have a good sense of humor, some do not—but in any case one's sense of humor can be exquisitely revealing and even at times embarrassing (Baker, 1993).[5] It is usually a mistake to try to affect a sense of humor when it is lacking, whether socially or analytically. Good humor flows easily; it cannot be forced or labored. The analyst who tries to be artificially humorous is enacting something and probably barking up the wrong analytic tree (Baker, 1993). Similar cautions apply to the analysand—some have a sense of humor and can respond receptively and perceptively to the analyst's humorous initiative; some do not and cannot. It is hard to draw lines of discrimination in this area, but generally more obsessional patients do not respond well to humor.[6]

Any and all patients, whether gifted with a good sense of humor or not, are less receptive to humorous input when they are caught up in

---

[5] On the differences in sense of humor and humorous themes between men and women, see Zippin (1966).

[6] Rosenheim and Golan (1986) studied the reactions to humor in 36 outpatient psychotherapy patients. Regardless of type of humor, none of the patients systematically favored humorous over nonhumorous interventions. They were equally divided between those rejecting humor and those having no preference. Obsessives consistently rejected humorous interventions; hysterics and depressives were roughly two-thirds negative and one-third neutral.

intense transference interactions or when they are relatively more defended or vulnerable, especially in the face of regressive transference pulls (Levine and Redlich, 1955). Freud himself had commented that receptivity to humor could be short-circuited by unfavorable conditions—serious intellectual work or strong affect, for example, both common enough in analytic work. I recall one intellectually gifted woman, who was capable of quite sophisticated illusions and picturesque metaphors as long as, in my role as analyst, I did not do or say anything that impinged on her resistances or defenses. Any attempts at humor on my part were met by a stubborn silence and a wall of pseudostupidity that was unyielding. Humor had little or no place in that analysis.

To the extent that a sense of humor is part of the analyst's real person as he or she engages in analysis,[7] we can also take into consideration the comic vision of life that Schafer (1976) included in his psychoanalytic vision of reality. He called it "comic" in a generic sense, but it lies closer to the heart of what I am calling "humor" here. As he put it, "The comic vision seeks evidence to support unqualified hopefulness regarding personal situations in the world. It serves to affirm that no dilemma is too great to be resolved, no obstacle too firm to stand against effort and good intentions, no evil so unmitigated and entrenched that it is irremediable, no suffering so intense that it cannot be relieved, and no loss so final that it cannot be undone or made up for. The problem is reform, progress, and tidings of joy" (p. 26).

As it stands, it serves as an expression of one aspect of the optimal goals of analysis; maturing of the patient's sense of humor may be a beneficial side effect of successful analysis (Poland, 1990; Christie, 1994). Such an outcome speaks to the realistic expectations tempered by the prevalence of the reality principle over the pleasure principle, by modifying pathological narcissistic demands to fit personal limitations and capacities, and the achievement of an optimistic and hopeful outlook reasonably attuned to the slings and arrows of outrageous fortune, even as it looks beyond the obstacles and difficulties, to regain or maintain the necessary initiatives required to overcome them, to seek and cherish more hopeful alternatives, thereby recognizing the effort and determination necessary to achieve hoped-for results.

The whole psychology of hope is embedded here, the distinction of hope as realistically oriented and applied from wishful fantasy, the dialectic of hopefulness and hopelessness.[8] The analysand, after all, comes

---

[7] Greenson (1967), for one, seemed to think of a good sense of humor as a mark of a good analyst; he wrote: "My own personal observations seem to indicate that among psychoanalysts, the best therapists do seem to possess a good sense of humor, do have ready wit, and do enjoy the art of story-telling" (p. 386). See also Baker (1993).

to analysis dissatisfied with himself, particularly his inner life shaped around the pathogenic configuration of introjections and identifications. The whole is permeated with conflict, but the comic resolution offers a fresh perspective—that this inner world can be reconsidered and revised to bring about a new perception of oneself and a fresh approach to social relations and life involvements. As Poland (1990) put it, "The ability to tolerate uncertainty and ambiguity and the ability to integrate into one's view of oneself and the world the vast mix of contradictory urges, feelings, and ideas are accepted goals of successful character analysis. They are, at the same time, the requisites for the gift of laughter. Mature humor is a reflection of analytic work successfully done" (p. 204).

I would emphasize that this comic vision represents a significant aspect of the analyst's personal participation in the analytic effort. The analyst undertakes the analysis with hope where the patient may have little or none; he maintains hopefulness in the face of the analysand's discouragement or frustration. When the analysand is immersed in painful affects and tortured anguish, struggling with his conflicts and self-limitations, the analyst remains empathically attuned to the patient's inner turmoil, but he does not join in it. Part of his essential neutrality is his capacity to see the problems in a different light, to maintain an attitude of calm, holding out the possibility of resolution and surcease of pain, of optimism over pessimism, of hopefulness over hopelessness. Where the patient tends to become overwhelmed by discouragement and to yield too readily to hopelessness, the analyst remains hopeful, directing his effort to engaging the patient in a process of self-scrutiny and exploration of meanings and motives that offer the possibility of change in perspective and understanding and to open the way to new possibilities and resolutions that the patient had never seen before. This balance in the analyst, while it facilitates reworking of inner processes in the analysand, also provides a model for identification facilitating internalization of the comic vision leading to correlative modifications in his self-concept and his approach to the external world and its difficulties.

HUMOR IN ANALYSIS

To move on to the question of the use of humor in analysis, I would like to consider the issues in relation to the components of the analytic relation—transference/countertransference, real relation, and therapeutic al-

[8] For an enlightened discussion of these issues, I call attention to the insightful discussion of hope by Lynch (1965). See also Meissner (1973, 1987).

liance. The use of humor has different impacts and implications in each of these aspects of the analytic involvement and interaction.

Transference and Countertransference

In the same way as any aspects of the analytic interaction—verbal, non-verbal, enactments, affective, motoric, behavior—can be drawn into or caught up in transferential processes, the analyst's use of humor is open to the same vicissitudes. Humor, especially in the form of joking, is not only a vehicle for expressing instinctual impulses, usually unconscious, but both making and getting a joke carries a narcissistic surcharge in the service of self-esteem (Schimel, 1978). Positive transference can endow the most pedestrian witticism with wondrous insight, while the most penetrating and humorous remarks may come to naught in the face of negative transference. Freud's perspective on the dynamics of jokes and joking should serve as a potent warning of the potential dangers in these waters—regarding jokes and humor as potential vehicles of transferential expression and enactment.

A major cautionary statement in this regard came from Kubie (1971), who argued that to take the position that humor was always destructive or that therapists should never use it would be extreme, but nonetheless the use of humor was always potentially risky and carried with it certain inherent dangers. Most of his cautions involved some form of transference or countertransference vicissitude, although (as I will comment later) other difficulties can arise in relation to the alliance or the real relation. Among the dangers in the use of humor are the possible collusion between analyst and patient in avoiding painful feelings and fantasies and the imposition of the analyst's personal reactions on the patient, usually to his detriment. Kubie contended that patients are exquisitely sensitive to implicit or masked hostility in the therapist's humor and that the joking context prevents expression of the patient's own resentment and anger at the therapist. Humor provides a convenient vehicle of defense against the therapist's own anxieties, as well as fending off the patient's anxiety or pain.[9] And to that extent it would have to be regarded as a countertransference enactment (Kubie, 1971; Baker, 1993).

Every patient has a history of exposure to humor. No analyst ever knows, certainly at the beginning or in earlier phases of therapy, what

---

[9] The same defensive dynamic of avoiding anxiety can play a role in child analysis as well; see Mahon (1992) for a case in point, Jacobson (1946), and Clowes's (1996) discussion of castration, oedipal, and feminizing themes in farmer's daughter jokes among latency-age boys. Joking in children can also serve expressive and creative motives, even as a form of sublimation (Loewald, 1976).

the patient's previous experience of joking, teasing, or mockery might have been, experiences that can influence the patient's experience of and response to humor in analysis or therapy. As Kubie (1971) observed:

> The therapist inherits a patient's buried reactions to earlier humor. Only at the end of long analytic study will the therapist discover that some of the most destructive people in the story of a patient's life may have been those who always found something to smile about whenever the patient was in pain. This predecessor may have been a father or mother or an older or younger brother or sister, or it may have been a friend or even some relative of a friend or a teacher. All of this confronts us with complicated problems that have far-reaching importance and should be explored separately [p. 863].

Even if the therapist tries to use humor to ally himself with the patient against his "opponents," there may be some gain in drawing analyst and patient closer together, but the risk is not only a collusive pseudo-alliance that implicitly endorses the patient's conflictual or distorted view, but leaves open the uncertainty in the patient's mind that he himself is not in some unspecified way the butt of the humor. These are obviously risks that fit quite neatly with any possible paranoid preoccupations in the patient's mind—concerns that are more than likely to be hidden from the therapist. This reaction can be fed by a smoldering resentment that the therapist takes lightly or casually what is so overburdened and painful to him. Any way you slice it, therapy is not fun.

Rosen (1963) reported a case of a woman suffering from phobic and obsessional difficulties, who was disappointed with the progress of her treatment and complained that she did not want to come to her sessions but felt forced to by having to pay for missed sessions. When she came, she protested repeatedly that she was there in body only and not in spirit. On each such occasion, on leaving she would say, "I'll see you tomorrow if I'm still alive." On one occasion, Rosen quipped, "And if not, come in spirit and leave your body at home." The patient did not think his comment funny and came the next day, feeling depersonalized and finally expressing her anger. Only later, Rosen realized that the depersonalization was a way of saying, "If you do not treat me the way I wish, I will leave both my body and my spirit at home."

On occasion, the analyst can become the object of a joke, which can trigger an emotional response, sometimes transference related, sometimes not. In any case, the analyst is confronted with another dilemma—to laugh or not. Laughing can collude with the patient and misses the opportunity to gain further insight into the patient's use of humor as a weapon. Not laughing can become an implicit rebuff and criticism of the patient for joking. There should be room for enjoying the patient's humor when it is appropriate, but the trick is to laugh with the patient and not at him. Kubie also noted that a dour or humorless approach carried its own burden of risk. If the patient had humor-compromised parents or parents who were incapable or reluctant to engage the child in humorous or playful ways and in the process convey a sense of enjoying the child, these elements will come into play in the transference—the transference perception and the character of the analyst will find common and mutually reinforcing ground.

A recent experience comes to mind from supervision. The patient, a young man in his twenties, asked the analyst for a tissue to blow his nose. The analyst, noting that the box was empty, got up to get a fresh box and handed it to the patient, commenting somewhat playfully, "Here are the supplies." The patient then went on to associate to a common joke about a store owner who hired three men—in one variant a German, a Spaniard, and a Chinese man. He put the German to work on the books, the Spaniard in charge of sales, and taking the Chinese man into the warehouse, put him in charge of supplies. When he returned the next month to check on things, he found the books neatly and carefully kept and up to date. The Spaniard was actively taking orders and making sales. But both complained that there was a problem in getting supplies to keep up with the orders. The owner went to the warehouse looking for the Chinese man. Suddenly the Chinese man jumped out from behind a carton and cried, "Supplies! Supplies!" The joke obviously pivots around the connection of "surprise" with the oriental pronunciation "supplies."

Further exploration of the joke led to some interesting findings. The patient was the son of a competitive, domineering, and authoritarian father and a mother who had little empathy or affectionate involvement with her son. A pervasive issue in the analysis had to do with the patient's transferential submission to the analyst's presumed authority and his trepidation and anxiety over any self-assertion or autonomy, especially if he thought it might infringe on the analyst's territory. His asking for a tissue was in itself a mark of considerable progress in his analysis. The joke reflected the analyst's responding to his request, a surprise in itself, and resulting in the analyst giving him "supplies." By the same token, the analyst's interpretations were another form of supplies that often came as a surprise insofar as the patient had not anticipated or expected them.

But from another perspective, there was a question of who was the Chinese man—the patient or the analyst? The patient would have been the ineffectual Chinese man who couldn't get it right, but who might surprise the analyst-owner if he were able to provide any supplies for the analytic process. Or the analyst might be the Chinese man who tries to offer supplies in his interpretations, but these turn out to be surprises that are ineffectual and do not work the magic the patient expects to solve his difficulties and make his analysis successful. In the former case, the owner-analyst might well fire such an ineffectual Chinese-patient; in the latter, the patient could well feel dissatisfied with his ineffectual analyst, who could then be reasonably blamed for the limitations in the outcome of the analysis. These adversions were all redolent of transference implications, the pervasive questions about whether he was an inadequate and ineffectual son or whether he was the victim of inadequate and ineffectual parents.

Real Relation

Humor has the potential for drawing the analytic interaction into the real relation. To begin with, every analyst has his or her own constellation of personal characteristics that, along with his sense of humor (Bader, 1993), includes mannerisms, style of behavior and speech, habits of dress, sex/gender (Lester, 1990; Appelbaum and Diamond, 1993), way of managing the therapeutic situation, attitudes toward the patient as a human being, prejudices, moral and political views, and personal beliefs and values (Klauber, 1968; Greenson and Wexler, 1969). Other personality attributes impinging on the analytic process may include the analyst's competence as an analyst, his commitment to the process, his values; ideals; training and education; use of language; habits; interests; physique; life experience; and tendencies to be active or passive, action-oriented or reflective, enthusiastic and alive or dull; tendencies to see events in positive or negative light; tendencies to be stiff or flexible, gruff or tender, cautious or risk taking, even-tempered or moody, patient or impatient, and authoritarian or not (Ticho, 1972; Cooper, 1986). The same list of characteristics applies *mutatis mutandis* to the patient. Both parties may react to the personality characteristics of the other in ways that are outside alliance and transference (Stone, 1961).

Baudry (1991) raises the question of whether and how the analyst's character influences his technique. He offers three possibilities:

> (1) general self-syntonic beliefs and attitudes which permeate all aspects of the analyst's functioning both personal and professional: pessimism/ optimism, degree of permissiveness, activity vs. passivity, degree of warmth vs. distance, rigidity/ flexibility, authoritarian tendencies, and so forth; (2) aspects of the style of the given analyst—tone, manner, verbosity, use of humor, degree of irony; (3) the analyst's characteristic reactions to various affects of the patient or to problems in the treatment, such as stalemated situations [p. 922].

While all of these possibilities can influence the interaction between analyst and patient, these are not necessarily aspects of countertransference.

Countertransference dynamics may enter the picture, but these qualities belong to the analyst's personality, exclusive of transference. Distance or warmth, for example, are matters of the degree of affective relation between patient and analyst. There is an optimal distance that facilitates meaningful communication consistent with demands of the alliance— excessive closeness or intimacy can lead to potential seductiveness and the risk of transgression of therapeutic boundaries, and excessive distance can lead to heightened defensiveness, resistance, and feelings of rejection. Both alternatives open the way for transference distortions and misalliances, and both are important discriminators in the use of humor.

Frequently enough, humor can serve the patient as a device for drawing the therapist out of his therapeutic role into one more akin to a real relation. I have argued repeatedly (Meissner, 1996a, b), that the therapeutic role and therapeutic action take place within the alliance sector but that inherent forces of resistance and defense are continually at work in all analyses to draw the action in one direction or another, either into the transferential sphere or toward a more real-relational basis. Humor can serve these purposes, but often enough the pull is toward the real. The patient may offer a joke, not as emerging meaningfully from the flow of associations, but as an effort to entertain the analyst and to engage him in another modality of interaction than that of analysis, to redress some perceived inequality or imbalance in the relationship.

The quality of such jokes approximates the telling and exchanging of jokes in the social setting; if the analyst engages in this process, by laughing without at the same time hearing the joke as a meaningful and therapeutically related communication, or by allowing himself to get caught up in joke swapping, he allows the analytic process to be drawn into the real sector and foregoes the therapeutic purchase of the alliance. In Baker's (1993) terms: "If a tendency arose whereby the analyst was compelled to be humorous, had to tell a joke, or needed to respond to a joke with another one, as individuals do in social groups, then it is apparent that the analyst would have lost his way. It might be a countertransference acting out or a wish on the analyst's part to gain gratification: certainly, it would not be analysis" (p. 956).

Another variant on the theme has to do with the sense of the comic. The patient may introduce an element of the comic in order to dissipate the intensity of analytic influence or diminish the level of anxiety experienced in the process, or—as Freud (1905) pointed out as one use of the comic—to diminish the authority and effectiveness of the analyst or his interpretations. One of my patients was an intelligent and gifted man with a jovial sense of humor. My tendency is often to put things in a trenchant or metaphorical way that might at times pass for wit. This patient was unusually appreciative and responsive to such interventions, a demeanor that I found encouraging. But it soon became clear that he was using his analytic experience as a device for increasing his sense of specialness among his friends and associates, describing to them in caricaturing and amusing detail the humorous events that transpired in his sessions, and painting a picture of me as a uniquely humorous, fun-making analyst—by implication making him special as my patient. In other words, he was attempting to turn the analytic process into something comic as a means of both defending against the inroads of the process, especially impinging on his narcissism, and retrieving his narcissistic losses by making his analysis a topic for general amusement and merriment, feeding his narcissistic need to be special and not the ordinary run of analytic patient. Drawing the analysis into the realm of the real where it could be dealt with in terms of a minimizing comical reduction served to undermine the alliance and serve multiple defensive needs.

As Poland (1990) observed, to appreciate a joke one must be willing to be taken in, but also alert not to be taken in. If there is risk of real enactment posed by a joke, fear of enactment should not compromise our spontaneity or affective engagement. But instead of the affective response of only laughter, we also offer the perspective of understanding. To quote Poland's bon mot, "The patient who starts to make a point can thus end by getting the point" (p. 218). In the previous example of the joke about "supplies," both the analyst's gesture of offering supplies and the patient's joking rejoinder could have served to draw the interaction in the real direction; seeking understanding that makes a therapeutic point keeps the process in the alliance sector.

Alliance

The argument for the role of humor as contributing to the alliance and promoting the analytic work was made by Poland (1971) and sustained by others (Rose, 1969, 1992; Rosenheim, 1974; Olson, 1976; Bader, 1993; Christie, 1994).[10] In an effort to balance Kubie's relatively negative view, Poland recounted two examples of humor in analysis. The first patient was a middle-aged woman who had recalled her father's prohibitions against reading certain books by saying, "No, that's a man's book!" The patient then complained about the course of her treatment and wondered whether Horney's approach to self-analysis might be more helpful. She then saw Horney's book in the analyst's bookcase and asked whether she could borrow it. Poland responded with, "No, that's a man's book!"

---

[10] Poland (1990) and Rose (1969, 1992) both also appealed to the model of the Fool in Shakespeare's *King Lear,* whose jesting conveyed meanings that Lear could not otherwise hear. The connotation of affective and expressive freedom in humor was stressed by Pasquali (1986).

Patient and analyst enjoyed a good laugh together, reinforcing the alliance and allowing a greater degree of perspective regarding her transferential ghost. The second case was a man described as a "Yes, but" character. The patient's early positive attitude and enthusiasm gave way to a negative reaction to the analyst, along with hostile critical attacks on the analyst. At one point in this onslaught, the patient commented, "I used to hang on your every word." And with a laugh Poland quipped, "And now I hang on my every word!"

Both these examples came at a point when transference dynamics were active and overburdening the analytic relation. Humor played the role of intersecting the transference vector and redirecting the analytic interaction along alliance lines. There was a risk involved in Poland's gambit, since the intensity of the transference response would have diminished the patient's capacity for and receptivity to his humorous intervention. As he is careful to note, humor has its best chance to facilitate the analytic work when the alliance is relatively strong and positive. But humor can serve to recover a weakened or tentative alliance or to break through an overriding transference dynamic—as in these cases.[11] Along similar lines, another therapist, noted for his gentle and kindly manner, was listening to the repeated complaints of his patient regarding how no one ever listened to her, never paid any attention to her difficulties and problems, never took her seriously, and on and on. Finally, at a judicious moment, with a smile on his face and a laugh in his voice, he said, "So what does that make me—chopped liver?" The patient was taken back for a moment and then laughed. She got the point—after all, he had spent many hours patiently and empathically listening to her complain and had taken her seriously. The therapist's remark brought her back to a more self-observant perspective and reengagement in the alliance.

Bader (1993) comments on the impression the analyst's use of humor makes on patients. The meanings to the patient are multiple but often touch on the patient's sense of the analyst's humanness as well as connoting a sense of alliance and partnership (Sands, 1984). To this extent they can help deepen the analytic process and promote healthy growth in the patient. Among the possible productive meanings, Bader includes the analyst's tolerance for and mastery of elements projected onto him by the patient in the transference, his avoidance of a countertransference

---

[11] Haig (1986) came up with a list of constructive aspects of humor in therapy: forming or reinforcing therapeutic alliance, breaking through resistance, diminishing anxiety, release of affect, fostering self-observation, providing an acceptable outlet for the patient's hostility, assisting diagnosis, revealing countertransference, building ego strength, serving communication, promoting transitional experience, encouraging free association, reassessing sacred cows and taboos, improving receptivity to interpretation, and helping the therapist outside therapy. Several of these would be directly involved in the therapeutic alliance.

response whether by depressive withdrawal or hostile traumatizing of the patient or by defensive one-upmanship, and finally the analyst's pleasurable engagement with and appreciation of the patient. Poland (1990) made the point that a mature and healthy sense of humor was a product of psychological development. The patient's ability to laugh at himself, at his foibles and weaknesses, to regard even his analyst and the analysis with a degree of humorous perspective is one of the outcomes of successful analysis—an aspect of Schafer's (1976) comic vision of reality—as well as an index of the positive or constructive state of the alliance.

Patients generate active fantasies about the analyst, his personality, and his thinking. The tolerant balance and perspective implicit in the analyst's humor provides an antidote to the patient's pathogenic fantasies. As Bader (1993) notes, "In these cases, the patients responded better when the analyst's tone and style conveyed humor, playfulness, irony, and a readiness to openly express genuine pleasure in the patient" (p. 27). While there are risks in drawing the analytic interaction into the real relation, there are also contributions that humor can make to the alliance. As Bader notes, "I chose to make my humor available to the patient with the belief that it would help the patient feel safer, provide an alternative model of mature relatedness with which he could identify, and expand his capacities for self-analysis" (p. 48).

The opposite side of the coin was discussed by Kubie (1971). Among the potential dangers of the use of humor, he pointed to several that seem to involve creation of misalliances that undermine rather than facilitate the therapeutic effort. The therapist's humor can often divert or abort the patient's spontaneous flow of associations and even more poignantly leaves the patient in the confusing dilemma of whether the analyst is being serious about what he is saying or "only joking." This can introduce a measure of misalliance that distorts the therapeutic alliance and reflects an inadequacy of the analyst's empathic attunement to his patient, often causing consternation and distress to the patient (Sands, 1984). As well as defending against anxiety, patients can use humor to defend against accepting the seriousness of their difficulties; should the analyst step into this trap, he would be colluding with the patient's need to escape such confrontation and engaging with the patient in a misalliance that only reinforces the patient's defenses rather than analyzes them.[12]

---

[12] A particular focus for these concerns are Jewish jokes, especially about psychoanalysts, which one often hears from the couch. The tension between separate registers of anti-Semitic accusation and Jewish self-defense can present any analyst with a technical dilemma. They can pose a problem for Jewish analysts insofar as the patient might use them to gain a footing on real terms with the analyst. See the discussion of such jokes by Meghnagi (1991) and Schlesinger's (1979) discussion of the connections of Jewish humor with Jewish identity.

At times, the humor can be at the patient's expense, but even then patients may feel constrained to act amused, if only to show that they have a sense of humor, but the hurt feelings are concealed. The facade of humor makes expressing anger impossible. Kubie also applied this to any attempts on the part of the analyst to use mimicry—what may be well intentioned therapeutically is more often experienced by the patient as mockery. As Sands (1984) noted, "It is the patient's humor and not the therapist's that, in the long run, is likely to be most useful to the patient" (p. 459).

But these aspects of the analyst's real personality—humor, for example—may become a vehicle for countertransference dynamics and undermine the alliance (Kubie 1971) or strengthen the alliance and promote analytic work (Poland, 1971, 1990; Christie, 1994). Schafer (1976) included the comic among the visions of reality inherent in the psychoanalytic outlook. Again, humor within the context of alliance can serve therapeutic purposes, not outside of it. As Jacobson (1993) observes, "Our real task is to maintain the optimal tension for analytic experiencing, learning, and change, to provide enough human connection to facilitate the process, but not on occasions or in ways where it will interfere with the development of the internal experiences the patient must come to know and understand" (p. 537).

HUMOR AND NEUTRALITY

Kubie (1971) had noted the inherent difficulty created by humor in maintaining the "analytic incognito." Neutrality, in his view, was meant to protect the patient from the therapist's frailties, but humor presented a subtle way to circumvent such protective restrictions. Against the background of presumed analytic authority, if not actual at least in the patient's experience of the relation, the analyst's humor tends to make the patient more vulnerable and exposed. The analyst requires careful self-monitoring and self-scrutiny to preserve his therapeutic role, keeping it centered on the alliance. But, Kubie argued, humor blunts our self-observation and self-corrective efforts. Elements of self-display, exhibitionism, or wooing can enter the process all too easily and subtly.

Bader (1993), who is otherwise positive about the use of humor, also cautions against the aspect of self-display that may turn out to be seductive or impose obligation on the patient, while his rationale is to modify the transferential distortion of the patient by humorous self-exposure, especially modifying the patient's sadistic superego. The risk here, as I would see it, is that the analyst's intervention is only too likely to draw the interaction into the real sector, not into the alliance. This is not to say that it should not be done; in some cases this approach may be necessary. It is to say, however, that to the extent that the interaction is drawn away from the alliance base and into a real interaction, it presents further difficulties for the analytic process. If there were a gain for the therapeutic effort, as Bader contends, there is a price to be paid in relation to the alliance and its subsequent role in the analytic work. Neutrality, in such instances, is more a matter of maintaining perspective, staying observant of the deviations from the alliance, and finding ways to recover the alliance footing.

Humor is entirely consistent with neutrality and a stance of abstinence, as long as it is clear that the analyst does not seek narcissistic gratification from his patient. But humor also excludes a view of abstinence as excessively rigid or neutrality as expressionless. Current efforts to define the role of the analyst as participating personally in the analytic process tend to advance such a caricature of neutrality and abstinence that would leave little room for humor (Meissner, 1996a, in process). Clearly, abstinence and neutrality, properly understood, do not call for the exclusion of humor (Baker, 1993), and, in my opinion, any rendition of them that does so would be mistaken and misleading.

Neutrality should not be confused with a lack of emotional expressiveness or affective involvement. Even for Freud, neutrality did not connote emotional distance or coldness or a dehumanizing lack of human warmth and sympathy, but rather an approach that was nonjudgmental, nonmoralizing, not imposing one's own personal attitudes or values, not intruding on the patient's personal life, staying impartial and objective (Blum, 1981). It is the position of equidistance from id, ego, and super-ego recommended by Anna Freud (1936), as well as a stance that an intelligent and attuned patient could respond to as reasonable and appropriate (Stone, 1981). As Stone (1981) observed, "To the extent that 'neutrality' with an affirmative affective tone is genuinely achieved, it is an excellent contribution both to the legitimate principle of abstinence and to the high tolerance and acceptance which characterize the analytic work in its best sense" (p. 101). As Bader (1993) notes, the humorless analyst is a caricature of analytic abstinence and neutrality; even humor has a place. He writes: "The unique feature of depression and affective rigidity among analysts is that we have a theory of technique that can be misread as justifying our neuroses, and we can enact them under the guise of abstinence and neutrality. . . . Misalliances or impasses can be the end result of what, to us, looks like a treatment based on good technique" (p. 49). The humorless mask can hide the analyst's anxiety, depression, or obsessional character and provides another model for misalliance.

What then do neutrality and abstinence come to in this regard?

Clearly, they do not connote lack of affective responsiveness and involvement or avoidance of humor. Rather, I would argue, the touchstone of humor within the bounds of analytic neutrality and abstinence is the therapeutic alliance. To the extent that humor is implemented within the perspective of the alliance, rather than in the framework of transference or the real relation, it is more likely to be therapeutically beneficial and constructive. To the extent that it veers into transference or the real relation, it exposes itself to the potential risks that others have been quick to caution against. In this context, then, abstinence calls for the avoidance, on the part of the analyst, of hidden emotional gratifications, especially of a narcissistic variety, from his display of wit or good humor, thus exploiting the patient to his own psychic benefit. Neutrality, in turn, calls for the degree of self-reflective introspection that keeps the impulse to the use of humor and the potential impact of humor on the patient in constant perspective—the most useful guide being the impact on the alliance, whether facilitating and reinforcing or not.

LAUGHTER

Laughter as a form of affective communication (Kris, 1940; Meerloo, 1966) comes in for consideration here. Laughter covers a broad range of behavioral enactments, from a quiet chuckle to a hearty guffaw. It may also find a place in dreams with much the same implications as in the waking state (Grotjahn, 1945). But it remains a bit of a mystery why people laugh. Millar (1986) quotes W. C. Fields to the effect that "the funniest thing about comedy is you never know why people laugh. I know what makes them laugh, but trying to get your hands on the why of it is like trying to pick an eel out of a tub of water" (p. 547). No doubt humor and pleasure are inherently connected. From early childhood, laughter carries the naive connotation of expressing pleasurable satisfaction and engaging a playmate in play (Piddington, 1963). Laughter in this elementary sense conveys a mood in which no further need is felt to adapt to the social environment beyond that in the present moment. Laughter in this sense is its own reward.

But by the same token, laughter even in its communicative guise may conceal more than it reveals. It can readily serve defensive purposes, acting as a device for avoiding conflict, whether intrapsychic or interpersonal. In Piddington's (1963) terms, "The neurotic and the laugher are using the same psychic device for the avoidance of conscious conflict, the only difference being that the former is acting along antisocial lines, whereas the latter is adopting a socially determined pattern of behaviour" (p. 130). Within analysis, laughter often serves to communicate affects, usually of a less than intense variety. Mild emotional reactions accompanied by laughter are usually more attuned to humor than to the comic, and intensification of the affect usually inhibits laughter.

The patient's laughter can express any and all of these possibilities and more. It may take the form of an appreciative chuckle, mingled with thoughtful mulling of the point of the analyst's joke, or it may take a more defensive path, fending off unwanted meaning and trying to reduce the analyst's humor to the comic or ludicrous. In such instances, any effort to analyze the laughter exposes the underlying affects, anxious, depressive, and so on (Brody, 1950). Or it may take the form of an invitation to play, that is to engage in a playful exchange that circumvents any serious thought or reflection—a collusive group of two (Kris, 1940). Since laughter can be contagious, the risk of the analyst's being drawn into a more reality-based exchange is considerable. I recall in one relevant supervision, the patient was a bright young man whose use of language tended to the colorful and witty, largely in the service of fending off his anxiety and maintaining a modicum of narcissistic superiority against threatening dependence on his analyst. His female analyst found this engaging and entertaining and, at one point, found herself giggling. We were able not only to trace the impact of the giggle on the patient, both in its overtones of colluding with the patient's defensive use of humor and in communicating a sense of triviality or levity that left him feeling both that he was getting away with something and that he was not being taken seriously. Both these aspects turned out to have important transference and countertransference implications.

The way in which the analyst responds to the patient's humorous efforts also becomes communicatively overburdened. There is always the conundrum of laughing with the patient as opposed to laughing at him. Our conscious intent is not always congruent with the patient's perception, conscious or unconscious.[13] Personal style plays an important role here, along with a generous measure of tact, all within a context of good empathic attunement (Rose, 1969). I can't remember ever having laughed outloud in response to a patient's joking—my own stylistic tendency is to respond with an appreciative chuckle if I feel that some positive affective response is called for; if not, I may respond with a more thoughtful "Hmm," or a question. This often has the effect of disengaging the pull toward playful exchange and brings the dialogue more toward meaningful inquiry.

HUMOR AND PLAY

Winnicott (1971) gave rise to the idea that therapy takes place in the intersection of two areas of play, whether in the treatment of children or adults. As Bader (1993) further observed, humor can readily assume the form of playfulness, but always with the intention of helping the patient. In his dealings with his patient John, Bader recounts his feeling pressured by the patient's transference pulls and pushes and his increasing awareness of his own countertransference. As I would view his account, his adopting a more relaxed, playful, and humorous stance reflected the degree to which he was able to resolve the countertransference difficulties and engage the patient more in terms of the alliance. His use of humor was such that his patient could respond to it and engage in the analysis more in alliance terms than had been the case when the interaction was driven by transference derivatives.

This does not mean that playfulness is always conducive to the alliance, since play and humor can also take less productive forms, especially if they become the vehicle for unconscious hostile, sadistic, or defensive motives (Kubie, 1971; Christie, 1994).[14] It seems clear that Bader's efforts to remain "neutral" played into the patient's transference based on the image of his mother whom he could never please or satisfy and who could never enjoy her relation with him—a good example of how an artificial and rigid neutrality or abstinence can become a form of therapeutic misalliance (Meissner, 1996a). Rather, adopting a more playful demeanor had the effect of disconfirming the transferential expectations and fantasies and allowed the patient to develop a new form of relatedness that proved analytically more productive. I would argue that it became more productive precisely because it reinforced and facilitated the alliance; if it had drawn the analytic interaction off into any other sector, the results would not have been as gratifying.

Efforts have been made to clarify the role of interpretations in analysis and to elucidate those aspects of the process that may have therapeutic effect but are not interpretive. Picking up Winnicott's (1971) notion of play in the analytic process and Huizinga's (1944) analysis of play, London (1981) drew a distinction between the ludic and the nonludic aspects of analysis. In these terms, the transference neurosis would take place in a context with the formal qualities of a state of play—a ludic context. These playlike qualities would include that the activity is voluntary and free, affectively absorbing, tending to repetition, limited by distinct boundaries of time and space, and governed by inviolable rules. The magic of play can be easily interrupted, however, if it becomes too stimulating or if it leads to uncontrollable regression. The transference neurosis shares these qualities in its own fashion, particularly that the playlike quality of

---

[13] To quote the Bard: "A jest's prosperity lies in the ear of him who hears it / never in the tongue of him who makes it."

[14] Oberndorf (1932) had noted the sadistic quality of kidding.

transference involvement is made possible by adherence to the rules of the game; if these inviolable rules and rituals are disregarded or not accepted by both parties, the transference play is disrupted and can readily become destructive.

With respect to the alliance, the interaction can have a ludic or nonludic quality, but the accent, more often than not, falls on nonludic aspects, but these aspects are less clear-cut. Nonludic interpretations, as Loewald (1976) suggested, would acknowledge the significance of the patient's infantile needs and at times regressive state. This requires an empathic grasp on the part of the analyst of the regressive aspect of the patient's experience based on regressive aspects of the analyst's own experience. For many analysts the regressive aspects of their own experience on the analytic couch can come into play in meaningful ways—as well as aspects of their own more regressive involvement in many life contexts. The extent to which the interpretive process can link the patients' experience with other meaningful contexts and bring them to verbalizable focus helps to draw the process back to ludic levels, but not necessarily in transference terms.

For example, an idealizing patient demands practical advice and problem solutions from her analyst. He maintains his abstinence, does not respond to the demands, but works at clarifying the nature of her demands, her consequent disappointment and anger. He also supports and acknowledges her increasing competence in managing the difficulties in her life. The analyst's response in this instance is not to work within the confines of the transference, but to deal with the ongoing interaction between himself and the patient in the immediacy of the here-and-now. These interventions may have less the character of interpretations than of clarification and even confrontation (Meissner, 1987). To the extent that the intervention can be made in a playful or humorous way, the easement of the interaction into an alliance perspective may be facilitated and the difficulties inherent in a countertransferential—supposedly superego derived—response or a reality-based enactment avoided.

Certain aspects of these nonludic parameters have been articulated in terms of the therapeutic or working alliance (Zetzel, 1956; Greenson, 1965; Meissner, 1988), as well as the holding environments (Winnicott, 1971; Modell, 1976, 1990). These are necessary preliminaries providing the patient sufficient security to allow him to enter the state of play. Such security depends on a sufficiently nonthreatening environment and a sense of sufficient self-cohesion to sustain regressive pressures without loss of self-integration. Technical abstinence is as necessary for these nonludic aspects as for the ludic, but in this realm abstinence cannot be too rigid since this may stand in the way of recognizing and accepting the patient's infantile needs. Within these parameters, humor tends to engage the patient more on ludic than nonludic terms.

CONCLUSION

My conclusion from this meandering reflection is that humor is indeed a funny thing. It is a complex, variegated, heterogeneous, multidetermined, and multifunctional dimension of the analytic interaction. These qualities of humor have given rise to the problematic aspects of its engagement in the analytic process. I have argued that the differentiation of the role and effects of humor in terms of its function within the component elements of the analytic relation, that is, in relation to transference/countertransference, real relation, and therapeutic alliance, offers an advantageous perspective within which to discern and discriminate the effects and purposes of humor in facilitating the effectiveness and progression of the analytic process. Humor enacted within the transferential sphere or in the context of real relationship carry certain disadvantages that largely outweigh their potential benefits. Humor within the context and framework of the alliance sector is where the benefits and therapeutic effectiveness of humor in the analytic interaction can be most readily identified.

REFERENCES

Appelbaum, A. & Diamond, D. (1993), Prologue. *Psychoanal. Inq.*, 13:145–152.

Bader, M. (1993), The analyst's use of humor. *Psychoanal. Quart.*, 62:23–51.

Baker, R. (1993), Some reflections on humour in psychoanalysis. *Internat. J. Psycho-Anal.*, 74:951–960.

Baudry, F. (1991), The relevance of the analyst's character and attitudes to his work. *J. Amer. Psychoanal. Assn.*, 39:917–938.

Blum, H. P. (1981), Some current and recurrent problems of psychoanalytic technique. *J. Amer. Psychoanal. Assn.*, 29:47–68.

Brody, M. W. (1950), The meaning of laughter. *Psychoanal. Quart.*, 19:192–201.

Christie, G. L. (1994), Some psychoanalytic aspects of humour. *Internat. J. Psycho-Anal.*, 75:479–489.

Clowes, E. K. (1996), Oedipal themes in latency: Analysis of the "farmer's daughter" joke. *The Psychoanalytic Study of the Child*, 51:436–454. New Haven, CT: Yale University Press.

Cooper, A. M. (1986), Some limitations on therapeutic effectiveness: The "burnout syndrome" in psychoanalysis. *Psychoanal. Quart.*, 55:576–598.

Freud, A. (1936), *The Ego and the Mechanisms of Defense*, Rev. ed. New York: International Universities Press.

Freud, S. (1905), Jokes and their relation to the unconscious. *Standard Edition*, 8:9–236. London: Hogarth Press, 1960.

———— (1923), The ego and the id. *Standard Edition*, 19:1–66. London: Hogarth Press, 1961.

——— (1927), Humour. *Standard Edition*, 21:159–166. London: Hogarth Press, 1961.

Greenson, R. R. (1965), The working alliance and the transference neurosis. *Psychoanal. Quart.*, 34:155–181.

——— (1967), *The Technique and Practice of Psychoanalysis, Vol. 1*. New York: International Universities Press.

Greenson, R. R. & Wexler, M. (1969), The non-transference relationship in the psychoanalytic situation. *Internat. J. Psycho-Anal.*, 50:27–39.

Grotjahn, M. (1945), Laughter in dreams. *Psychoanal. Quart.*, 14:221–227.

——— (1957), *Beyond Laughter*. New York: McGraw-Hill.

Haig, R. A. (1986), Therapeutic uses of humor. *Amer. J. Psychother.*, 40:543–553.

Huizinga, J. (1944), *Homo Ludens*. Boston, MA: Beacon Press, 1955.

Jacobson, E. (1946), The child's laughter: Theoretical and clinical notes on the function of the comic. *The Psychoanalytic Study of the Child*, 2:39–60. New York: International Universities Press.

Jacobson, J. G. (1993), Developmental observation, multiple models of the mind, and the therapeutic relationship in psychoanalysis. *Psychoanal. Quart.*, 62:523–552.

Klauber, J. (1968), The psychoanalyst as a person. *Brit. J. Med. Psychol.*, 41:315–322.

Kohut, H. (1966), Forms and transformations of narcissism. *J. Amer. Psychoanal. Assn.*, 14:243–272.

Kris, E. (1940), Laughter as an expressive process: contributions to the psychoanalysis of expressive behaviour. *Internat. J. Psycho-Anal.*, 21:314–341.

Kubie, L. S. (1971), The destructive potential of humor in psychotherapy. *Amer. J. Psychiat.*, 127:861–866.

Lester, E. P. (1990), Gender and identity issues in the analytic process. *Internat. J. Psycho-Anal.*, 71:435–444.

Levine, J. & Redlich, F. C. (1955), Failure to understand humor. *Psychoanal. Quart.*, 24:560–572.

Loewald, E. (1976), The development and uses of humour in a four-year-old's treatment. *Internat. Rev. Psycho-Anal.*, 3:209–221.

London, N. J. (1981), The play element of regression in the psychoanalytic process. *Psychoanal. Inq.*, 1:7–27.

Lynch, W. F. (1965), *Images of Hope: Imagination as Healer of the Hopeless*. Baltimore, MD: Helicon Press.

Mahon, E. J. (1992), The function of humor in a four-year-old. *The Psychoanalytic Study of the Child*, 47:321–328. New Haven, CT: Yale University Press.

Meerlo, J. A. M. (1966), The biology of laughter. *Psychoanal. Rev.*, 53:189–208.

Meghnagi, D. (1991), Jewish humour on psychoanalysis. *Internat. Rev. Psycho-Anal.*, 18:223–228.

Meissner, W. W. (1973), Notes on the psychology of hope. *J. Relig. & Health*, 12:7–29, 120–139.

——— (1986), *Psychotherapy and the Paranoid Process*. Northvale, NJ: Aronson.

——— (1987), *Life and Faith: Psychological Perspectives on Religious Experience*. Washington, DC: Georgetown University Press.

—— (1988), *Treatment of Patients in the Borderline Spectrum*. Northvale, NJ: Aronson.

—— (1991), *What Is Effective in Psychoanalytic Therapy: The Move From Interpretation to Relation*. Northvale, NJ: Aronson.

—— (1992), The concept of the therapeutic alliance. *J. Amer. Psychoanal. Assn.*, 40:1059–1087.

—— (1995a), The economic principle in psychoanalysis. I. Economics and energetics. *Psychoanal. & Contemp. Thought*, 18:197–226.

—— (1995b), The economic principle in psychoanalysis. II. Regulatory principles. *Psychoanal. & Contemp. Thought*, 18:227–259.

—— (1995c), The economic principle in psychoanalysis. III. Motivational principles. *Psychoanal. & Contemp. Thought*, 18:261–292.

—— (1996a), *The Therapeutic Alliance*. New Haven, CT: Yale University Press.

—— (1996b), The therapeutic alliance and the real relationship in the analytic process. In: *Understanding Therapeutic Action: Psychodynamic Concepts of Cure*,

—— (in process), Further thoughts on neutrality and abstinence.

Millar, T. P. (1986), Humor: The triumph of reason. *Perspect. in Biol. & Med.*, 29:545–559.

Modell, A. H. (1976), "The holding environment" and the therapeutic action of psychoanalysis. *J. Amer. Psychoanal. Assn.*, 24:285–308.

—— (1990), *Other Times, Other Realities: A Theory of Psychoanalytic Treatment*. Cambridge, MA: Harvard University Press.

Oberndorf, C. P. (1932), Kidding—A form of humour. *Internat. J. Psycho-Anal.*, 13:479–480.

Olson, H. A. (1976), The use of humor in psychotherapy. In: *The Use of Humor in Psychotherapy*, ed. H. S. Strean. Northvale, NJ: Aronson, 1994.

Pasquali, G. (1986), Some notes on humour in psychoanalysis. *Internat. Rev. Psycho-Anal.*, 14:231–236.

Piddington, R. (1963), *The Psychology of Laughter: A Study in Social Adaptation*. New York: Gamut Press.

Poland, W. S. (1971), The place of humor in psychotherapy. *Amer. J. Psychiat.*, 128:635–637.

—— (1990), The gift of laughter: On the development of a sense of humor in clinical analysis. *Psychoanal. Quart.*, 59:197–225.

Rose, G. J. (1969), *King Lear* and the use of humor in treatment. *J. Amer. Psychoanal. Assn.*, 17:927–940.

—— (1992), *The Power of Form: A Psychoanalytic Approach to Aesthetic Form*. Madison, CT: International Universities Press.

Rosen, V. (1963), Variants of comic caricature and their relationship to obsessive-compulsive phenomena. *J. Amer. Psychoanal. Assn.*, 11:704–724.

Rosenheim, E. (1974), Humor in psychotherapy: An interactive experience. *Amer. J. Psychother.*, 28:584–591.

—— & Golan, G. (1986), Patients' reactions to humorous interventions in psychotherapy. *Amer. J. Psychother.*, 40:110–124.

Sands, S. (1984), The use of humor in psychotherapy. *Psychoanal. Rev.*, 71:441–460.

Schafer, R. (1976), *A New Language for Psychoanalysis*. New Haven, CT: Yale University Press.

Schimel, J. L. (1978), The function of wit and humor in psychoanalysis. *J. Amer. Acad. Psychoanal.*, 6:369–379.

Schlesinger, K. (1979), Jewish humour as Jewish identity. *Internat. Rev. Psycho-Anal.*, 6:317–330.

Stone, L. (1961), *The Psychoanalytic Situation*. New York: International Universities Press.

—————— (1981), Notes on the noninterpretive elements in the psychoanalytic situation. *J. Amer. Psychoanal. Assn.*, 29:89–118.

Strachey, J. (1934), The nature of the therapeutic action of psychoanalysis. *Internat. J. Psycho-Anal.*, 15:127–159.

Ticho, E. (1972), The effect of the analyst's personality on psychoanalytic treatment. *Psychoanal. Forum*, 4:135–172.

Vaillant, G. E. (1977), *Adaptation to Life*. Boston, MA: Little, Brown.

Winnicott, D. W. (1971), *Playing and Reality*. New York: Basic Books.

Zetzel, E. R. (1956), Current concepts of transference. *Internat. J. Psycho-Anal.*, 37:369–378.

Zippin, D. (1966), Sex differences and the sense of humor. *Psychoanal. Rev.*, 53:209–219.

PART III

Character and Creativity

8

Humor in the Freud–Ferenczi Correspondence

JUDITH DUPONT
translated by Susan Fairfield

Humor and psychoanalysis have always gotten along well together. Isn't the essence of many interpretations similar to that of the joke—a condensation that "clicks"? I, for one, have had occasion to tell a funny story by way of interpretation. An example is the following anecdote that draws the patient's attention to the fact that he is the author of his dreams, that the interior "factory" in which they are produced is himself:

> A woman dreams that she is lying in her bed when she suddenly sees the doorknob turning slowly. The door opens halfway and a huge black man slips into the room. He approaches her with outstretched hands, bends over her, and stares at her threateningly. Overcome by fear, the woman cries, "Oh my God, what are you going to do to me?" And the black man answers, with a kind smile, "I don't know, ma'am; its *your* dream."

(As it happens, this story tallies with a brief sociopolitical analysis made by Ferenczi in his letter of July 9, 1910: "The persecution of blacks in America reminds me of the case that Jung so sagely presented, according to which the blacks represent the 'unconscious' of the Americans. . . . Thus, the hate, the reaction formation against one's own vices." He goes on to say: "Along with the circumcision/castration complex, this

161

mechanism could also be the basis for *anti-Semitism*" (Brabant, Falzeder, and Giampieri-Deutsch, 1993, pp. 186–187).

My own analyst did not hesitate to resort to humor from time to time; he once offered me, by way of interpretation, his personal "interpretation" of a little aria from Mozart's *Marriage of Figaro*. Freud himself made ready use of humor, but he also took an interest in it on the theoretical level. He devoted an entire work to it, "Jokes and Their Relation to the Unconscious" (1905), in which he analyzes the place of humor in the psychic economy and the various mechanisms underlying the comic effect. Ferenczi (1911), too, wrote a paper on this topic, in which he presents Freud's work on humor to the public at large. But, as in his other writings aimed at setting forth Freud's ideas, his own personality and his own thought are abundantly evident here.

Humor also figures in other works of these two authors, as well as in the correspondence they carried on for a good quarter-century. But in these intimate letters they use humor much more freely, with the result that their respective characters find more marked expression here than in their writings destined for publication.

The Freud–Ferenczi correspondence makes a number of direct or indirect allusions to Freud's treatise on humor. "I wish you much humor in all of these difficulties," Ferenczi writes, adding: "After all, you invented the theory of humor yourself; you should also be able to apply it" (letter of October 29, 1910, in Brabant et al., 1993, p. 230). And in fact Freud did just that. The correspondence often repeats funny stories or jokes cited in Freud's work, such as the account of the undisciplined artilleryman Itzig whose commanding officer advised him to buy his own cannon and set himself up independently (Ferenczi's letters of December 20, 1912 [Brabant et al., 1993, p. 443] and July 23, 1914 [Falzeder and Brabant, 1996, p. 8]).

The long correspondence of Freud and Ferenczi, comprising nearly 1250 letters, has often been compared to a 25-year-long psychoanalysis—an analysis of Ferenczi by Freud, more rarely of Freud by Ferenczi, not to mention certain self-analytical passages (frequent, extensive, and detailed in Ferenczi's case, more sporadic, reticent, and brief in Freud's). In the course of this epistolary pseudo-analysis, one that is more or less mutual though definitely asymmetric, both men often use humor to make an interpretation, to convey their thoughts, or to touch on a weak point in the correspondent without appearing brutally frank. But when it comes to third parties, they quite often allow themselves forthright "interpretations" that are neither neutral nor kindly. Thus Ferenczi says in his letter of February 16, 1910: "If Riklin is boring, that proves that he hasn't changed" (Brabant et al., 1993, p. 141). Freud, in particular, has a knack for coming up with some especially devastating formulations in such cases as, for example, in a letter of April 6, 1911, in regard to Adler and Stekel:

I am constantly annoyed about the two—Max and Moritz—who are also developing with great rapidity in a backward direction and will soon have arrived at a denial of the unconscious. But I am quite powerless against them, especially as long as I can't throw them out of the Zentralblatt. Enemies are much more comfortable; you can at least ignore them [Brabant et al., 1993, p. 267].

Similarly, in his letter of April 29, 1916, Freud writes: "Rockefeller's daughter presented Jung with a gift of 360,000 francs for the construction of a casino, analytic institute, etc. So, Swiss ethics have finally made their sought-after contact with American money" (Falzeder and Brabant, 1996, p. 126).

But Freud and Ferenczi use humor for more than conveying interpretations. They also call upon it to give vent to their bad temper, their anger, and sometimes—especially in Freud's case—their scorn. And humorous expressions often serve to cloak overly intense emotions, as when a very personal confession is being made or a lament uttered, especially one concerning their health or some great sorrow. Thus Freud has to turn to a bit of black humor in order to speak of the death of his daughter Sophie, including it along with a whole group of problems and difficulties: "I think: the session continues. But it was a bit much for one week" (letter of January 29, 1920, unpublished).

Health problems and the idea of time passing, of aging, and of death play a large role in the concerns of the two men and are referred to throughout their correspondence in a series of witty formulations, most often with a feigned lightness of tone. These references are so numerous that they really deserve a chapter to themselves.

For both Freud and Ferenczi the humorous tendency is most often expressed through style: in turns of phrase, as when Freud reassures Ferenczi, who fears he had been too aggressive with a medical colleague, "Misfortune doesn't come to him without justification" (Brabant et al., 1993, p. 26), or in the choice of words—adjectives, for example—that are slightly inappropriate or have a double meaning and that present difficulties for the translator, since they are impossible to render without tiresome explanations that, of course, completely spoil any comic effect. Nevertheless, some of these unusual epithets are readily translatable. Thus Ferenczi writes on November 20, 1919: "Out of the ten patients expected, only four wholes and two halves have reported thus far" (Falzeder and Brabant, 1996, p. 368). And Freud, the great master of black humor, writes on August 24, 1922, in connection with his sister, whose daughter Judith had just committed suicide: "My sister, a virtuoso when it comes to despair" (unpublished).

The two correspondents tend to proceed by allusions, juxtapositions, unusual comparisons, and descriptions of people or events from an unexpected angle. They frequently illustrate their remarks with citations—as when Freud quotes Lichtenstein: "It is always better for an office to be lesser than its holder's capabilities" (letter of January 20, 1909, in Brabant et al., 1993, p. 39)—or simply with a discreet smile hidden behind their words. In such cases we would speak of "wit" instead of "humor." Sometimes the humorous effect stems from the fact that the quotation is in a foreign language. Both men make ready use of Latin, Greek, French, English, even Spanish, and often Yiddish: "Whatever you don't have coming to you is *Rebach* [an extra advantage]" (Freud, letter of November 17, 1911, in Brabant et al., 1993, p. 314).

Sometimes these citations are merely alluded to, their origin being clear to these two highly cultivated men, though their meaning may well escape even an educated reader of today. Freud, for example, often refers to his "poor Konrad"; any reader of *Imago* by Carl Spitteler, who won the Nobel Prize for Literature in 1919, would immediately make the connection with the painful intestines of Victor, the hero of that novel. But who would ever read Spitteler nowadays? And when Freud begins his letter of October 2, 1912, with "The beautiful days, etc." (Brabant et al., 1993, p. 408), his correspondent will immediately recognize the passage from Schiller's *Don Carlos*, Act I, Scene 1, in which it is said that the beautiful days in Aranjuez are now over.

While both men go in for humor, they do so in very different ways. Ferenczi's is sometimes so subtle, so lightly marked by a stylistic touch, that it is hard to give examples here that could be understood without a lengthy account of their context. Freud, less constrained by diffidence and respect than his young correspondent, allows himself more obvious jokes that speak for themselves; thus I am citing more of them in this chapter.

We must not forget that the position of the two correspondents is not symmetrical. Freud is the inventor of psychoanalysis, the older man, the master, in a sense the father. As it happens, this last title is repeatedly acknowledged by Ferenczi and sometimes overtly assumed by Freud. In his letter of November 17, 1911, Freud addresses Ferenczi as "Dear son" (Brabant et al., 1993, p. 314), underlining the infantile position that the latter found it so difficult to escape at this time; Freud repeats the term in his next letter (November 30, 1911), adding: "Until you object to this form of address" (Brabant et al., 1993, p. 316). Faced with this renowned master and imposing father, Ferenczi plays the younger brother, the pupil, the son. The nature of his humor naturally reflects this junior role.

But the style of wit evolves along with the relationship of the two men. At first, Ferenczi risks only tentative pleasantries, often at his own expense, whereas Freud feels free to needle the younger man, sometimes rather severely or with a clearly pedagogic aim. Toward the end of the correspondence, at a time when Ferenczi's investigations are moving in an increasingly independent direction, Freud's humor gradually changes to bitter irony; Ferenczi, for his part, is worn down by grief and illness and no longer feels like laughing at this point.

But the differing styles of humor depend just as much on character as on respective position. Ferenczi's, while more timid, is also warmer, happier, more lighthearted than Freud's. Freud, on the other hand, often uses humor as a weapon, from little provocations that are more or less well intentioned, depending on circumstance and interlocutor, to comparisons that are downright offensive (so-and-so is an ass or a pig). Ferenczi makes one such attempt, calling someone a dog, but he immediately apologizes—to dogs. Freud's humor can on occasion take a devastatingly ironic turn. Ferenczi can also be ironic with regard to his adversaries, but judging from his paper on humor, he does not hold irony in high esteem. In "The Psychoanalysis of Wit and the Comical" (1911), he writes that irony is a contemptible way of causing laughter. Though he was not above ignoring this virtuous principle from time to time, he was never as scathing as his elder correspondent. Thus he writes on April 27, 1910: "I was just thumbing through a brochure by *Frank*, which impudently calls itself '*the* Psychoanalysis,' . . . although it contains only *his* impoverished analysis, discarded by the authorities" (Brabant et al., 1993, p. 168).

As I have noted, Ferenczi often uses humor at his own expense, not only in order to convey his awkwardness and embarrassment vis-à-vis the venerated master, but sometimes also to take the edge off an aggressivity that he does not dare to express more directly. We know that Ferenczi reproached Freud for not having interpreted the negative transference in the course of his brief analysis with him. "Analysis Terminable and Interminable" (1937), written 4 years after the death of his friend, shows that Freud was never able to accept this criticism. But in fact traces of this negative transference can be found scattered throughout the correspondence, carefully veiled in mollifying circumlocutions tinged with self-irony but nonetheless unmistakable.

Yet above all, Ferenczi is eager to gain the affection and the respect of his master and friend. He brings him ideas and examples designed to illustrate the soundness of analytic principles, yet shyness or circumstances sometimes lead him to diminish, or actually to take back, the offering with which he had intended to honor Freud and psychoanalysis. Thus, on October 30, 1909, Ferenczi begins describing a symptomatic act of his friend Gizella Pálos, his intention being to publish this story in order to confirm an aspect of Freudian theory. He starts off enthusiastically: "Frau Isolde [the code name of Gizella, who, as a married woman, has to conceal her affair with Ferenczi], whom I am eagerly at work analyzing"

(Brabant et al., 1993, p. 90). But then he realizes that this fine clinical example that he would so much have liked to offer as a gift to his master cannot be published as is, since the protagonists would be too easily identifiable. But if he alters it, it will no longer make the intended point. And so he concludes that "it should . . . find its way to the wastepaper basket!" (Brabant et al., 1993, p. 91).

Ferenczi sometimes allows himself to show open cheerfulness, a rarity for the more bitter, more cynical Freud. On June 5, 1910, Ferenczi writes: "The day before yesterday it was so hot that I had to give the course on the upper deck of an omnibus and in the city park. Very peripatetic!" (Brabant et al., 1993, p. 179). Humor also informs some of his theoretical insights. On April 27, 1916, an idea about autotomy occurs to him: "If a worried person scratches his head, he perhaps removes—symbolically—the uncomfortable thought" (Falzeder and Brabant, 1996, p. 125). Or, on August 3, 1926:

> "I'm writing this time only to let you know about a little discovery. In the case of a patient who managed the feat of forgetting an entire day of his life (a day on which he at the same time experienced all kinds of things, especially of the sort that are otherwise "forbidden"), and who thus produced one of those famous cases of splitting of the personality, I've found out that this symptom was an indirect (and unconscious) communication addressed to me, namely that he had consciously concealed a great many things from me, or presented them in a dishonest manner. I'm convinced that all such cases can be explained in a similar way, that they are an admission of mendacity, that is, of the fact that these people, in different life situations or with regard to different groups of people, reveal only *parts* of their total character and conceal much of their conduct. This can of course be traced back to infantile lies concerning sexual matters—at the same time an imitation of the mendacity of adults [unpublished].

Sometimes these letters also contain a comic touch that is entirely involuntary. This is true primarily of Ferenczi, who driven by his desperate admiration for Freud, gets himself involved in effusions whose linguistic excesses can make us smile. Thus Freud writes in his letter of December 23, 1912, on the occasion of his conflict with Jung: "With deference to my neurosis, I hope I will master it all right" (Brabant et al., 1993, p. 446). On December 26, Ferenczi replies with an armful of flowers, perhaps not entirely without thorns, from which I shall excerpt a few lines that are of interest in other ways as well:

> *Mutual analysis* is nonsense, also an impossibility. Everyone must be able to tolerate an authority over himself from whom he accepts analytic correction. You are probably the only one who can permit him-

self to do without an analyst; but that is actually no *advantage* for you, i.e., for your analysis, but a necessity: you have no peer or even superior analyst at your disposal because you have been doing analysis fifteen years longer than *all* others and have accumulated experiences which we others still lack.—Despite all the deficiencies of self-analysis (which is certainly lengthier and more difficult than being analyzed), we have to expect of you the ability to keep your symptoms in check. If you had the strength to overcome in yourself *(for the first time in the history of mankind)* the resistances which all humanity brings to bear on the results of analysis, then we must expect of you the strength to dispense with your lesser symptoms.—The facts speak decidedly in favor of this.

But what is valid for *you* is not valid for the rest of us [Brabant et al., 1993, p. 449].

Thus Ferenczi almost never allows himself to make Freud the target of a joke. But we may note a rare instance of an attempt at teasing directed at Freud: "I do not want to give up hope that you will let a part of your withdrawn homosexual libido be refloated and bring more sympathy to bear toward my 'ideal of honesty.' You know: I am an unimpeachable therapist" (Brabant et al., 1993, p. 224). This is from a letter dated October 12, 1910, written shortly after the so-called "Palermo incident" in which Ferenczi had asked for a mutual analytic frankness that Freud was absolutely unwilling to grant. But Ferenczi allows himself some hints of humorous aggression towards adversaries or other third parties, as if following the example of Freud, who hardly denies himself such opportunities. Yet on the whole his respect obviously imposes a degree of constraint on his freedom of expression. He becomes freer as the years go by, but he never proves to be as scathing as Freud.

As we have seen, a typical form of humor for Ferenczi is self-mockery, as in the phrase with which he ends his letter of October 12, 1908: "You will, I fear, have many letters wash over you from your very obedient . . . Dr. Ferenczi" (Brabant et al., 1993, p. 21). Or, on February 15, 1913: "I am sending you a brief communication for the *Zeitschrift*, about which I have absolutely no idea whether it is worth the printer's ink" (Brabant et al., 1993, p. 470). And on February 5, 1910: "I evidently want to play the little *Freud* here" (Brabant et al., 1993, p. 131). Later, when his relationship to Freud becomes more strained, the self-mockery takes on a more bitter tone: "This all sounds very mystical— please don't let it scare you. As far as I can assess my own situation, I do not (or only seldom) overstep the bounds of normality," he writes on September 15, 1931 (unpublished), trying to win acceptance from Freud for the direction in which his investigations were heading, a direction in which Freud saw no merit.

Judging by the number of "Jewish stories," this self-mockery may well be considered to be a feature of Jewish humor. In this respect it is akin to the humor of blacks, in both cases a reaction of a people who have often been socially disempowered and relegated to minority status, a people who preempt aggression by cloaking it in their own formulations and thereby mock their aggressors. They seem to direct the aggressive remarks at themselves, but they do so in their own fashion. Ferenczi often has recourse to this comic strategy; no doubt he felt disempowered with regard to Freud. As for Freud, he is never much drawn to self-mockery, at any rate not in this correspondence. Ferenczi is his friend, to be sure, but also his pupil, his junior. In contrast, he occasionally yields to self-mockery in his correspondence with Fliess, where he is the one who shows endless admiration for his correspondent. Thus he writes to Fliess on June 30, 1896: "I am looking forward to our congress. . . . I bring nothing but two open ears and one temporal lobe lubricated for reception. I foresee important things—I am that self-seeking—also for my purposes" (Freud and Fliess, 1887–1904, p. 193). Today we are in agreement that this admiration was basically transferential. Nevertheless, its effects were clearly the same.

If Freud does not often engage in self-mockery with Ferenczi, this is not only because his position is the much more confident one; perhaps he also wants to protect his authority, the respect he hopes to inspire in his pupils and followers. On the other hand, he too is not without a certain fragility, the reasons for which are no doubt many. We know the problems he had to face over the years: attacks from various quarters, his university career blocked, his vulnerable position as inventor of a science that was still considered scandalous, not to mention what it meant to be a Jew in a largely anti-Semitic country. On the personal level, he lost people who were dear to him, his daughter Sophie and his beloved grandson, and then there was his long and painful illness. And we must not forget all the stresses and secret wounds that every human being carries within, what Michael Balint (1968) called the basic fault that everyone has, something that even a man who had carried self-analysis as far as Freud had could not escape. But in any event his character led him toward outright confrontation as opposed to the indirectness of self-irony. The only area in which he was able to joke at his own expense was that of age and illness.

Another vulnerable point, apparently never healed over, surely stemmed from his childhood. When Freud was around 10, his uncle Joseph was arrested and imprisoned for forgery. And here is the passage from Freud's letter of December 23, 1912:

A patient recently failed to bring up anything for a whole week because he couldn't allow himself the cruelty of reminding me that a brother or uncle of mine had been executed for larceny and murder. A Dr. Birstein from Odessa . . . wanted forcibly to bring a patient of mine to Adler and told him I was so ambitious because I was the son of a *Schames* [caretaker in a synagogue] and was suffering from agoraphobia, etc., etc. Similar kind things are coming out of Zurich. There is something nice and patterned about this thing, but it requires a strong stomach [Brabant et al., 1993, p. 446].

And in fact, even if Freud had not had an uncle who was a murderer, he had certainly had one who was a forger. Freud's brothers who lived in England were surely implicated in the counterfeiting affair that resulted in his uncle Joseph's imprisonment, as was perhaps his own father. The young Sigmund could not have been ignorant of what was undoubtedly a major trauma for the entire Freud family. Nicolas Rand and Maria Torok (1997) offer an extensive analysis of the likely impact on Freud of this event.

As far as Ferenczi is concerned, Freud often resorts to humor to convey a negatively toned message tactfully. An example is a passage from his letter of May 10, 1908, the tenth letter in the correspondence, in which he is trying to let Ferenczi know the appropriate distance to maintain. After inviting Ferenczi, who was looking forward to long-awaited exchanges with the master, to join him and his family on their summer vacation in Berchtesgaden, Freud is careful to add: "It is understood at the outset that you will not disturb me in my work and that I won't have to take any precautions against you" (Brabant et al., 1993, p. 11). He goes on to say that they will be able to share a meal from time to time and that Ferenczi will be able to go mountain climbing with Freud's sons.

On the whole, however, the tone tends to be jovial at the beginning of the correspondence. When, in connection with the planned trip to America of September 1909, Ferenczi announces: "I am even 'able' to follow you there" (letter of January 2, 1909, in Brabant et al., 1993, p. 30), Freud replies: "I would also be ['able'] to ask you to accompany me" (letter of January 10, 1909, in Brabant et al., 1993, p. 33; this author's translation).

While Freud often—though not always—tried to treat Ferenczi gently, he was also capable of being very harsh in the humor he directed at others. Thus with regard to Friedländer he writes: "I learned from Jung that Friedländer was with him 'sweet as sugar and wagging his tail.' He's a rotten character!" (letter of October 22, 1909, in Brabant et al., 1993, p. 85). And, on November 10, 1909: "A formidable attack, half demented, half clairvoyant, and dipped in holy venom, has been very deliberately directed against me by Foerster in the *Evangelische Freiheit*" (Brabant et al., 1993, p. 98). Or, perhaps a bit less cruelly, on March 30, 1922: "Tell her [Gizella] that I've recently read a number of old books by Groddeck . . . that are downright German and bad" (unpublished).

An entire chapter could be devoted to Freud's ironic comments on America and Americans, topics on which he held apparently unshakable prejudices. Thus on January 10, 1909 he writes:

> I do find the presumption to sacrifice so much money in order to give lectures there much too "American." America should bring money, not cost money. By the way, we could soon be "up shit creek" the minute they come upon the sexual underpinnings of our psychology. Brill writes, alternating between hopefulness and misgiving, that he thinks he will soon find this very hard [Brabant et al., 1993, p. 33].

And on June 13, 1909, he writes that "honesty will not be any more frequent a phenomenon in America than it is in Europe; progress is also not to be expected from that quarter" (Brabant et al., 1993, p. 66). Similarly, on October 22, 1909, he complains of "an entirely American exploitation" (Brabant et al., 1993, p. 84). And again: "I could also be better healthwise; America has cost me much" (letter of November 21, 1909, in Brabant et al., 1993, p. 108).

Freud was even critical of American bathrooms. It is said that he complained about the endless corridors and stairs one had to negotiate when one felt an urgent need in the street, and when a gentleman who, like Freud, had prostate trouble finally reached his goal . . . it was too late.

Malicious allusions to America and Americans return in the years 1926–1927, when Ferenczi was spending 6 months in the States. There are several reasons for this over and above Freud's preconceived ideas. Rank, after the crisis set off in 1924–1925 by his theory of birth trauma, had gone to live in America. He had distanced himself from Freud, who did not agree with the overly exclusive use he made of his theory, and he seemed lost to the "cause." Freud feared that Ferenczi, too, might become estranged from him, geographically if not scientifically, should he decide to remain in the United States. The political situation in Hungary was grim since the coming to power of the reactionary and anti-Semitic regime of Admiral Horthy, and Ferenczi had often considered emigration to various countries, including America.

Moreover, a crisis had just erupted within the psychoanalytic community, namely the problem of so-called lay analysis (analysis practiced by nonphysicians). Freud was strongly in favor of it, American analysts strongly opposed. Nor were they the only opponents; Jones, Abraham, and other European analysts held the same view. But the only group to adopt this position unanimously—and this was true until quite recently—were the Americans. Extremely annoyed at this situation, Freud lost no opportunity to express his sentiments. On September 19, 1926, before

Ferenczi's departure for the United States, Freud begins a letter to him with: "Before you entrust yourself to the sea in search of the land of the dollar-barbarians." And on March 23, 1927, congratulating Ferenczi on his work in the States: "What fine work, what an achievement! . . . And unfortunately just for Americans, who don't know the true value of anything and on whom nothing leaves an impression" (unpublished). He goes on to relate "personal news from me that you don't need to tell to the savages over there" (unpublished). On Ferenczi's return he observes sadly: "I find [you] more reserved than you were before America. Damn that country!" (letter of August 2, 1927, unpublished). In a letter written 6 days later, he calls America "Dollaria."

But America is not the only target of Freud's ironic wit. He is not without a certain misogyny, a feeling shared with many men of his time. Thus on January 10, 1910, he writes:

> I fear that not much new will result from an investigation of what is constitution and what is repression in the sexual character of women. The question will probably be answered with bisexuality and the knowledge that there are women who are capable of everything. A large piece of sexual repression is inextricable from the character of a woman of culture [Brabant et al., 1993, p. 122].

And in his letter of October 23, 1926, he writes of a woman physician, Dr. Powers, that "even among women and among doctors it's rare to find such stupidity, far above the human average" (unpublished). Still, his misogyny did not get in the way of his showing deep affection for women such as Gizella Ferenczi or admiration and respect for others such as Marie Bonaparte or Lou Andreas-Salomé, not to mention his own daughter Anna, who always occupied a privileged place in his esteem. Yet this high regard did not put admired women beyond the range of his mockery. In a letter of March 20, 1913, he writes: "Frau Lou Salomé wants to spend one or two full days with you . . . ; she is a highly significant woman, even though all the tracks around her go into the lion's den but none come out" (Brabant et al., 1993, p. 476).

But Freud could on occasion show a gentler kind of humor, as for example when he characterizes Pfister as "a charming fellow . . . , half Savior, half Pied Piper" (letter of April 25, 1909, in Brabant et al., 1993, p. 55).

As I have noted, two anxiety-arousing topics preoccupied Freud throughout his life and hence throughout his correspondence with Ferenczi: his age and his health. His sense of modesty usually leads him to veil these sources of distress in humor. On October 6, 1910, he writes that someone "who is not master of his Konrad [that is, his intestines] should not travel" (Brabant et al., 1993, pp. 221–222). And on May 12, 1914:

> At six in the evening, perhaps brought on by an excess of festivities, an acute intestinal condition set in, which Dr. Zweig examined with a proctoscope, and then he congratulated me. He then admitted that I didn't yet have the neoplasm that he suspected, but rather a very acute inflammation of the romanum. So I have been restored to life [Brabant et al., 1993, p. 552].

And on September 10, 1917: "Health quite uneven. He who has a talent for hypochondria can write all kinds of verses to it" (Falzeder and Brabant, 1996, p. 237).

As far as death is concerned, Freud cannot endure the thought of his priority being challenged or thwarted. On February 6, 1921, he writes about Anton von Freund's wife, who fantasized that she would find her recently dead husband again after her own death: "Explain to her that I, who am probably next in line for such a reunion, am prepared to convey greetings and undertake commissions" (unpublished). This feeling of rivalry is clearly expressed in his response to Ferenczi, who writes on July 24, 1921:

> I find that our friend Lajos [Lévy]—a former patient of mine!—is all too ready to emphasize the psychical; he clearly wants to pay me back in my own coin. . . . [H]e should above all know what is happening on the organic level, how I produce these attacks, in order wherever possible to take from my hands the weapons with which I (ucs.) want to commit suicide" [unpublished].

Freud replies on July 29:

> I believe you are carrying on an "unfair competition." Because, in every letter to you, I write about the prospect of death, . . . you take the hint and think you have to equal or outdo me. But as far as I'm concerned it's just a project, a preparation, not even a willingness, since I still have such a lively interest in many issues, and am so curious, that I'm not in any hurry, provided I can still lead a bearable life. . . . I hold fast to a lawful death, even if it is just a comforting illusion like immortality?" [unpublished].

At this time Freud's cancer was not yet evident; later on, his humorous comments about his health take on a more tragic tone. In the 1930s, fearing that he might die before he secured the future of his beloved child, psychoanalysis, he urgently hoped that Ferenczi would take charge of the destiny of the analytic movement by agreeing to run for the presidency of the I.P.A. On July 5, 1930, he writes: "If I hold out beyond September 31 it's really long enough. But if I last longer, I would not want anyone but you to deliver the funeral address" (unpublished). On September 16, 1930, after having received the Goethe Prize, he refers once again to his health:

> The dreadful newspaper reports about my health must have reached you as well. I find them very interesting as evidence of how hard it is to foist on the public and the community something they don't like. The reports are of course the reaction to the Goethe Prize and should warn us not to be fooled into thinking that the resistance to analysis has, in practice, eased up in any tangible way. The same reactionary attitude is shown in Bumke's speech, which I know only from a note in the N[eue Freie] Presse, and also in the heightened activity among Adler's bunch of monkeys, who are now publishing pieces there on the meaning of life (!) and on homosexuality. In short, the Goethe Prize will turn out to be costly for us.

And he notes on October 13 of the same year: "Living essentially for one's health has something unsatisfactory about it" (unpublished).

Ferenczi, too, is preoccupied with his health. He diagnoses himself as a hypochondriac and, like Freud, is able to joke about this subject even though he is often overcome by anxiety. On August 24, 1914, he writes: "I, too, experienced a recurrence of massive slips of the tongue (which I, in the manner of the hypochondriac schooled in medicine, jokingly interpreted as incipient paralysis)" (Falzeder and Brabant, 1996, pp. 14–15). And on October 27, 1914, when he was drafted at the time of World War I: "I learned that I would have to perform local duties. My unconscious seemed so gratified by this news that it immediately began substitutive gratification in the form of diarrhea" (Falzeder and Brabant, 1996, p. 19). Yet in the long declamations devoted to the state of his health, Ferenczi often uses a dramatic and anguished tone completely devoid of humor. Likewise, Freud is often overcome by anxiety or, when he is later stricken with cancer, by the effects of his illness. He cannot endure being thought to be in better health than he feels himself to be, and hence a kind of rivalry is established between him and Ferenczi in the matter of their respective illnesses. Right up to the end, he finds it difficult to admit that his young friend, whom he had wanted to make his successor, is beating him to the finish line and presuming to die before him.

In the 1930s, as is well known, differences arise between Freud and Ferenczi. After Balint devoted an entire chapter to this matter in *The Basic Fault* (1968), it was discussed in numerous articles, and I shall therefore say only a little about it. Above all, Freud wanted to understand the workings of the human psyche. Ferenczi's priority was ministering to patients' suffering, to the point where Freud accused him of *furor sanandi*. His research on technique frequently led him to violate one or another of the technical rules of psychoanalysis, rules established on the basis of treating neurotics. But when it came to caring for psychotic or borderline patients, something new had to be invented. In seeking to create the most favorable atmosphere for treating these difficult cases, Ferenczi often introduced measures that he later found he had to retract (for example, mutual analysis). His early death no doubt prevented him from pursuing his investigations to the point where they could win Freud's agreement. But a personal communication from Michael Balint leads me to think that Ferenczi might well have succeeded in doing so. In 1939, before Freud's death, when Balint had him reread Ferenczi's last articles (the ones that had prompted his most vehement rejection, such as "Confusion of Tongues Between Adults and the Child" [1933]), Freud reacted by commenting: "Nevertheless there are many interesting points there."

But beginning in the 1930s, illness and stress had increased to the point where a humorous manner was no longer appropriate. Light turns of phrase now become more rare in Freud. In the letters of Ferenczi, who suffered a great deal as a result of the dissention between them, hardly any are to be found; at this time he is more concerned to plead his cause than to make jokes.

Freud's last use of humor, a fiercely ironic humor, occurs in his letter of December 13, 1931, which is known as the letter dealing with the "kiss technique":

> You have never made a secret of the fact that you kiss your women patients and let them kiss you. . . . Now if you give detailed accounts of your technique and your successes, there are two paths you can follow. Either you report this or you hush it up. The latter option, as you can well imagine, is unworthy. One must be publicly accountable for whatever one does in the way of technique. Moreover, both paths would soon converge. Even if you yourself say nothing, it will become known, just as I knew about it before you told me.

> Now I'm certainly not one to outlaw such little erotic satisfactions out of prudishness or concern for bourgeois convention. And I know that at the time of the *Song of the Nibelungen* the kiss was an innocent greeting accorded to every guest. And further, I am of the opinion that analysis is possible even in Soviet Russia, where government policy sanctions complete sexual freedom. But that does not alter the fact that we do not live in Russia and that for us a kiss is an unmistakable sign of erotic intimacy. Up to now, in our technique, we have held fast to the principle that erotic gratifications are to be refused to the patient. . . .

Now imagine what would happen if you published your technique. There is no revolutionary who cannot be driven off the battlefield by an even more radical one. Any number of independent thinkers in matters of technique will say to themselves: Why stop at a kiss? Surely it's even more effective to add "cuddling," since after all you still don't make babies that way. And then even bolder ones will come forward to take the further step of looking and showing, and soon we'll have accepted the whole repertoire of doing-everything-but and petting parties[1] into analytic technique, with the result that there will be greatly heightened interest in analysis on the part of analysts and analysands. But the new ally will easily claim too much of this interest on his own behalf, our more junior colleagues will find it difficult to stop the new relationships they have formed at the point where they originally intended to stop, and Godfather Ferenczi, looking at the lively scene he has created, will perhaps say to himself: Maybe, after all, I should have halted my technique of maternal tenderness *before* the kiss [unpublished].

Ferenczi is quite unable to reply to this letter in the same tone. He tries instead to explain the aim of his investigations and to defend their interest; then, in the very first note in his clinical journal, dated January 7, 1932, he mentions all the reasons that might have led the patient who had boasted to Freud that she could kiss "Papa Ferenczi" whenever she felt like it to have somewhat exaggerated the frequency of these occasions.

From then on, there is not much place for humor in the Freud–Ferenczi correspondence; the tone is rather one of deep emotion. Both men find their disagreement painful. Freud, for his part, is too hurt by what he experiences as an abandonment to resort to irony, which he is nonetheless quite able to deploy when he is simply angry. Moreover, the world around them is becoming more and more sinister. The gradual rise of fascism and nazism are creating a looming atmosphere of anxiety that is difficult to escape. Ferenczi is more sensitive to it than Freud, and he also proves to be more perceptive. In one of his last letters, a few weeks before his death in 1933, he urges his master to leave Austria, which he feels will follow in the tracks of Germany. He advises him to take up residence in England with his family and several patients. Freud does not even want to contemplate leaving Vienna, where he has always lived. He cannot believe that the danger will involve him. Ferenczi finally admits that his own poor health, by constantly wearing him down, is perhaps making him view things in a negative light.

In the final letters there is scarcely any more humor, but there is also no longer any bitterness. Now the old, warm friendship reappears on

---

[1] Translator's note: "Petting parties" is in English in the original, as is "Godfather," below.

both sides. We know, however, that Freud never quite got over the tensions and disagreements that marked the last years of their relationship. As we have seen, he was able to revise some of his overly negative judgments about the last works of his pupil and friend. But it was an unhappy, bitter, and disillusioned man who, on September 23, 1939, asked his physician to put an end to his suffering.

In conclusion, this is how I would characterize these two men and, therefore, the type of humor each employed. I would say that Ferenczi is an optimist in despair: against all odds he expects that things will turn out for the best and that, despite their weaknesses, people will in the end prove capable of positive achievement. When he makes fun of himself, he nevertheless does so with the idea that he will manage to produce something of value after all.

Freud, however, is what one might call a cheerful pessimist. Each time he notes to his displeasure that everything is going poorly, that people do not understand him, that his supporters are leaving him or even betraying him, he can at least comfort himself with the pleasurable thought that, at any rate, once again things turned out just as he expected.

REFERENCES

Balint, M. (1968), *The Basic Fault.* London: Tavistock.

Brabant, E., Falzeder, E. & Giampieri-Deutsch, P., eds. (1993), *The Correspondence of Sigmund Freud and Sándor Ferenczi, Vol. 1, 1908–1914,* trans. P. T. Hoffer. Cambridge, MA: Harvard University Press.

Falzeder. E. & Brabant, E., eds. (1996), *The Correspondence of Sigmund Freud and Sándor Ferenczi, Vol. 2, 1914–1919,* trans. P. T. Hoffer. Cambridge, MA: Harvard University Press.

Ferenczi, S. (1911), The psychoanalysis of wit and the comical. In: *Further Contributions to the Theory and Technique of Psychoanalysis.* New York: Brunner/Mazel, 1980, pp. 332–344.

——— (1933), Confusion of tongues between adults and the child. In: *Final Contributions to the Problems and Methods of Psychoanalysis,* ed. M. Balint (trans. E. Mosbacher). London: Karnac, 1980, pp. 156–167.

Freud, S. (1905), Jokes and their relation to the unconscious. *Standard Edition,* 8:9–236. London: Hogarth Press, 1960.

——— (1927). Humour. *Standard Edition,* 21:159–166. London: Hogarth Press, 1961.

——— (1937), Analysis terminable and interminable. *Standard Edition,* 23:216–253. London: Hogarth Press, 1964.

——— & Fliess, W. (1887–1904), *The Complete Letters of Sigmund Freud to Wilhelm Fliess,* ed. & trans. J. M. Masson. Cambridge, MA: Harvard University Press.

Rand, N. & Torok, M. (1997), *Questions to Freud.* Cambridge, MA: Harvard University Press.

9

Winnicott's Laughter

F. Robert Rodman

I: YOUNG DONALD

Donald Winnicott's early letters[1] are a portrait of English enthusiasm in the early 20th century.

> The Leys School
> Cantab.
> 23rd November 1913
>
> My Dear People:
>
> [He asks that his family write to his nurse who has had an operation for appendicitis. He describes a few athletic injuries, including one around the eye, which renders the skin "utterly senseless and dead to this moment."]
>
> Dr. Hindle told me on Friday that I had made a very good dissection of a frog. He's going to write to the manager of the Plymouth Aquarium (whom he knows) to ask him to let me look round etc. Topping of him I think. I dare say father could have got me in, but it would be much more profitable to get an intro from a co-scientist and biologist.
>
> I seem to have written a lot in 13 minutes. Perhaps it is not so much fun to have read.
>
> [. . .]

---

[1] Donald Winnicott's letters are reproduced with the kind permission of The Winnicott Trust and Mark Paterson copyrights.

Less than four weeks from now and I shall be home at this time having our Sunday supper. I do like our Sunday supper at Rockville [the name of the Winnicott home in Plymouth], although I don't know why. I perhaps do not like it so much at the time, only it is a nice meal to look back upon. So cool, with mint sauce and cold meat.

I am acting Queen in an awfully funny play the litterary [sic] and Debating Society is getting up, next Monday.

Donald is 17 here. Perhaps there is something to be made of his preference for "an intro from a co-scientist and biologist" in the context of his relationship to his influential father. His reflections on Sunday supper show an attempt to differentiate between pleasure in the moment and pleasure in retrospect. There is an anecdote told by Rosa Taylor in a 1988 interview in London with Madeleine Davis and me about Winnicott and James Taylor, his first wife's brother. They were taking a train. This was in the days of steam engines and the engineer was getting it ready. Jim said: "He's happy, isn't he?" Donald said: "Yes, but he doesn't know it." At boarding school, he is already thinking about this subject.

November 30, 1913 (one week later)

Well my home circle:

[. . .] [He lists what he wants for Christmas, lots of books.] I don't want much do I! HA! (?) I hope I don't get everything I want; I am sure it is not good for me.

Yes, well I am longing to get home now. It seems very wonderful that the time is flying so quickly. I am having a wonderfully good time here, too good did I hear someone say? Well that may be. I hope not. I am starting another sheet, but I will not have time to fill it, I am afraid.

I am sitting at the back of the hall, and a chap to the right has very dexterously taken off his coat, changed his collar and waistecoat [...] and put on his coat again. This was done without his being spotted, but now he looks exactly like a parson and is doing all manner of antics imitating the Head, the Bursar and anyone who occurs to his mind. He is really a rather humourous lad....

December 9, 1916. Jesus College (twenty years old)

Hullo At last, my dears!!!

[. . .]

... We have an annual bust up in my rooms, this year surpassing all others in row and hilarity. It was simply fine.

We sang songs, did acrobatics, played rugger—polo—golf—soccer—hockey with walking sticks, and my old top hat (that I bought for 2/-). Also we made awful noises, and owing to the beautiful arrangement of my rooms no damage was done. If I had had burnished tables, glazed pictures, and Turkey carpets we should have done about 7 pounds worth damage. But as it was we did none.[2] And yet my room looks quite nice. A lot of people tell me they like it. . . .

I have been absolutely mad lately, rushing about and then sleeping and then doing silly things in fits and starts.[3] Yesterday I went into a very fine shop to order some handkerchiefs for H. O. Lee (who is ill again, but not so bad), and the man in there seemed so frightfully staid that I could not resist giving him a shock. So when he asked if Lee wanted a good quality, I quoted Lee's words verbatim and said: "It doesn't matter as long as they don't blister his nose when he blows it." I then watched him carefully, and derived infinite enjoyment from seeing the way he treated the departure. He didn't even smile. "Fancy and he an undergraduate too!" HA !!!!! However this is only naughty childishness. The joke won't appear as such to you, but it had reference to certain conversations and discussions which have lately been waged at Jesus.

November 15, 1919 Jesus

My dear Violet [his sisters, both older, were Violet and Kathleen]: [After describing the nature of psychoanalysis, a new-found enthusiasm] . . . I shall probably be accused of blasphemy if I say that Christ was a leading psychotheraputist. (I don't know why, but Violet is fond of saying that what I say is blasphemy, when there is no connexion whatever between what I had said and the term.) It is no less true that extreme sects and religious revivals and obsessions are an exact counterpart of these mind disorders, and by psychotherapy many fanatics or extremists in religion can be brought (if treated early) to a real understanding of religion with its use in setting a high ethical standard.[4]

. . . Even if I do not take up any subject which allows of psychotherapy in my work, the knowledge will always be useful as a hobby. . . .

I hope this letter has not bored you. I have enjoyed trying to say a few facts about my hobby since it is always good to crystallise one's thoughts a little.

---

[2] "Objects" that survive aggressive attack are central to "The Use of an Object" (Winnicott, 1968).
[3] Shades of Marion Milner's (1989) "Catherine Wheel" (see footnote 9).
[4] Thirty-three years later he will take this point of view toward the group activity around Melanie Klein.

7 New Square
Cambridge
Sept. 10th 1916

My dear Mother[5]

This letter of over 2000 words is of interest primarily because it is one of the few surviving documents that bear upon the relationship to his mother. After a beginning marked by evident conflict, he regales her at great length about how he managed to put on an entertaining program with his scout troop dressed as Indians. We see him at age 20 enjoying himself and trying to give enjoyment to his mother, who "would do anything for him" (Ede, 1988, interview in Edinburgh with Madeleine Davis and me) and for whose very death, in 1925, 9 years later, he would blame himself. She had a heart ailment, and he had not urged her not to walk up stairs.

His father had advised him to "decline a bad offer," but he took it anyway and made a hilarious success out of it. There is a possibly snide reference to her forgetfulness early in the letter, but Donald goes on to make her a gift of an eyewitness account of an amusing struggle with a successful outcome. In volume it provides Mother with a great deal. Shall we infer that he turns away from his father's advice toward his mother? He does not take credit for his success. He is only the organizer, more or less as he would describe his analytic work much later. He is a facilitator. World War I is raging at this time of the amusing skit, which features cowboy-and-Indian killings. He is socially concerned (as was his father and as he would always be)—helping scouts, praising the Serbian boys. At one point, apropos of nothing (in other letters he asks for books as gifts and presents long descriptions of the books on his shelves), he says, "It was so infinitely better than a book to me, and such a revelation of the powers of imagination of the boys." Perhaps in his enthusiastic unguarded state, he spontaneously compares reading to action, the shared gestural world, and chooses the latter. This comparison must have been readied in his thinking prior to this moment. Perhaps it was in his genes.

Winnicott's writing, in which he attends to what I am calling the gestural world, is compelling and real. When he turns to a verbatim account of analysis, as in *Holding and Interpretation* (1986), much of the writing, in my opinion, is lifeless. It does not sound like Winnicott. He dictated this work, probably not from notes and not always immediately after a session (Joyce Coles, 1988, in an interview with Madeleine Davis and me).

---

[5] The complete text of this letter may be found in Appendix 2.

The Leys School
Cambridge
3rd May 1915

My dear Parents and Sisters:

(a very long letter). . . . After shaking hands with one of the servants
on the station and with an Old Leysian who was up having brought
his brother as a new boy, I made a hasty retreat from the depressing
station and jumped onto a 'bus. The buses are doing a good trade in
the absense of trams, but I dreamed that night, 'mongst other thing,
that Cambridge had started electric trams! Only a dream![6] . . . [much
detail on his return to school and then the visit of the King] It was
great fun watching the top hatted fathers and old Leysians in their
frock coats, and the hobble skirted ladies, wives and mothers of
Leysians past and present, arriving from the special trains in cars,
cabs and handsome cabs. And by 10.00 o'clock the Leysian Mission
band had struck up some enlivening music which stirred our hearts to
the auricles and ventricles, (how many of each V. & K.?), and our
bone to the marrow. Why were we thus stirred? What great event was
to happen? Why, we were to be visited by royalty, one of the long line
of kings of dear old England, a man who has in his arteries the very
blood of Alfred and Egbert and what others not. No wonder we felt a
thrill. We should indeed lack imagination if we did not experience
that feeling under such circumstances.

. . . At dinner I could get up no game of tennis, nearly everyone was
away. Went over to B, and wrote an a/e of the events of the day. Then
I went to the the [sic] Post Office, to the offices of the Cambridge
Chronicle, to the P.O. again and to the offices again. I learned on the
whole what was best to do, and so proceeded to do it, although I
knew it to be fearful cheek.

I went down to the station, sent off the letter addressed to the London
Office of the Mercury, by train letter, which cost 3d. Then I sent two
telegrams: [here he inserts two drawings of telegrams as rectangular
pieces of paper on which he wrote] "West Mercury, Fleet Street London. Meet 5.15 train Liverpool Street for account of King's visit to
Cambridge. Winnicott." AND "Mercury, Plymouth. Telephone to
London Office for account of King's visit to Cambridge. Winnicott."
so that it all came to about 1/6. But I did not say who I was, so they
may think I sent it wishing it to be printed as an advertisement for the

---

[6] The "depressing station" in the dream probably provoked wish-fulfilling "electric trams"
in Cambridge. This is notable because of the transparency of reference and because he is
attending to his thought process, just as he does when reflecting on the Sunday night meal
at Rockville. He is a nascent psychoanalyst already, and somewhere in the mix of thoughts
there is fun. Also, he is a writer with enough ambition to attempt to get his description
published in a newspaper. I do not know if he succeeded.

Leys. Then I should get no money. Booh! If they do not send any I
shall write them for something. HA!

H.M.S. Lucifer
c/o G.P.O.
London
July 10th 1917

Dear V. & K.[7]

Altho' I address my letter to you today I don't mean that I love you
any more than usual. In fact I mean nothing except that I am conscious that one should not be able to claim more of my regard than
the rest.

I wonder how you would like the heaving main, my sisters: in how
many hours would you be sick? The poor Snottie is ill as usual, lying
beside me doomed to feel like nothing on earth till to-morrow evening.
I have just taken his temperature, at his request, and regret to state it
is normal. Ill people, as you have probably found out, like to have
something to show. Not even a tenth of a degree up or down.

. . . My healthy crew [is] different from the army that one finds in
hospitals. The stokers tend to get fat round the Mary like chefs. One
man has the shivers, and I can't make out what is the matter with him.
If he looks at you he shakes all about, and his hands shake as he
splices ropes. He takes it back to Pneumonia, because he used to shake
then when he was feverish, but I doubt the verity of that. As a matter
of fact I think he has something like a cerebellar cyst or some such.
But then I always diagnose such awful things when really the condition is simple if one only knew.

II: HUMOR IN THE CONTEXT OF HIS LIFE

Increasing biographical access to Donald Winnicott (C. Winnicott, 1978;
Rodman, 1987; Phillips, 1988; Goldman, 1993; Kahr, 1996) reflects an
ever-intensifying interest in a man whose work has changed the face of
psychoanalysis. This was evident in the last 2 decades of his life (1896–
1971) and has continued unabated, partly because a large number of
posthumously published books has drawn attention to him, but more so
because his ideas have appealed to psychoanalysts and academicians alike.

We know that Donald Woods Winnicott was an only son, after two
girls, born into a wealthy nonconformist family in Plymouth, that he was

---

[7] He is a Surgeon-Probationer, only a medical student, but seems to be entirely composed
and capable of laughter, at himself and others.

sent to boarding school at 14 at the behest of his father who owned a large hardware business, was elected mayor, and eventually knighted for civic work. He studied at Jesus College, Cambridge, and learned medicine at St. Bartholemew's Hospital. His mother was probably depressed, and Donald felt it incumbent upon himself to enliven her. A poem called "The Tree" (see Appendix 2), written a few days after his sixty-seventh birthday, portrays his personal struggle as Christ-like. He had analysis with James Strachey and Joan Riviere, was much taken with Melanie Klein's theories, and eventually insisted upon his own highly original point of view. That he was one of the Middle Group, now the Independents, in the British Society characterizes his stance as one who could tolerate differences. True to his origins, he was a nonconformist and enjoyed being so. His Englishness, with its pragmatic and empirical components, contrasted with the Germanic characteristics of the psychoanalysis that he inherited.

His pediatrics practice was counterpart to a wide experience in the analysis of children and adults, neurotic and psychotic, and his psychiatric consultations with essentially normal children. This was the clinical background that led him to suggest revisions that took greater account of actual experience in our understanding of the life of children and adults. He believed that the rediscovery of principles for himself or herself was essential to an analyst's lively engagement in thought and practice. This made adequate room for his own unique contribution and for anyone else's.

We can ask whether his humor, clowning, irony, or comedy was related to the task of enlivening his mother, but we can never know. He wanted to be surprising. He sometimes came into a room and fell down on the floor. People wouldn't know if it were serious or not (Coles, 1988). He would drive off in his car with half his body, from the waist up, out the window, waving, and looking in the opposite direction from the one in which he was driving. During the War in Oxford, Clare remembered him with his feet on the steering wheel and a walking stick on the accelerator (Coles, 1988). He was physical, in a state of motion, which made him a verb rather than a noun, or, rather, exhibited the principle that no life can be trapped in words. He would not be "fixed with a formulated phrase" any more than he would fix his patients similarly.

In his writing we can discern what might be called his perceptual pleasure and his enjoyment of understanding and interacting with his patients. "The test of these case descriptions will hang on the word enjoyment. If they are a labour to read then I have been too clever; I have been engaged in displaying a technique and not in playing music. I am of course aware that this actually does take place from time to time in the case descriptions" (D. W. Winnicott, 1971, p. 6).

Speaking of one of the children in *Therapeutic Consultations in Child Psychiatry* (1971), he wrote: "This sense of humour is evidence of a freedom, the opposite of a rigidity of the defences that characterises illness. A sense of humour is the ally of the therapist, who gets from it a feeling of confidence and a sense of having elbow-room for manoeuvring. It is evidence of the child's creative imagination and of happiness" (p. 32).

His lifelong friend Stanley "Jimmy" Ede and his wife had two little girls that Donald and his first wife Alice looked after for more than a year, while the Edes traveled abroad. The girls (Elizabeth and Mary née Ede in a 1988 interview with Madeleine Davis and me) remember with delight that he quacked like the Donald Duck they called him, leaped up flights of steps, and stood up in the driver's seat of his large convertible and drove around Richmond Park with the use of a walking stick to manipulate the controls, just as Clare had remembered in Oxford. The Edes were strict, clean and controlling parents and, by contrast, Donald was free. He explained things about his patients and told them not to be concerned if they were very angry with their parents, and they loved it. At one point, the Winnicotts tried to adopt the girls (Stanley Ede interview, 1988).

Marion Milner (1972) describes her first sight of him by making a comparison to a Catherine Wheel, and in their consultations, he characteristically rushed around, upstairs and down, before settling into their work. She thought this was a necessary prelude to the deeply serious concentration that inevitably followed.[8] She thought (Milner, 1989) the

---

[8] "One night driving through France, there was a crowd in the market place of a little town, all grouped round an arc lamp, where a trapeze had been set up by travelling acrobats. Several were there, star performers, in spotless white, doing wonderful turns and handstands on the bar. Down below was a little clown, in a grey floppy coat too big for him, fooling around while the others did their stuff, occasionally making a fruitless attempt to jump up and reach the bar. Then, all of a sudden, he made a huge leap and there he was, whirling around the bar, all his clothes flying out, like a huge Catherine Wheel, and with roars of delight from the crowd. I knew this was my image of Winnicott, because often, over the years when we had a gap of time and we had arranged to meet and discuss some theoretical problem, he would open the door, and then be all over the place, whistling, forgetting something, running upstairs, a general sort of clatter, so that I would be impatient for him to settle down. But, gradually, I came to see this as a necessary preliminary to the fiery flashes of intuition that would follow, when he did finally settle down. I even found the logic of it described in one of his papers, where he talks of the necessity, when doing an analysis, to recognise and allow for phases of nonsense, when no thread must be looked for in the patient's material, because what is going on is the preliminary chaos that is the first phase of the creative process. And after the whirling clown on the bar came another image; an actual Catherine Wheel firework, nailed to a tree and lit by a small boy, in the still dark of the countryside; the wheel first splutteringly misfiring, and then getting going as a fizzing fiery ring of light, sending off sparks into the darknes around.

word *frolic* is a good one for Winnicott. Margaret Little (1989) thought the word *quicksilver* characterized him. Two speakers at the British Society's Commemorative Meeting in 1972 descibed him as gnome-like.[9] He was also said by Harry Karnac (in Kahr, 1996), the book dealer, to resemble a garden "gnome" (p. 103). A gnome is defined in the *Oxford English Dictionary* as "one of a race of diminutive spirits fabled to inhabit the interior of the earth and to be the guardians of its treasures." In a 1988 interview with me, Pearl King described Winnicott's capacity to make the unexpected comment as "like the knight in chess, exasperatingly unpredictable." She said that he liked to shock people, in order to open them to new ideas. Peter Giovacchini spoke of his "impish self" (Kahr, 1996, p. 109). Serge Lebovici (Clancier and Kalmanovitch, 1987), describing his behavior in the Paddington Green clinic he maintained for 40 years, said, "He stayed with a family and a child for ten minutes, for example, then went to join another family jumping over the seats" (p. 133). As we listened to him, it seemed to us that he was clearly a man inspired. The French analyst Evelyne Kestemberg (Clancier and Kalmanovitch, 1987) said that "almost always Winnicott gave the impression that he was asleep when he was listening. . . . He had such an unconventional side to him that he sometimes seemed strange, odd: to my great fright, I have seen him cross a street when nobody else would do so and felt sure he would be run over—he wasn't. I think the drivers saw that he was not looking, for indeed he gave the impression that he was not looking, as if he were moving in a world of his own. . . . He withdrew into himself with total contempt for the outside world" (p. 127). Raymond Cahn (Clancier and Kalmanovitch, 1987) comments: "I saw Winnicott shortly before his death, at the Congress of Child Psychiatry at Edinburgh. I was fascinated by his face, by a sort of light that radiated from it" (p. 115). Dr. Josephine Lomax-Simpson, a psychoanalyst, described him as an "elf-like ethereal man (Kahr, 1996, p. 109). Paul Roazen, a historian, said he was a "wonderful pixie of a man" (Kahr, 1996, p. 109). In an obituary, someone (C. Winnicott, 1971) wrote: "As fragile as Donald looked, his face seemed chiseled out of rock and this gave him the appearance of timelessness."

Has there ever been another psychoanalyst except Freud who

I was to think of this dark disc at the centre whenever I read in his writings about the unknowable fore of the self"(Milner, 1972).

The firework nailed to a tree suggests to me a Christ figure. This is supported by his poem "The Tree," in which he is clearly identified with Christ, as well as of an incident during his analysis of a woman, when he left behind a small crucifix, with the slumping head of Christ, which he had fashioned out of matchsticks and a rubber band. The tragic and the comic Winnicott are combined in the Catherine Wheel.

[9] "This gnome of a being," "gnome-like charm."

commanded such descriptive efforts? Gnome, elf, imp, pixie, clown, chess knight, ethereal, inspired, frolic, quicksilver. His small physical stature (5'6"), bright blue eyes, deeply lined face, wide range of expressive capacities do not quite explain the use of words for figures who are not exactly of this world. There is humor in these words, humor implied, but also some parahuman quality, which seems to have lent him an extraordinary outside view of human life, objective, but magically involved. Kestemberg's comment gives us one aspect of it, one who turns away from the outside world, but on the other hand a gnome "is fabled to inhabit the interior of the earth" and is the guardian of its treasures. Perhaps it is a paradox that deserves to be in the Winnicottian lexicon that a man who seemed to show contempt for the outside world should have been the one most responsible for bringing the influence of the outside world into the heart of psychoanalytic thinking. He kept hold of the Freudian emphasis on the intrapsychic while adding, in his own way, the crucial importance of actual experiences, particularly with the mother, in the development of the child. After Ferenczi, who is only lately receiving due appreciation, he was the forefather of today's heightened recognition of the environmental factor in child development and psychoanalysis as both theory and therapy.

It is the unique nature of his contributions and his very evident bodily and emotional presence,[10] for which observers and readers have attempted to find the right and telling words. In this endeavor they have tried to catch Winnicott's spirit, the true self, which as he believed, was, in anyone, always hidden. Words can give us only brief glimpses into a complex person who was gifted with words that bordered on gestures, used language as gesture and thereby reached his readers and listeners with the liveliness of patients and himself.[11] Essential to that liveliness was movement, his own mind (and body) in motion, and continuous awareness of the fluctuating motions within the mind (and the body) of the patient.

---

[10] "Winnicott listened with the whole of his body, and had keen unintrusive eyes that gazed at one with a mixture of unbelief and utter acceptance. A childlike clownish spontaneity imbued his movements" (Masud Khan, 1982, p. xi).

[11] It would be fruitful to study language in the psychoanalytic setting from the point of view of the extent to which it borders on gesture. The poetic element in Winnicott's work is related to this. In so many ways, as others have noted (Phillips, 1988; Turner, 1988), he seems to have derived from the English romantic poets, perhaps especially Byron who, unlike the others, could laugh at himself. Winnicott was a visionary whose views were tempered by respect for empirical reality, with a dialectic between imagination and reason always evident. Other analysts have discussed the same dialectic as part of the process of observation, but they do not *demonstrate* it to us in the visible and convincing way that Winnicott did.

At the initiative of his friend Jimmy Ede, the two boys used to rearrange the furniture in Donald's home—this was perfectly fine with his mother.[12] There are echoes here of Ede's future career as an aesthete and designer of interior places, echoes as well of Winnicott's interest in space and his habit of writing papers and then rearranging the parts again and again. And in the composition of his published papers, according to his secretary (Coles, 1988), he would start off by dictating in perfect English, an hour at a time. Then he would alter the order of the text in extreme ways, as if it were a jigsaw puzzle. Undoubtedly, the form followed the content, which was usually surprising. Winnicott was preoccupied with the new, the unexpected, the unsuspected, and the revealing. This was himself brought to bear on his subject matter. We see his forays on reality, stroboscopic sometimes in their split-second illumination, extended at other times in their development of major themes. Always there is the sense of movement, the evidence of the lived life of the speaker and writer, and often, his evident delight in these forays, a delight that delighted his audiences.

In a chapter of *Winnicott and Paradox* (Clancier and Kalmanovich, 1987), we read: "His physical presence, his ease, his squiggle games, in which his dazzling intuition was combined with a technique rooted in theory and experience—everything about him was reminiscent of the circus clown, defying balance without appearing to do so" (p. 89). My own experience in reading his work coincides with that of a colleague who, having read "The Child, The Family, and the Outside World," said she had never before had "such personal contact with an author" (Ford, 1971). His humor, the various pleasures manifest in his writing, are linked to his insistence on expressing himself unlike any other, not with nonconformity as an end in itself, but as a personal requirement that could be inhibited only at the cost of living his life at all. The history of psychoanalysis until his time did not lead naturally to an understanding of enjoyment in life, except in relation to erotic experience. Largely neglecting the erotic in his writings, he brought us to an awareness of experiences of pleasure rooted in the ego. He defined analysis as a form of playing. His humor is most evident in his child consultations (1971), including the extended one, which is the basis of *The Piggle* (1977).

Much of his work can be read with a view to understanding how he tried to protect people, that included himself, from incursions that would damage the capacity for play. He was a spokesman for a point of view that put playing and spontaneity at the center of human life. In 1952, he wrote to Melanie Klein about a paper he had given to the British Society

---

[12] In his first marriage, he "brought home people who threw the furniture around," and like his mother, "his wife Alice accepted it" (R. Taylor, 1988, interview by Madeleine Davis and Robert Rodman).

(Rodman, 1987): "What I was wanting Friday undoubtedly was that there should be some move from your direction towards the gesture that I make in this paper. It is a creative gesture and I cannot make any relationhip through this gesture except if someone come to meet it. I think that I was wanting something which I have no right to expect from your group, and it is really in the nature of a therapeutic act, something which I could not get in either of my two long analyses although I got so much else" (p. 34). Here he is both a writer about analysis and a kind of patient in need of a therapeutic act. In the light of his writings, it is not difficult to say that he is also a baby in need of a receptive mother. He is making a gesture that requires a positive response, which he does not get, on the Friday of his presentation, in either of his two long analyses or, one wonders, in his childhood. His childhood was described by his second wife in glowing terms (C. Winnicott, 1978), but by now we can see that, like all other childhoods, it bore its own unique stamp of conflict.

Madeleine Davis,[13] one of the Board of Editors that published Winnicott's huge posthumous output of writings, thought that his mother's clapping of her hands together as she came down the steps to breakfast each morning (reported to us by Jim Ede, 1988) might have been an effort to deal with depression. It seems possible that Winnicott's playful rearrangements and attempts to surprise people were a part of his effort to cure that depression.

Winnicott devoted his life to the subject of mothers and babies. The father is rather dramatically ignored. Whatever interferes in the rapport of mother and baby is regarded as disruptive of the going-on-being of the child and, by implication, possibly the adult. This is a complex subject, which Adam Phillips has addressed (1989). Here, I would only call attention to the father, all but totally scotomatized in Winnicott's writings, as the principal culprit. Freud and the intellectuals of psychoanalysis—although he was always careful to express his real appreciation of Freud and a number of others—represent the paternal, potentially destructive world of interpretation, and he would hold them at bay in order that the true selves of himself and patients may survive. Because of his mistrust of

---

[13] She and her husband, Cambridge pediatrics Professor John Davis, were personal friends of Donald and Clare. It was Clare Winnicott who granted me access to her late husband's letters, a selection of which (out of the large number with professional and personal content that were photocopied in her home), I edited for publication (Rodman, 1987). From her I learned a great deal about their life together. After her death, Madeleine took over. In 1988, we interviewed a number of people about Winnicott as preparation for a biography. She was a great Winnicott scholar, perhaps the very greatest. Every one of her papers shows her incisive and gracefully expressed understanding. Her letters to me, and our frequent telephone conversations, showed me paths of insight I did not suspect. She died in 1991.

interpretation, his point of view is revolutionary. He saw an unrestrained urge to interpret (apotheosized in Klein) as misguided penetration into the internal life of the patient. One may speculate about the phallic implications of this point of view.

The analyst was a kind of mother-substitute who presented the conditions in which a patient could resume growth in an atmosphere of safety. This was not a sentimental love. He was aware of the inherent, useful, and indispensable fact of human aggression. His interpretations were given to let the patient know the limits of his undertanding, a way of foregoing the illusion that the analyst knew everything. These "doses of reality" fed the process he eventually described in "The Use of an Object" (1968), that is, the external as the object of destructiveness (because outside the area of the patient's omnipotence) and the destructiveness as the creator of the external (which survives). This gave the patient something to destroy, which then survived and could be used.

For Winnicott, the threatening power of the paternal is illustrated in his own life. We know that he could not divorce his first wife and marry Clare Britton until his father had died. One may speculate that divorce was not part of his father's expectation for his only son, that Sir Frederick was an elderly widower during this period, but it makes more sense when we note that his decision to become a doctor, rather than his father's successor in business, was also something he could not directly communicate to his father. He gave the task to Jimmy Ede who wrote the letter for him (Ede, 1988).[14] Two big life decisions—the choice of a profession and the choice of divorce and remarriage—could not be communicated to his father. How fearful he must have been!

The pursuit of a life of his own seems to have been a pressing matter not to be taken for granted. Even later on, during his successful second marriage, when he had become a famous psychoanalyst, he wondered aloud what would happen if he never had another original idea (C. Winnicott, 1979, personal communication). He thought that, if he moved his practice out of Central London, he might never be referred another patient (C. Winnicott, 1979, personal communication). Winnicott studied problems associated with authenticity and wrote about them as he understood part after part. The private preoccupations found expression in his choice of topics of interest and in what he wrote about his work.

I have quoted his 1952 letter to Melanie Klein. In 1945, a year after meeting and working with and starting an intimate relationship with Clare Britton, he introduced a paper called "Primitive Emotional Development" (1945) to the British Society this way: "By listening to what I have to say, and criticizing, you help me to take my next step, which is the study of

---

[14] This matter is discussed by Clare Winnicott in her memoir (1978).

the sources of my ideas, both in clinical work and in the published writings of analysts" (pp. 145–146). He has cast his audience in the role of helpers of the development of his ideas. Then, however, instead of criticizing Klein for failing to respond, he is in a nearly defiant mood. Instead of conforming with the accepted custom that a writer has studied the sources of his ideas and gives due credit to his predecessors, he leaves it to last, leaves it to the audience to guide him. In fact, he goes further. "I shall not first give an historical survey and show the development of my ideas from the theories of others, because my mind does not work that way. What happens is that I gather this and that, here and there, settle down to clinical experience, form my own theories and then, last of all, interest myself in looking to see where I stole what. Perhaps this is as good a method as any" (p. 145). The pursuit of his own development is glaringly evident here. And the reference to stealing is probably related to his recent work on delinquency, undertaken during World War II in Oxfordshire.

Later on, in "The Antisocial Tendency," (1956) he will see stealing as a sign of hope in the child who at first had good-enough mothering and who, deprived, makes a delinquent gesture toward anyone who can understand it, hoping to be seen as one who has a right to mothering of the sort that has been interrupted. The children he studied were evacuees who had been separated from their families to avoid the bombs falling on London. The fact that he and Clare had begun their affair during this period suggests a link to his own life, as if the fulfilment he now enjoyed were the resumption of what he had once had and lost. There is a masculine, possibly post-war victorious, swagger in his introduction to "Primitive Emotional Development" (1945), which probably expresses his newfound happiness, although it was to be a secret from almost everyone for several years. Subsequently, still married to Alice Taylor, who was a disturbed woman 6 years older than he, he suffered heart attacks, which led Marion Milner to urge him to leave her because, as she told him (Milner, 1988, interview in London with me), he would die unless he did.

Breaking the news to a friend (informant, 1993a), he wrote: "It seemed to me clear that we were doing each other harm, and that the future had nothing better for us in our relationship, only worse. This is awful when one remembers how much Alice and I have experienced together, and have as common memories. Nevertheless, when two people live together, either the body warms or cools when there is contact, and for me there had come a feeling of strain that is indescribable. For Alice too I'm sure there should eventually be relief. There is a third person, someone who has a different effect on me, but I don't really believe I'd have allowed this to break things up if I had not been bothered by certain dominating trains of thought (in Alice) that wrecked my relation to Alice.

The strange thing is that I'm awfully fond of Alice, deeply attached, always shall be, but can't bear the idea of a return to actually living with her." This letter was written at the end of October 1950, 8 weeks after a heart attack. His father's death at the end of 1949 had given him the freedom to divorce and remarry.

A friend of Donald and Alice throughout their marriage, the recipient of his letter announcing that he had "abandoned" Alice, reports (informant, March 23, 1993b) that, during World War II, when she lived with them in Hampstead for 6 months, she and Donald "always had breakfast together, Alice arriving late, never looking as if she had washed or bathed and while eating would fall asleep. Donald said once, have you ever seen anyone sleep and eat at the same time (with a smile)?" She also says: "I found Donald easy to live with, we had great fun, maybe a relief from Alice, we did many things together, Alice having other things to do. They both took on the role of Wardens in their road when raids occurred, donning their tin hats and out, one of the garages they turned into a First Aid Post, fully equipped for any casualties. On one evening off they went at the sound of the Siren, and after about two hours Donald came in, and I said 'Where's Alice?' His answer was 'Oh! she's plying for hire,'—terrific laughter, Oh what have I said? Then we'd have coffee" (4/24/93). She writes: "On one of their visits (I was very overdue) Donald had just bought a second hand Rolls—2 seater, it was like a chariot, he said 'Come on, I'll bump you around the countryside and get you moving.' Well of course it did it, one feels nothing in a Rolls, but it was a lovely experience and how he enjoyed that car. He had a passion for Golden Syrup for his breakfast toast, not the usual English Marmalade and we were rationed, so I would send him my coupons, on Sundays breakfast was a real treat, relaxed, reading the papers and Donald eating the whole of his Butter ration in one go, I think one ounce. In so many small ways he was childlike, enjoying simple pleasures and enjoying these so much. Once arriving for a visit, he opened the door to me and said 'How nice—I almost kissed you. He could be so funny'" (Informant, 1993a).

III: THE COMEDY OF MAN'S PRETENTIONS

More than any analyst, Winnicott recognized the limitations inherent in verbal accounts of experience. His rapt and relaxed attention was given over to the gestural world, which was both a supplement to words and a universe of communication unto itself. Never losing sight of the body as inherent in the mind, he was anti-Cartesian in a still Cartesian world. His serious attempts to sketch out ideas were very often something like a dumb show in which he tried to point toward the ineffable. The squiggle game, which embodied his genius for communicating through line draw-ings, illustrates his appreciation of the limits of words, even if words are appended and indispensable to the outcome of his encounters with chil-dren. His paper on communicating and not communicating takes us into an entirely new universe of thinking, where the true self is permanently incommunicado. While he was working to see into his patients and to show others the details of his experience and the lines of reasoning that issued from that experience, he came to realize that the deepest part of himself and of his patients was a sacred location beyond anyone's reach. His regret about interpreting too soon (1967) underscores the earned realization that what he provided as an analyst was a context for per-sonal development, arrived at by the patient and not by clever insights, no matter how indispensable insight might be.

In his written work and lectures, Winnicott says just what he thinks, without any authoritarian pressure to believe. In his book on therapeutic consultations (1971) he writes: "I hope it will be recognised that in pre-senting these cases I am not trying to prove anything. The criticism that I have failed to prove my case would not be appropriate as I have no case" (p. 11). And this: "As I have already stated, the work cannot be copied because the therapist is involved in every case as a person, and therefore no two interviews could be alike as they would be carried through by two psychiatrists" (1971, p. 9). And this: "I cannot say whether this was right or wrong but I felt like doing it" (1971, p. 18).

"I have no case." "The therapist is involved in every case as a per-son." "I felt like doing it." The reader is invited to think about what is on the page without an intellectual struggle, and Winnicott is therefore ex-cellent company. Reading him, we overlap with him. Separateness of view, where present, will develop in slow reflection, but for the duration of reading, the usual strain of maintaining a line between the writer and the reader tends to be absent. It may be that it is this characteristic that baffles the many analysts who say they don't "get" Winnicott. The only other writer to whom I can compare him in this respect is Harold Searles. When next one encounters a patient, the residue of the human contact transmitted through words from such writers informs the analyst, opens the way, perhaps because the overlap between analyst and patient is fos-tered, rather than the tendency to objectify, which is more typical of the analytic attitude generally.[15]

By the year of his death, Winnicott had achieved his place as unlike

---

[15] Certainly this is an oversimplification, which runs the risk of dichotomizing those who find value in the overlap and those who tend to maintain a strict and constant awareness of the separateness of patient and analyst. All analysts have both attributes, but the ratio within a given hour, for better or ill, and as a general characteristic must vary enormously.

any other and in some ways not even a continuation of anyone else, except Freud and Klein. He had failed to pay due heed to a good many others, for which he was apologetic, as in his 1967 speech to the 1952 Club. "I can't cover all that I want to. I will just say that I don't know whether you'd like to discuss any of this or would like to help me in a letter to try and make amends and join up with the various people all over the world who are doing work which either I've stolen or else I'm just ignoring. I don't promise to follow it all up because I know I'm just going to go on having an idea which belongs to where I am at the moment, and I can't help it" (Winnicott, 1967).

For an analyst like myself, reared in the medical tradition of competitive striving, and probably for all who arrive through many academic waystations to the inspiring air of psychoanalysis, it is refreshing to read someone who "has no case." He does make way for others to express themselves as they can, not in a formalized style acceptable to the establishment, but merely by example. This is one of his great triumphs. And in his persistence, dating from early in life, he gave heart to contributors to psychoanalysis who wished to include the personal element, which is an indispensable element, in every bit of work.

Being himself, evident in the full range of his often startling contributions,[16] is encoded, I think, in his emphatic attention to the value of paradox. Respect for defenses and proper timing of interpretations had been early hallmarks of psychoanalytic work, but Winnicott's plea to let paradox stand unresolved was entirely new. His own personal struggle to maintain his capacity for enjoying life is at the center of his clinical recommendation: Do not ask the child if his transitional object was found or created. In traditional parlance, taking account of reality as we have been trained to know it, the child found an object that was provided and invested it with meaning. But for Winnicott, the object was also created. On the scale of his life, the creator of the object seems to me to be identical to the formulator of the paradox. And one of the messages in this entreaty may be translated: "Let me exist. Do not resolve me out of existence." Intellectual ambition can be pernicious unless tempered with restraint.

Winnicott's aim was to enjoy his life and to foster a similar capacity for enjoyment in his patients. This meant that in the deepest way, he would have to be allowed not to be known: analysis, for all its potential for helping, would have to keep from penetrating and therefore exploiting

---

[16] When I first read *The Maturational Processes and the Facilitating Environment* (1965), the "true and false self" concept seemed to cram too much into a few simple words, but I recognized in the excitement with which I encountered them that they resonated as a new location of reflection, a new refuge for the mind. For me, this same description applies to almost everything he wrote.

the true self. At such a moment, the analyst would show his instinctive awareness that sometimes restraint is more important than resolution.

He was the creator of his own world, the "omnipotent" master relating to us the workings of his unique mind in dialogue with external reality, which was the data of his own personal life and his vast experience of patients. He provided us with the rudiments of a theory of the creation of and survival of external reality. His "Use of an Object," (1968) and much of *Playing and Reality*, seem to me to have been thrown down on paper in the shadow of his impending demise, his final effort to tell us what he had learned.

He had succeeded against considerable odds. He had been ostracized for long periods in the British Society, limited in the number of lectures he could give the candidates, coldly set apart from Melanie Klein and her followers, never fully accepted by Anna Freud. Yet he persevered in his own way and found his audience, which continues to grow 25 years after his death. Never willing to be the leader of a movement, he was found and revered by innumerable people in all walks of life around the earth, because he spoke to them in a language that was itself an expression of the value of personal freedom, untethered by institutional ambition. He succeeded in being himself within the constraints of a science that demands certain kinds of conformity. He gained acceptance for a style of self-expression at a considerable distance from every previous and subsequent version of psychoanalytic scientific writing.

I think he had a view of human struggle, which could be seen as tragic or as comic, depending upon his mood and perspective. Certainly he knew tragedy, as "The Tree" and a good deal more tells us. Phillips (1988) has written that "his work, in a sense, initiates a comic tradition in psychoanalysis" (p. 31). Winnicott is reported by him to have said "on more than one occasion that if he hadn't been a psychoanalyst he would like to have been a comic-turn in a music hall" (p. 31), but Phillips gives no sources for this and does not clarify what he means by "a comic tradition in psychoanalysis." To initiate a tradition is oxymoronic unless seen in retrospect. If there are others who followed, I don't know who they are.

It is the infant within each of us, the never-relinquished omnipotent core, constantly colliding with an external world that tells us the limits of that omnipotence, which gives Winnicott the greatest delight. He knew that it was the core of liveliness that needed protection and affirmation in order to thrive and express itself spontaneously, and he also knew that the shape of its more complex utterances would only grow out of collisions with an unyielding external world and that this struggle would continue throughout the lifespan and be cause for laughter and for tears. Thus, he attained a unitary grasp of the human odyssey, which was, first and foremost, the sense of himself as a unit navigating the shoals of life. Not having succumbed to the pressure for shaping himself into a false representation of what he was, he could serve as a stalwart ally of all others who wished a similar outcome for themselves, patients, other analysts, parents and children. His sentences and his papers and books were the gestures by which he communicated his example and his reflections on the conflict, which is part of achieving authenticity. His laughter is the expression of delight in being alive and himself.

The striving for the power of verbally based understanding, so inherent in psychoanalytic ambition, no matter how successful, was a doomed enterprise if completeness or perfection was its goal. Yet he was the foremost protector of the delicate world of omnipotence carried over from fetal life into postnatal development. Toward the end, as he formulated the collisions between that life and the external world with all its limits, in "The Use of an Object," (1968) he paid due heed to omnipotent fantasies of destruction as a backdrop for emerging awareness of the truly external. Without such omnipotent aggression directed at an external world that survived these fantasies, there could be no appreciation of its existence and therefore no benefit to be derived from experience with it. Life was a long challenge to omnipotence, on the basis of which the external world could provide nourishment for an evolving acquaintance with it. The comedy was in the ceaseless struggle between our impulses and the external world. At our best, we could enjoy the battle that we are doomed to lose.

He had a taste for humor from the beginning and throughout his life. He was a very ambitious man, a writer in boarding school before he became interested in psychoanalysis, one who tackled the most difficult problems, with faith in his qualifications to do so, yet he never lost sight of the ridiculous nature of human ambition. His willingness to risk making a fool of himself was a form of courage inherent in his raids on the inchoate.

Madeline Davis and I interviewed Jimmy Ede and his daughters at their home in Edinburgh in 1988. He was something of a double for Winnicott, with an April 7 birthday, a year earlier than Donald's. At 93, dressed in a blue sweater and tweedy light blue pants, he was a handsome man with an erect carriage and a shock of gray-white hair. His head was bent arthritically forward at the neck, like a lead soldier that had been broken and repaired. As we were leaving, I asked him if he ever dreamt of Donald. He said he hadn't. I asked him then: "If you imagine him, what do you see?"

"He's coming toward me and laughing."

"Indoors or outdoors?"

"He's coming through the front door. He was a very brisk person."

I liked to think of Winnicott's laughter still alive in the mind of his oldest friend. And to think of the man himself right where he had always been, in a state of transition.

APPENDIX 1

7 New Square
Cambridge
Sept. 10th 1916

My dear Mother,

I said that I had a lot to tell you in my letter this week, but that was partly because [it] was written in the middle of it all and when I was full of it. But now that it is all over there seems to be no very great surplus to report.

By the way, thank you for your letter, and for news of Aunt Delia's recovery from the indigestion attack; I hope you are having good weather to allow her to move outdoors into some garden.

Although you have noticed no great change between this paragraph and the last, 4 hours really separate them, and between them I have had time to drop my pen on the nib, whereby altering its writing.

Two commands and one answer [This tone of authority is the same one he uses with V & K]: Firstly will you write as soon as possible to let Nurse Aston know of any nice lodging at Newquay. She wants to get right away from the place, and as she has no home, has to choose some such place. She is either going there or Hyracombe (?) or Llandodno or some such. What is Newquay like now? I am afraid when you saw her you did not get a very good impression any more than one would get of V. or K. if they met them one evening when they are on night-duty—and when they had not slept for about two days, and nights. She was really looking ill, and I was glad when she was taken off night-duty. She can't sleep in the day.

Secondly, will you send to Mrs. Charlesworth the receipt you have for tomato chutney. She asked me to ask you ever so long ago, and I forgot.

Then for the answer, the names are Halliwell and Bertram. When you first asked me I sat straight down and wrote you a post card with the names and descriptions of the lads on it. This I sent off, and whether you have never received it or whether you have simply forgotten will probably remain a mystery.

I left my sponge—talking about post cards—at the Dennisons, and when I asked them to send it on they sent me a lovely one, slightly bigger than my own and much softer. I am glad I left my own, now.

When I was home, Father may remember, I had a post-card asking me to assist at a Garden Party with the scouts. Father told me I must learn to decline a bad offer, but in spite of that I accepted.

Well, last Thursday week we started to rehearse some play of sorts, and obviously it was perfectly hopeless; I wished I had taken Dad's advice. On Saturday we went to the Cherryhinton Spinney and tried the same again, this time with so little success that I gave up the idea and we had games instead. Moreover I had to come home early because I was singing at a concert at hospital. It was hopeless, and on Sunday I went down to tell Mr. Wright we want to cry off. However I could not let him know that night as he was out, and had to tell him on Monday. That was last Monday, and the Garden Fete and Saled (?) Work was to be last Thursday—so it was rather a humiliating job.

Well, on Wednesday [Tuesday is crossed out] (!) morning Mr. Wright came along to New Square and said I really must do something as lots of things had fallen thus, and they were at a loss. "All right," said I, "it shall be done, even if we only drill."

This was Wednesday - you realize, and something had to be done for the Thursday Fete.

Well I went and secured each boys' [sic] promise to turn up that evening on the square outside my rooms, with the intention of doing some drilling—very uninteresting and bad work, indeed. The last boy I found on a bicycle, and when I told him, he said he did not think people would enjoy drilling. I said I quite agree with you, but we must do something. And then he started talking. We cycled to New Square and stood talking outside No. 7 while Mrs. Grant shouted for me to come in to tea, until the whole scheme had been settled, and some of the details decided on and arranged. I had tea; the lads came along and we explained the scheme, and told those who were to be Indians what to get and do, and with that and another little conference with this lad of ideas (and some supper!) we went to be in fear, hope and quivering. Next day at 1:30 we had our first and last rehearsal, which ended in the middle owing to the fact that the people had arrived and that the opening ceremony was in progress.

It was now 3:0 P.M. and I had to keep the boys amused, without letting them be nuisances till 6.0 P.M. when our display was to start. This was no easy job. However as soon as the speechifying was over I went home to get some things and to get some tea down and to rest awhile for the greater exertions of the evening. At about 4.30 P.M. I returned, and had to fight the 18 boys for 3/4 hour till they could have tea (which they let us have for 3d a piece) to keep them amused. This was rather tiring work, but quite necessary, else they would have lost heart and would not have been so good at the actual display.

After the tea—fight—much enjoyed by the onlookers since most of the boys had already painted themselves all colours of the rainbow—after the tea, I left them to dress themselves (having learnt that this is the best way to get them to do things well, and went in for a tug-of-

war. We all tugged against each other and I won and was allowed a 1'
dip free! I got a lovely box of chalks.

Then, as ours was the next item, I flew to our apportioned plot and
surveyed the landscape. It teemed with Indians and cowboys. May I
describe an average Indian? He is a slender lad of huge vivacity and
some 12 years, with no shoes and stockings, and with his little pants
tucked up as high as they will go and hidden by a small wooley mat,
tied with string. Shirt is likewise absent and the only other garment—
if so it may be called, is a piece of tape round the head with feathers
stuck in by means of two holes. (I got the feathers from the poultry
man on Peas Hill.) You may expect from this that there was much
flesh showing, but you are wrong. A dozen burnt colours and 10 1/2 d
worth of red brown and yellow theatrical chalk had hidden the pink
bareness of nature, and the effect was such that one started and fled,
and then recovered one's senses. Did I laugh? I nearly wept! I almost
split my sides. Since each boy had no help whatever from me, each
one was absolutely different from the others, and half the charm lay
there.

Before the show, when the people had gathered round, I explained the
situation to the audience in a speech. Now, strange to say I find no
difficulty at all in talking to the crowd when I have something to say.
There is such a difference in trying to find something to say because
you must speak, and trying to find a moment to speak because you
have something you must say. I said that it was only fair to the Troop
to say that the Troop leader was on his holiday. A patrol leader and
two seconds were helping the Serbian Boys at their camp, and another
patrol leader was at work and could not get off—also another second
was on the land helping the farmers, and so any work done today
would be done without the mainstays of the Troop. I also thought it
right to explain that the scheme, and all the costumes—or lack of
costumes, in fact all was the idea of the boys of the Troop and I had
done nothing except collect all the ideas into a pot and serve up the
stew. The rest—I said—I should leave to their imagination, and I only
hoped it would not require too much.

Then the fun began. You see I had told the audience that the scene was
near midnight, and you saw the cowboys come home from rounding
up the cattle. They came and sat round the fire over which a kettle
was hanging on a tripod made of three scout poles, near the tent—
which we had pitched before; and as night drew on, these went to bed.
Before doing so the Sheriff installed a small cowboy as sentry and
went into the tent too. All was quiet—and dark (imagined). The sentry was pacing up and down the side of the tent with an air-rifle. But
lo! meanwhile an Indian scout had been dispatched to make a detour
and to kill the sentry. This caused great amusement and was done
awfully well by a lad called Wilfred Carter. He made the people shriek

with laughter. The sentry paces his steps in apparent oblivion. Suddenly the wiley and silent-treading Indian darts to the front and stabs the sentry. In dying, the latter makes an ugg sound which wakes the other sow-boys in the tent. They rush out with their air rifles and 100 shot pistols, making an awful row—just like at the front, and the Indians come up with their war-whoop.

Well to cut a long story short; the cowboys retire leaving two dead and one captured. The Indians have two dead also—at least one was evidently badly wounded for he was making all sorts of. . . , writhing with pain. The Indians take the captured one and torture him horribly at a tree. They cut him, and red ink flows out of fountain-pen filler all down his bared chest and arms. Then a war dance is danced round the victim, And just as he is about to be lit up in flames, a whistle is heard, the cowboys come to the heroic rescue, all the Indians are killed, the hero saved—all serene etc. etc. etc. . . . . Cheers, etc. etc. Then I marched them round for the people to see them, and the play had ended.

I am afraid I am boring you with this, but it was so infinitely better than a book to me, and such a revelation of the powers of imagination of the boys that I shall never forget the day. We finished the evening by picking up every little scrap of paper—much to our own . . . (advertiament?), and by giving 3 cheers to the Salvation Army band and to Councillor Smith. (I was chosen because I had a large voice and 19 boys with elefantine bellows to back me up). I have since been congratulated all round, but I put all this praise onto the Troop, for I left it all to them. Mr. Smith did not see the display—I think, but if there is an account of it I am sure he will send it you. If I find one I will send it too! HA!

Then I also wanted to tell you about the Serbians, but I must cut that short as I have already written enough to fill two envelopes I am sure.

Well, I had a note last week asking me to supply three scouts to go to camp or rather holidays with 50 Serbian boys, to make an English atmosphere and to encourage the speaking of our nation's tongue. This I did. Last Friday, I went out to see them, and found them having a fine time, and in close friendship with lots of the Serbian boys. This is of course a fine experience for these boys from the slums of Cambridge. The Serbians are all classes mixed, and as they could not tell class in the scouts by the manner of speaking they all mixed without a thought in that direction and got on in a wonderful way. I spent Friday night there and made some friends amongst that awfully decent lot of Serbian Boys there, and was very pleased with myself. I came home here to Breakfast at 8.15 as they are only 7 miles out of Cambridge. It was fine. Am going out again. (several Serbian words translated: be quiet, sun, moon, owl, sun shines very nicely, good, not good.)

With love to all. Donald.

APPENDIX 2

THE TREE

(April 11, 1963)

Someone touched the hem of my garment
Someone, someone and someone

I had much virtue to give
I was the source of virtue
        the grape of the vine of the wine

I could have loved a woman
                Mary, Mary, Mary
There was not time for loving
I must be about my father's business
There were publicans and sinners
The poor we had always with us
There were those sick of the palsy
        and the blind and the maimed
        and widows bereft and grieving
        women wailing for their children
        fathers with prodigal sons
        prostitutes drawing their own water
            from deep wells in the hot sun

Mother below is weeping
                weeping
                weeping

Thus I knew her
Once, stretched out on her lap
                as now on a dead tree
I learned to make her smile
                to stem her tears
                to undo her guilt
                to cure her inward death

To enliven her was my living
So she became wife, mother, home
The carpenter enjoyed his craft
Children came and loved and were loved
Suffer little children to come unto me

Now mother is weeping
She must weep

The sins of the whole world weigh less than this
    woman's heaviness

O Glastonbury

Must I bring even these thorns to flower?
    even this dead tree to leaf?

How, in agony
Held by dead wood that has no need of me
    by the cruelty of the nail's hatred
        of gravity's inexorable and heartless pull

I thirst

No garment now
No hem to be touched
It is I who need virtue
Eloi, Eloi, lama sabachthani?

It is I who die
    I who die
        I die
        I

REFERENCES

Clancier, A. & Kalmanovitch, J. (1987), *Winnicott and Paradox: From Birth to Creation*, trans. A. Sheridan. London: Tavistock.

Ford, J. (1971), A Tribute to Donald Winnicott. Unpublished.

Goldman, D. (1993), *In Search of the Real: The Origins and Originality of D. W. Winnicott*. New York: Aronson.

Informant. (1993a), Letter to F. R. Rodman.

Informant. (1993b), Letter to F. R. Rodman.

Kahr, B. (1996), *D. W. Winnicott: A Biographical Portrait*. London: Karnac Books.

Khan, M. (1982), Introduction. *Through Paediatrics to Psycho-Analysis* by D. W. Winnicott. London: Hogarth Press.

Little, M. (1989), Phone conversations with F. R. Rodman, April 25.

Milner, M. (1972), *Sci. Bull. Brit. Psycho-Anal. Soc. & Inst. Psycho-Anal.*, Vol. 57.

—— (1989), Letter to F. R. Rodman. April 25.

Phillips, A. (1988), *Winnicott*. Cambridge, MA: Harvard University Press.

Rodman, F. R. ed. (1987), *The Spontaneous Gesture: Selected Letters of D. W. Winnicott*. Cambridge, MA: Harvard University Press.

Turner, J. (1988), Wordworth and Winnicott in the area of play. In: *Transitional Objects and Potential Spaces: Literary Uses of D. W. Winnicott*, ed. P. L. Rudnytsky. New York: Columbia University Press, 1955.

Winnicott, C. (1971), Compilation of parts of 60 obituaries made into a single one, unpublished.

—— (1978), D. W. W.: A reflection. In: *Between Reality and Fantasy*, ed. S. Grolnick. New York: Aronson.

Winnicott, D. W., Letter to "My Dear People," November 23, 1913.

—— Letter to "My Home Circle," November 30, 1913.

—— Letter to parents and sisters, May 3, 1915.

—— Letter to his mother, September 10, 1916.

—— Letter to "my dears," December 9, 1916.

—— Letter to Violet and Kathleen, July 10, 1917.

—— Letter to Violet, November 15, 1919.

—— (1945), Primitive emotional development. In: *Collected Papers: Through Paediatrics to Psycho-Analysis*. New York: Basic Books, 1958.

—— (1956), The antisocial tendency. In: *Collected Papers: Through Paediatrics to Psycho-Analysis*. New York: Basic Books, 1958.

—— (1960), Ego distortion in terms of the true and false self. In: *The Maturational Process and the Facilitating Environment*. New York: International Universities Press, 1965.

—— (1963), Communicating and not communicating leading to a study of certain opposites. In: *The Maturational Processes and the Facilitating Enviornment*. New York: International Universities Press, 1965.

—— (1967), Postscript: D. W. W. on D. W. W. In: *Psychoanalytic Explorations*, ed. C. Winnicott, R. Shepherd & M. Davis. Cambridge, MA: Harvard University Press, 1989.

—— (1968), The use of an object. In: *Playing and Reality*. London: Tavistock, 1971.

—— (1971), *Therapeutic Consultations in Child Psychiatry*. New York: Basic Books.

—— (1977), *The Piggle*. New York: International Universities Press.

—— (1986), *Holding and Interpretation: Fragment of an Analysis*. London: Hogarth Press.

10

This Scherzo Is [Not] a Joke

STUART FEDER

SCHERZO

Scherzo means joke in Italian. It is the musical term that most defini-
tively indicates that humor is at the heart of a musical entity and may
therefore be anticipated by the listener. A related term, scherzando, is an
adjective suggesting a degree of playfulness, which is also characteristic
of the classical scherzo, a "movement-type generally swift and light in
character and commonly in triple time" (Sadie, 1980, p. 634). It was
Beethoven who established usage as a regular alternative to the symphonic minuet, although the term had been current since the early 17th
century. Before Beethoven, instrumental music—not to mention opera—
was hardly lacking in the humorous dimension. For example, Haydn's
music was full of a jocularity and playfulness without formal symphonic
scherzi (Sadie, 1980). Later, while the scherzo remained a fixture of symphonic form, practice underwent many changes in the latter part of the
19th century and into the 20th. By the turn of the century the scherzo
might be replaced by a movement incorporating a national dance (as in
Dvorak) or ballet-type movement (a waltz, for example, in Tchaikovsky).
Also, subtly related affects insinuated traditional scherzo humor, for example, irony or frank grotesquerie in the music of Prokofiev,
Shostakovitch, and Mahler. (I have written elsewhere [Feder, 1990] about
the song-inspired scherzo of Mahler's *Second Symphony,* which, while
humorous in another sense, harbors serious psychological, as well as
formal, implications.) Such extensions of the classical and relatively naive

and "swift and light" nature of the scherzo are consistent with the postmodern temper and among the variations in humorous affect; irony, in particular, plays a significant role (see Feder, 1996).

In this study we will consider a scherzo by Charles Edward Ives (1874–1955). Not only does humor in its myriad forms mark Ives's music but is an element of the "high" and the "low"—a quest for the representation of both the temporal and the spiritual. In pursuit of these goals the utilization of vernacular materials in music plays a meaningful role. In addition, song is a significant feature, not only in those Ives wrote but in the multiple quotations of other songs (mostly from the 19th century), which, quoted in his own music, characterize his style. Self-revealed programs, marginalia, and frank autobiography suggest the biographical background to such musical quotations and to a creative life in music. Further, a consideration of this background suggests the ways in which childhood experience may be the determinant of both style and content in the work of the mature composer. Of particular importance is the influence of the early auditory environment of the composer (Feder, 1992). Finally, Ives was a successful businessman as well as composer. Leading a double creative life, he was also an innovator in the then burgeoning field of insurance.

CHARLES IVES AND *TSIAJ*

Ives's scherzo, the middle movement of his *Trio* for violin, cello, and piano, was probably started in 1904 when Ives was on either side of 30, written (or at least sketched out) in connection with his sixth college reunion (Yale '98).[1] On a sketch for a title page, Ives scrawled, "Trio . . . Yalensia et Americana (Fancy Names)—Real name: Yankee jaws at Mr. Yale's School for nice bad boys!!" (Ives, 1972, p. 158). The title on the first manuscript page reads: "*TSIAJ*" (or Medley on the Fence . . . Campus) (Figure 1, Ives, n.d.). The letters stand for: This *Scherzo Is A Joke*. Ives indicates the work's manifest gaiety by frivolously transforming the quotation marks of the title into decorative musical notes.

Despite his chronological age, Charles Ives had only just begun to accomplish the passage from adolescence to maturity. The results were not confined to the intrapsychic but were specifically artistic as well. The

---

[1] Ive's own dating of the work was 1904–1911. Recent analysis by Gail Sherwood suggests that the surviving sketches are in Ives's handwriting of 1907–1914. It was Ives's habit to work on a piece over some period of time, thus a characteristic ambiguity: Did he actually start it in connection with his reunion, or did he merely conceptualize it then and recall the occasion in music later, or did he simply misremember?

FIGURE 1. Title page from "*TSIAJ*" by Charles Edward Ives (1874–1955). (Reprinted by permission of Yale Music Library.)

joking, back-slapping heartiness of the above "Medley on the Fence" comments reveals the considerable vestige of postadolescence, which Ives was long in shedding. The "Fence," incidentally, was that place on campus where individual classes would gather in what was the late 19th-century equivalent of "hanging out." More than this, one's place *on* the fence was one's "turf" and accordingly vigorously defended. Despite a tendency to moodiness and a degree of aloof withdrawnness, which only increased as he grew older, Ives greatly valued comradeship in an almost idealized and intellectualized manner. The phrase "we boys" was nostalgically and tenderly mentioned in several of his prose passages in the autobiographical *Memos*. The long-sought esteem and approval of friends would be cast in a new light as he entered his creative period of "innovation and synthesis," which marked the years 1902–1908 (Burkholder, 1985).[2] In Ives's case, self-doubts dogged creative innovation. "I felt (but only temporarily)," he wrote, "that perhaps there must be something wrong with me. . . . Are my ears on wrong?" (Ives, 1972, p. 71).[3] Thus college friends and postcollege housemates constituted a forum for innovation, some of which Ives cast in the guise of "jokes," "take-offs," or "stunts." In his marginalia he would occasionally quote the approving comments of friends who could have known little of what he was attempting musically beyond the superficial.

The year 1902 had been a watershed year. Ives (1972) joked that it was then that he "gave up music," as he put it (p. 57). Fours years out of college and working in the actuarial department of Mutual Life, Ives was also organist and choir director at Central Presbyterian Church in New York. In addition he seemed to be pursuing the possibility of the more conventional musical career of his Yale professor, Horatio Parker. In fact, it was shortly after the New York premiere of the cantata *The Celestial Country*, a work in which Ives emulated his teacher, that he decided to "give up" music—this despite the fact that the reviews, if not raves, were at least acceptable and even encouraging. Far from abandoning music, however, Ives privately and intensively pursued composition, cultivating now the less conventional and more experimental trends he had begun to explore.

I have suggested elsewhere an interpretation for this paradoxical behavior in the form of an enactment. By far the most important object in Ives's life was his father, George Edward Ives (1845–1894), a village

---

[2] Burkholder (1985) appropriately calls the above-mentioned adolescent and postadolescent periods "the years of apprenticeship" (1894–1902, p. 58).

[3] The comment dates from 1914. Interestingly, it was provoked by a visiting musician (the violinist Franz Milcke) who, looking over some of Ives's music, chanced upon the scherzo, "stared at [it], then threw it [down]" (p. 70) and left.

bandmaster, music teacher, and sometime small-town impresario in Danbury, Connecticut. Idealized by his son, the more so for a legendary, if distorted, view of his role as Civil War bandmaster, the elder Ives was actually somewhat of the black sheep of a distinguished, prosperous, and well-established local family. Young Charlie was the favorite of George's two boys, father and son remarkably alike in musical endowment. George was his earliest teacher and musical mentor, and his death at the age of 49, when Charles was 20 and in the throes of adolescent separation, was devastating to the son. Among the sources of ambivalence was a rivalry in which the younger man was poised to prevail, owing to a superior gift. Among the sources of guilt was Charles's struggle to separate at the time of his father's death, moving into social circles at Yale, which George's life choices had closed for him. In addition, knowledge of a sacrifice weighed heavily: George, too, had given up music, his motive to earn sufficient money for the boys' educations. Indeed, it was this sacrifice that enabled Ives to move in the circles that were beginning to open to him—now fraternities, later a promising business career. As for music, it had been George's devotion that made Ives's early musical development possible and laid the groundwork for current creative life in more ways than either might have anticipated. The "giving up" music in 1902 constituted an elaborate psychological compromise in which Ives, manifestly emulating his father in some punlike literal sense ("I resigned as a nice organist and gave up music") (Ives, 1972, p. 57) entered a private mental creative compartment in which his father was very much present in fantasy as a part of a prolonged mourning. It was in this context that Ives, as his first biographer put it, "has written his father's music for him" (Cowelll and Cowell, 1955, p. 12).

While other of Ives's music, in particular his great Civil War pieces, are more obviously related to the idealized George Ives (who was in fact among the Union's youngest bandmasters), Ives's *TSIAJ* scherzo falls into the category of "his father's music" in another sense.[4] It is a musical "stunt" and George with his keen sense of humor, fresh manner of listening, originality, and alertness to new sounds and combinations was fond of musical stunts. For example, he would divide his band into spatially separated groups in order to hear new combinations of sound or direct two separate bands passing each other in order to create ever-shifting and clashing musical combinations. Ives recreated many such musical events in his own works transforming memory and the vernacular into musical art.

"Stunt" is a distinctly American term, initially used in late 19th

---

[4] Ives's Civil War music includes *Decoration Day* of the *Holidays Symphony* and *The Saint-Gaudens in Boston Common* of *Three Places in New England*.

century college athletic slang (*New Shorter Oxford English Dictionary*, 1993, p. 3110). Its aim is to attract attention and to entertain, perhaps by "stunning" feats or events. A "take-off" is a related effort, and in both, humor often plays a role with the element of surprise and the unexpected eliciting an amused, "Wow!" on the part of the observer. Ives composed or performed many musical stunts during his college years. It was a way to curry favor with classmates while at the same time carrying on the composer's private, auditory experimentation, which in Ives's case was of an innovative nature. The two endeavors came together in Ives's earnest desire for his peers to approve and endorse creative activities, which might be considered effeminate on one hand or crazy on the other. He tried picturing a football game in tones, as for example in *A Yale–Princeton Game*, in which the offensive wedge formation was pictured in a musical take-off in tone, graphically represented, however, in a wedge-like pattern on the orchestral score. Performing for fraternity shows, Ives tried "some similar things . . . not so successfully." Better, said he, were "marches with college tunes in the trio [final section] against the original themes" creating an amusing "off-key and off-time" agglomeration of sound (Ives, 1976, p. 41).

Such efforts were avowedly "half in fun, half serious." But I suggest that the "fun" regularly screened elements, which were of the greatest seriousness in Ives's mental life. Two in particular are considered here. The first relates to the vicissitudes of mourning, which we have already discussed. The ongoing and near-endless work of mourning made constant demands on the creative process, even as it lent impetus to the entire endeavor in the intrapsychic creative collaboration noted above. The presence of George Ives in Charles's music manifested itself in both form and content. In *TSIAJ*, for example, the vernacular "stunt" takes the form of a kind of medley of tunes of the general type that might find its way unto George's band programs but was uniquely transformed by Charles. The tunes themselves were characteristic of Ives's musical quotations, for as we will see later, mixed with the fraternity tunes, which were of course related to the manifest occasion for the piece, were the tunes of his father's times.

The second "serious" element screened by the "fun" of *TSIAJ* is a gender issue relating to Ives's shaky discomfort with his own creative psychological bisexuality. Ives, as Judith Tick (1993) put it, "stands out as the prime example of an artist who ascribed a masculine ideal to music" (p. 83). From childhood on, when he confessed to "feeling partly ashamed" of his musical interests—a feeling he considered to be "wrong . . . but one typical of boys in small towns" of the America of his times—Ives was concerned about the effeminate taint of music. The conflict, revived later in life, gave rise to some idiosyncratic fantasies about a virtual, fantasized, masculinized, yet powerfully bisexual "ear," which I have written about elsewhere (Feder et al., 1990, p. 155). Tick (1993) keenly notes that his "statements about effeminacy and music, which do not appear until after 1905, seem to be correlated with the evolution of his radical experimental style, which crystallized at the same time" (p. 99). Ives was at the brink of this departure when the *Trio* was in concept, and he was deeply involved in the radical endeavor during its development and completion. Diverse strivings served as context to its composition: social bonding with fraternity peers and a strong need for acceptance; confirmation that his creative direction was not crazy and the autonomous artistic requirements of that direction itself, which was often innovative, hence difficult to comprehend. Still other strivings join the creative compromise observed earlier, including his identification with his father via musical stunts, as well as the rich citation of his father's life and times in the multiple quotations of associated tunes.

On a deeper level Ives sought the company and love of men. He had written of the emptiness he experienced after his father's death and of how he sought to fill it with other musicians and later an older man, his father-in-law, who might understand his needs. Profoundly sentimental, he feared the feminine implications of frankly expressed affect: the "sissy" in boyhood, the unspeakably homoerotic in manhood, warded off in tirades against the musically emasculated. "Music is a nice little art just born, and they ask 'Is it a boy or a girl?—and one voice in the back row says, 'It's going to be a boy—sometime!'" (Ives, 1972, p. 30). That was Ives's own "voice" of course, and it became the composer's voice as it penetrated the boundaries of the substance of the music, motivating and endowing the experimental style he now cultivated. Thus, among its stylistic features, dissonance itself, long associated with masculinity, played a prominent role, and Ives experimented with it richly, both playfully as we will see in *TSIAJ* and with the utmost seriousness as well, often at the same time. An extreme would at length be witnessed when, late in Ives's life, the composer Elliott Carter observed him "adding dissonant notes" to a score he was revising. Carter "got the impression that he might have frequently jacked up the level of dissonance of many works as his tastes changed" (Perlis, 1974, p. 138)—"as his tastes changed," yes, but also by then as the issue of musical masculinity became more compelling to an artist with failing creative potency.

But the work at hand is still a youthful one, and sentimentality is warded off not only with dissonance but with a driving "masculine" speed and quasiprecision. As noted, tunes were typically quoted in the creation of Ives's music but rarely in so simple a form that might elicit tears or such frank affects as sadness, love, or the *sehnsucht,* which is the amalgam of the two. Overall, Ives's music encodes a nostalgia that is undeniable, and the very employment of old tunes constitute an act of commemoration (Feder, 1990). However, in the quoted melodies of *TSIAJ*, we may observe with eyes and ears how Ives re-forms old tunes by obscuring, fragmenting, layering, distorting, and even reinventing to the degree that one is not quite sure that he is in fact quoting an old tune. (Peter Burkholder [1995] has written brilliantly and in detail about the use of quoted materials.) In *TSIAJ* they appear at moments to be not merely disguised but fairly obliterated. I suggest simultaneous and contradictory motives for the use of such tunes and their treatment: to both experience and to deny strong affects.

Before going on to a discussion of the music itself and some guidelines for study and listening, a word about the "transcendental" Ives is necessary. Indeed, the amalgamation of the above vernacular considerations and these philosophical and spiritual elements go a long way in characterizing the man and his work. Ives's fascination with the New England Transcendentalists goes back at least as far as the time of George's death when he found solace in the writings of Thoreau (Ives, 1961). It culminated in his masterpiece, the *Concord Sonata,* and the spiritual and mystical *Fourth Symphony.* A projected and unfinished *Universe Symphony* would explore its farthest spiritual reaches in a reenactment of Creation (Feder, 1992). Transcendental philosophy and conventional religion converge in Ives's belief in an afterlife characterized by a reunion with loved ones. The breaking through the curtain of reality into another, spiritual world constituted part of Ives's creative ethos. It is striking to encounter it in his "joke," *TSIAJ.*

TSIAJ: THE MUSIC

With the foregoing biographical and interpretive remarks in mind, an actual "hearing" of the music might at first be disappointing. *TSIAJ* does not make for easy listening nor for easy performing. Except for two formally significant and emotionally poignant moments and a penultimate time-suspended cadenza, the pace is fast and rhythmically complex and the texture dense. A "stunt" and tour de force it might be, but as entertainment there are demands on the listener. The performer who must keep up a breathless pace in the midst of technical demands is nonetheless immersed in the surprises of realizing the quoted tunes, an experience that the listener might share. Some may wonder if Ives is not posthumously laughing at their struggling over rhythmic complexities that are hardly casual (Robert Martin, personal communication, 1996). The "fun" to the fraternity men would have been in the encountering of these familiar college songs embedded in the rush and thicket of overlapping, obscured, or dissonantly blending tunes and fragments of tunes that make up its texture. The uninitiated might discern the humorous distortions of familiar 19th-century parlor and patriotic tunes heard as if through the auditory equivalent of funhouse mirrors. Perhaps it is the modern listener who might receive a different impression in catching one's breath musically when the headlong impulse relents for the two contemplative moments of adagio noted above and in the brief experience of timelessness just before the final cadence.

Overall, the progression of melodies might suggest something along the lines of a medley, as defined by Burkholder (1995) as the statement of "two or more existing tunes, relatively complete, one after another in a single movement" (p. 3). However, Burkholder relates this movement more specifically to the ancient *quodlibet* (Latin term meaning "whatever you please"), which involves "combining two or more existing tunes or fragments in counterpoint on in quick succession, most often as a joke or technical tour de force" (p. 3). Interestingly, the close formal relationship to techniques of patchwork, paraphrase, and especially collage relates this apparently casual work of the early 20th century to postmodernism.

In rapid succession one hears fraternity songs *A Band of Brothers in DKE* (Ives's junior fraternity, Delta Kappa Epsilon) and *Few Days* (of Psi Epsilon). But in the background there sounds a haunting fragment of Ives's favorite Civil War *Marching Through Georgia* and surprisingly, the adolescent *The Worms Crawl In, The Worms Crawl Out*. The movement will end citing this macabre joke. Soon over a repeated figure in the violin, two "old" tunes are heard: the nostalgic *My Old Kentucky Home* and *That Old Cabin on the Hill*. Introducing a sudden adagio, the piano sounds the first line of *In the Sweet Bye and Bye*, the words of which are: "There's a land that is fairer than day. . . ." (Were it to continue, the text would read: "and by faith we can see it afar, / For the Father waits over the way / To prepare us a dwelling place there." The refrain: "In the sweet bye and bye, / We shall meet on that beautiful shore.") There follows a reverent chorale-like echo in the strings reminiscent of similar Ives moments, as for example in the adagio cantabile third movement of his *Second Symphony*. Here it seems to musically spell out the final phrase of *My Old Kentucky Home*. (This is the first of the two poignant episodes noted above, the second of which will appear near the end of the movement.)

The pace is resumed with a curious simultaneity of the *Sailor's (or College) Hornpipe* and the trio section of a march dear to both Charles and George Ives, Reeves's *Second Regiment Connecticut National Guard March*, quoted in extenso by Ives in his *Decoration Day*. It continues with episodes that include the catalogue of songs that follow: (the interested reader will find a detailed analysis in Burkholder[5]): *Pigtown*

---

[5] The foregoing analysis is drawn from Burkholder (1995, pp. 373–374).

Fling, The Campbells Are Coming, Long Long Ago, Happy Day (also known as *How Dry I Am*), *Ta-Ra-Ra Boom De-Ay, Dixieland, Hold The Fort McClung is Coming* and *Reuben and Rachel*. Finally, a full quotation of a hymnlike secret fraternity song, *The Gods of Egypt Bid Us Hail,* is followed and balanced by a comparably near-full rendition of the hymn *Fountain ("Are you washed in the blood of the lamb?")* prominent in what would become perhaps Ives's greatest song, *General William Booth Enters into Heaven,* of 1914.

With an interruption and elision of the last line of *Fountain* the "Sweet bye and bye" adagio returns with the quoted, "There's a land that is fairer than day..." with its reciprocal string "answer." What follows at this point is a musical idea that is unanticipated and without precedent in this work, a mass of sound in a series of grand piano arpeggios incorporating a crescendo which starts triple-piano (ppp) and extends to triple-forte (fff). Arriving at the climactic point, the piece ends with a four-measure unison rendition of *The Worms Crawl In, The Worms Crawl Out.* It is rendered in a dissonant presto and the piece ends on that nose-thumbing note.

Noted at the outset were some of the composer's verbal comments scrawled on the manuscript of *TSIAJ.* Ives frequently covered his scores with marginalia of various kinds ranging from directions to the copyist to personal reminiscences and associations to frank diaristic entries. This manuscript is no exception, and here and on the third from last page of the manuscript, on the bottom of the page, Ives writes, "Greek Day ends with Sun Rise over East Rock." On the final page in the measure where the cadenza starts, Ives writes "Sunrise Cadenza."

WHERE WILLIAM JAMES MEETS SIGMUND FREUD

Several writers have commented on a "stream of consciousness" quality in the music of Ives (Perry, 1974; Burkholder, 1995). Indeed Perry (1974) writes of "Ives's *attempt* to create human consciousness in music" (p. 106; italics added). Burkholder writes further of the "multi-layered feel of life" rendered by the composer commenting further on his characteristic "collage of half-heard and half-remembered tunes that is a wonderfully true musical evocation of the way human memory works" (Burkholder, 1995). In an earlier article I considered the issue of memory, its layering, and the nature of associations (Feder, 1989). Perhaps the most immediate and graphic picture of the process is provided by the composer himself:

Throughout his life, Ives had been known by many in the family to improvise endlessly at the piano, carrying on a running commentary as if music and word blended in reminiscence and free association. The tunes would remind him of people and places and of the events and experiences of the past; and as he recalled them, the memories stimulated recall of still more tunes, which then emerged in musical association [Feder, 1992, p. 350].

Two terms, William James's (1842–1910) "stream of consciousness" and Sigmund Freud's (1856–1939) "free association," are not identical although they are often cited in conjunction with one another, frequently as if describing interchangeable phenomena. James's *Principles of Psychology,* published in 1890, is not in the Freud bibliography although Freud actually did meet James in the course of his American sojourn at Clark University in 1909 (Freud, 1925, p. 52). It is instructive to both music and psychoanalysis to distinguish certain aspects of the two phenomena. First, James emphasizes the flow of "mental life" (another of his terms) in contrast to the alterations or transformations of its content. He writes: "Consciousness, then, does not appear to itself chopped up in bits. . . . It is nothing jointed; it flows. A 'river' or a 'stream' are the metaphors by which it is most naturally described. In talking of it hereafter, let us call it the stream of thought, of consciousness, or of subjective life" (James, 1890, p. 239). Freud (1925), on the other hand, in writing of "free association" seems to take for granted that some temporal process exists but is chiefly interested in the aspect of subjective experience relating to the "free" and literal report of it clinically, that is, without "conscious direction" or "critical objection" to any of its content (p. 40). It is thus, he writes, that the fundamental rule "should have achieved what was expected of it, namely the bringing into consciousness of the repressed material which was held back by resistances" (p. 40). James hardly ignores discontinuities in flow or range of content for that matter, but the emphasis is on the conscious experience of the flow itself.

Above all, music is the temporal art par excellence. Ives's musical temporality frequently mimics and recreates the flow of human mentation from a formal point of view. This may, in fact, be said to be one of the stylistic features of his work. In such instances as the scherzo, music is created that is apparently isomorphic with the subjectively perceived flow of thought in all its complexity. Thus there is a continuity of ideas such as described above, with Ives improvising at the piano but a network and layering of association as well. This Jamesian notion of "stream of consciousness," however, does not preclude the dynamic implications of "free association" such as the institution of defense mechanisms in the course of association. It is here that James and Freud may be said to meet again.

The musicologist may join this particular aspect of the discourse in calling the scherzo a quodlibet. Stemming from the Renaissance, the humorous quodlibet form is distinguished from "more serious works in which pre-existing material has a constructive or symbolic function" (Sadie, 1980, p. 514). But in the case of Ives the very selection of tunes—words as well as music—implies a symbolism of its own, which may be interpreted in its biographical context. Quodlibet creates a framework for both "stream of consciousness" *and* "free association."

AN INTERPRETATION

To say that there is a network and layering in Ives's musical associations, which begins in the superficial and penetrates to the deepest level, is to say something about his music in general, for the banal and the humorous frequently serve as psychological defense yet portal to more profound meanings. *TSIAJ* starts as a joke, its occasion a fraternity reunion; it ends a commentary on mortality and the transcendental. In its course there are allusions to personal history (in particular early life), as well as the history of America. Behind the breezy, carefree affects associated with fraternity life are those associated with the sentimentality inherent in everyday family life, religion, and mourning. With regard to the last, the spirit of Ives's father, George Ives, is present in several transformations. And finally, there is embedded a striving toward the spiritual and the universal of the kind that would lead eventually to the conception of Ives's never-to-be-completed *Universe Symphony.*

The camaraderie of men and acceptance into their company provides the manifest motivational background to *TSIAJ*. Issues related to masculinity, in particular, acceptance of the normally bisexual, let alone its intensification in artists, hover as conflict in the background as discussed earlier. More than this, there is the longing for the company of men, the restoration of a lost object in Ives's father, and the fantasized childhood utopia. The fraternity songs provide the manifest musical framework while the entire endeavor smacks of George Ives's humorous "stunts." College tunes of a pious, reverential nature are balanced with the frivolous, redolent of adolescent exuberance, rebelliousness, drinking, burlesque-house sexuality, and just plain silliness.

Peering through the musical thinking are associations to everyday 19th-century life in the musical quotations of sentimental parlor songs and the two songs from the Civil War, one from each side. The sentiment inherent in these are obscured by the dense musical texture, a density that not only screens but *means*. It is in itself an arcane reference to childhood, representing as I have suggested elsewhere (Feder, 1992, pp. 75

and 280), a re-creation and mastery of the chaotic musical experience, which characterized Ives's early auditory environment. The quotation of the Reeves march, beloved to both father and son, opens a window on yet another later layer of musical experiences shared by both. In addition, it relates to early perceptions of the pleasures of the gathering of men as exemplified in the bands that George Ives led and that Charles experienced at home and elsewhere. There is a body image component as well—the sense of men moving together: In Charles's own late childhood, he played in one of George's bands. Men moving together in fraternal revelry and men *singing* together in fraternity chorus would serve as the adolescent equivalent for Ives.

A deeper religious note is struck toward the end in the hymn *Fountain,* which balances the piously pompous *Egypt*—the Christian following the pagan. Ives (1972) wrote reverentially about his father's leading the hymn-singing at camp meeting, yet another early community that preceded college and fraternity: "There was something about the way Father played hymns" (p. 46). It was for this reason that gospel hymns were particularly meaningful to Ives. The gospel tune *In the Sweet Bye and Bye* has particular aesthetic and structural significance in *TSIAJ.* Its nostalgic, yet other-worldly, rendering parallels the words' meaning in a fantasy of reunion ("we shall meet on the beautiful shore"). The father "who waits over the way" is both temporal and spiritual father. The answering refrain in the strings sentimentally echoes the closing phrase of the parlor song *My Old Kentucky Home.*

The foregoing casts light on the enigmatic "Sunrise" cadenza. Manifestly, Ives is programmatically picture-painting in music: Greek Day (more likely all-night) revelry ending with dawn breaking over East Rock, a 350-foot outcropping not far from Yale. The cadenza essays a mystical, timeless quality free of the multilayered quotation-filled scurrying that preceded. Its open and negative space is reminiscent of Ives's "signature" piece, *The Unanswered Question,* while its geographical association with New Haven's East Rock (although not quite so awesome) presages his sketches toward a *Universe Symphony.* Although a transcendental element is thus introduced in the suggestion of yet another reality beyond everyday reality ("There's a land that is fairer than day"), one wonders as always about the incorporation of the all too real. By Ives's college days a Soldiers and Sailors Monument had been built on the summit of East Rock commemorating those who had lost their lives in every American war through the Civil War, which for Ives was the war of wars—that in which his father served. The nose-thumbing ending is a musical memento mori in the form of a denial. In the midst of youthful play, the tune quoted is *The Worms Crawl In, The Worms Crawl Out.*

IVES AND HUMOR: "I WAS ONLY JOKING"

If Ives's *TSIAJ* can be said to be a musical joke, it is also *not* a joke at the same time as it touches upon layers of meaning and human experience. Humor was the mode in which the composer frequently expressed himself. Among its many functions, humor served to ward off the depression from which Ives suffered periodically, "slumps," as he called them. During his youth it is likely that the demands of good fellowship dictated he not appear too seriously reflective, let alone depressed. The combination of depression and idiosyncratic originality was a dangerous one with its taint of the "crazy." Humor could be a mitigating and socially redeeming factor. Not only was Ives's esteem at stake but in a sense his future as well, for college relationships would become the social contacts that would determine future success in business and life in general. For example, Ives's roommate's sister was to become his wife. Yet Ives's contemplative mode was very much a part of his withdrawal into private composition when he "[gave] up music" after 1902. Contemporary with the *TSIAJ* was his pair of "contemplations": "A Contemplation of a Serious Matter," which was his *The Unanswered Question,* and "A Contemplation of Nothing Serious," *Central Park in the Dark.* But in *TSIAJ* contemplation is eschewed in childhood's simplistic denial of anything serious: "I was only joking."

REFERENCES

Burkholder, J. P. (1985), *Charles Ives: The Ideas behind the Music.* New Haven, CT: Yale University Press.
——— (1995), *All Made of Tunes: Charles Ives and the Uses of Borrowing.* New Haven, CT: Yale University Press.
Cowell, H. & Cowell S. (1955), *Charles Ives and His Music.* London: Oxford University Press.
Feder, S. (1981), Charles and George Ives: The veneration of boyhood. In: *Psychoanalytic Exploration in Music,* ed. S. Feder, R. Carmel & G. Pollock. Madison, CT: International Universities Press, 1990.
——— (1981), The music of fratricide. In: *Psychoanalytic Exploration in Music,* ed. S. Feder, R. Carmel & G. Pollock. Madison, CT: International Universities Press, 1990.
——— (1981), The nostalgia of Charles Ives. In: *Psychoanalytic Exploration in Music,* ed. S. Feder, R. Carmel & G. Pollock. Madison, CT: International Universities Press, 1990.
——— (1989), Calcium night light and other early memories of Charles Ives. In: *Fathers and Their Families,* ed. S. Cath, A. Gurwitt & L. Gunsberg. Hillsdale, NJ: The Analytic Press.

———— (1992), *Charles Ives: "My Father's Song."* New Haven, CT: Yale University Press.

———— (1992), "Vox Humana": A Composer's Childhood. In Chapter 5, *Charles Ives: "My Father's Song."* New Haven, CT: Yale University Press.

———— (1992), Universe. In Chapter 20, *Charles Ives: "My Father's Song."* New Haven, CT: Yale University Press.

———— (1996), Gustav Mahler: The mind of the ironist. In: *Colloque Gustav Mahler 1996.* Montpellier, France: anticipated 1999.

Freud, S. (1925), An autobiographical study. *Standard Edition,* 20:71–74. London: Hogarth Press, 1959.

Ives, C. E. (n.d.), Manuscript page (Copyflow #3114), Yale Music Library.

———— (1961), *Essays Before a Sonata and Other Writings,* ed. H. Boatwright. New York: Norton, 1961.

———— (1972), *Memos,* ed. J. Kirkpatrick. New York: Norton, 1972.

James, W. (1890), *The Principles of Psychology, Vol. 1.* New York: Dover.

New Shorter Oxford England Dictionary (1993). Oxford: Clarendon.

Perlis, V. (1974), *Charles Ives Rememberd.* New Haven, CT: Yale University Press.

Perry, S. (1974), *Charles Ives and the American Mind.* Kent, OH: Kent State University Press.

Sadie, S. (1980), *New Grove Dictionary of Music and Musicians, Vol. 15.* London: Macmillan.

———— (1980), *New Grove Dictionary of Music and Musicians, Vol. 16.* London: Macmillan.

Tick, J. (1993), Charles Ives and gender ideology. In: *Musicology and Difference,* ed. R. Solie. Berkeley: University of California Press, 1993.

Conclusion

JAMES W. BARRON

"Human kind cannot bear very much reality"
—Eliot, 1952, p. 118

As the authors contributing to this book have amply demonstrated, humor is multilayered and multifaceted. It exists at many different developmental levels and can be primitive or sophisticated in its blending of sexual and aggressive impulses or fantasies. At the extremes it can function as a sadistic attack or masochistic abasement or, in more modulated forms, can facilitate empathic recognition of the limits of self or other. Perhaps most importantly, it can be used in the service of avoidance and denial or can be used to accept and integrate threatening aspects of reality.

In his chapter, Bergmann calls our attention to a central theme in Freud's work:

> the difficulty we all have in the transition from the pleasure principle to the reality principle. This change takes place slowly, painfully, and incompletely. Humor helps us make this transition with less pain and allows to relinquish the reality principle in favor of the pleasure principle in a way that does not endanger our capacity to test reality.

Although it is possible to view humor as a defense, at its most mature level of development, humor is akin to sublimation, a transformation and reorganization of experience that is valuable to the individual and society.

219

As artists have known intuitively since first portraying the human drama, tragedy and comedy are closely allied. Each is a complex response to the unbridgeable gap between the real and the ideal, between our ongoing experience of ourselves in the world and our unrelinquished wish for our condition to be otherwise. In our conjurings of paradise, we create a world where all our needs would be met. There would be no suffering and therefore no tragedy. An equal, although perhaps unintended, consequence would be the absence of humor or comedy, which, like tragedy, is contingent upon loss.

Richard Gilman (1995) describes the intertwining of tragedy and comedy, each dealing with similar content, but each having distinctive attitudes. He cites two examples in the Western canon, Dante's *La Divina Commedia* and Balzac's *La Comédie Humaine*.

> Both, after all, enclose more than enough suffering, evil, and death, everything grievous, somber, and cruel. . . . The word "comedy" suggests the answers to the following questions: What is our state of mind or spirit supposed to be after we finish these works? How are we to understand them, to "take" them, as we like to say? [p. 73].

As Gilman points out, we can view Dante as offering us relief from spiritual anxiety through an appreciation of God's difficult, yet loving, "joke." Balzac appropriates Dante's use of the term *comedy* but sheds its religious meanings and offers us hope from a secular perspective, closer to our contemporary sensibilities:

> But though it may be a black farce at times, a comedy we sigh over, whose humor is often of the gallows variety, it isn't in the end conducive to despair. . . . It's to offer hope through privileged perception, a "cure" through a well-wrought description of the disease. Even the darkest moments in Balzac, the particular novels or sequences within them that recoil most strongly from being called comic, take their places in the general easing of anxiety which occurs whenever experience is recovered from shapelessness and made less inexplicable [p.74].

The humor lying at the heart of comedy, and I would argue at the heart of psychoanalysis, allows us to look at ourselves and the context in which we are embedded and to recover our experience from shapelessness, to render it less inexplicable, without our resorting excessively to denial on the one hand or being overwhelmed with despair on the other. Humor, while being deeply pleasurable, has a serious purpose. In his study of the plays of Chekhov, both those that Chekhov labeled as serious dramas and those that he categorized as comedies, Gilman (1995) describes this artfully disguised seriousness of purpose:

The resulting "lightness" in the noncomedies is nothing like a diminution of seriousness, and in the comedies it's nothing like frivolity. In their different ways both kinds of play offer us something like breathing room, space in which we can maneuver, take emotional or intellectual steps of our own, set matters in order, compare, *recognize*. All this is an act of freedom from what deconstructionists would call a programmed response" [p. 75].

HUMOR AND LOSS

In the midst of the cataclysm of the first world war, Freud wrote "Mourning and Melancholia" (1915a), followed a few months later by his brief essay "On Transience" (1915b) in which he described a walk through a "smiling countryside" during the previous summer in the company of a despondent young poet:

[The poet] was disturbed by the thought that all this beauty was fated to extinction, that it would vanish when winter came, like all human beauty and all the beauty and splendour that men have created or may create. All that he would otherwise have loved and admired seemed to him to be shorn of its worth by the transience which was its doom [p. 305].

Despite his best logical argumentation, Freud was unable to alleviate his companion's despondency and failed to persuade him that the transience of what is beautiful did not involve any diminution of its worth, nor did Freud succeed in convincing him to relinquish his implicit demand for the unending continuation of this paradisiacal moment.

As Freud observed, the young poet was unable to accept that what is painful may nonetheless be true. Freud attributed his companion's simultaneous melancholia and rebelliousness to his turning away from the truth, resulting from his inability and/or unwillingness to engage in the necessary process of mourning. I would add that his turning away from the truth also resulted from his incapacity, at least at the time of the described encounter, to experience the interplay of the tragic and the comic, to find or generate humor in the gap of the real and the ideal. Without that capacity, we cannot bear very much reality.

REFERENCES

Eliot, T. S. (1952), Four quartets: Burnt Norton. In: *T. S. Eliot: The Complete Poems and Plays 1909–1950*. New York: Harcourt Brace, p. 118.

Freud, S. (1915a), Mourning and melancholia. *Standard Edition,* 14:243–258. London: Hogarth Press, 1963.
———— (1915b), On transience. *Standard Edition,* 14:303–307. London: Hogarth Press, 1957.
Gilman, R. (1995), *Chekhov's Plays.* New Haven, CT: Yale University Press.

Index

232 Index